G000296530

QUESTIONS
ON
BANKING PRACTICE

Revised and issued under the authority of the
Council of The Institute of Bankers

ELEVENTH EDITION
1978

PROBUS ET FIDELIS

LONDON
THE INSTITUTE OF BANKERS, 10 LOMBARD STREET, EC3V 9AS

First published in 1885
Second edition   1887
Third   ,,   1889
Fourth   ,,   1892
Fifth   ,,   1898
Sixth   ,,   1909
Seventh   ,,   1921
Eighth   ,,   1930
Ninth   ,,   1952
Tenth   ,,   1965
Eleventh   ,,   1978

Published in 1978 by
THE INSTITUTE OF BANKERS
10 Lombard Street, London EC3V 9AS

ISBN: 0 85297 045 5

©

THE INSTITUTE OF BANKERS

Printed and bound in England by
STEPHEN AUSTIN AND SONS LIMITED
at Caxton Hill, Hertford

PREFACE

This edition of 'Questions on Banking Practice' has been prepared with the collaboration of a special Institute committee which included senior representatives of leading British banks. Their work is gratefully acknowledged by the Council.

Revision of the last edition, published in 1965, has called for a very careful scrutiny of the 'old' questions and answers, some of which have been quite substantially revised, with many obsolete questions being omitted, for example those dealing with stamp duty on bills of exchange and various other instruments. New material has been added where this was thought to be useful, some of it suggested by the banks and some originating from the valuable 'Question and Answer' series regularly published in the Institute's *Journal*.

A new departure is the recommendation, which appears occasionally, for the branch banker to refer to his head office or other higher authority. This arises in some difficult situations where it would seem imprudent for the branch manager to proceed without legal guidance, or where it is evident that practice in the particular circumstances varies as between the different banks.

Of special note are the references to the 4th edition of 'Leading Cases in the Law of Banking' by Chorley and Smart, published by Sweet and Maxwell in conjunction with the Institute in 1977. This book has in part superseded the series of volumes of 'Legal Decisions affecting Bankers' (containing full reports of cases) which the Institute has now ceased to publish because of its limited appeal. Most of the cases referred to in QBP are to be found in Chorley and Smart's digest. For readers interested in the legal background to much of today's banking practice, 'Leading Cases' could well be considered a useful companion volume to QBP.

Students of earlier editions will notice the disappearance of the occasional reference to some of the older banking text-books. In these cases it was felt that the answer to the question could well stand on its own, and there seemed little point in referring readers to publications not likely to be readily available in bank branches.

However, there is one quotation in this book, transposed from earlier editions: it is from 'The Law of Banking' by Heber L. Hart, K.C., 4th (1931) edition: 'Within the scope of his business, the banker is bound to exercise the degree of skill, care and diligence usual in the ordinary conduct of banking business, and reasonably necessary for the proper performance of the duties undertaken by him.' It is hoped that QBP, as a guide to banking practice in England and Wales, will enable its readers to conduct their banking in the spirit of this *dictum*.

GEOFFREY DIX
Secretary-General

The Institute of Bankers,
10 Lombard Street,
London EC3V 9AS.
November, 1978

CONTENTS

GENERAL ARRANGEMENT OF SUBJECTS
(The references are to the questions)

ABBREVIATIONS

The following abbreviated references are used throughout this volume:

BILLS OF EXCHANGE ACT   Bills of Exchange Act, 1882.

CHEQUES ACT   .   .   Cheques Act, 1957.

CLAYTON'S CASE .   .   Devaynes *v.* Noble, Clayton's Case (1816) 1 Mer. 529. (Leading Cases, 4th ed., page 143.)

LEADING CASES, 4th ed.   *Leading Cases in the Law of Banking*, by Lord Chorley, Q.C., LL.B., M.A., and P. E. Smart, LL.B., A.I.B., 4th (1977) edition.

THE CUSTOMER

MINORS

1 Is there any objection to conducting an account with a minor,
  (a) if the account is kept in credit, or
  (b) if it is allowed to be overdrawn?

Answer: (a) There is no objection.

(b) Money lent to a minor cannot be recovered from him, even after he attains his majority (Infants' Relief Act, 1874, sec. 1), even if he obtained the advance by a false representation that he was of full age (*Leslie* v. *Shiell,* [1914] 3 K.B. 607; Leading Cases, 4th Ed., p. 163). Any security given by the infant for the advance is void.

2 In a case where a minor is not personally liable to repay an advance made to him, can a guarantee for such an advance be enforced against the guarantor?

Answer: It appears from the case of *Coutts & Co.* v. *Browne-Lecky,* [1947] 1 K.B. 104, (Leading Cases, 4th Ed., p. 164) that such a guarantee cannot be enforced.

If the guarantee is solely a contract of suretyship, the guarantor would not be liable under it because of the legal principle that there cannot be a surety without a principal debtor. As the minor cannot make himself liable as principal debtor, so the intending guarantor cannot make himself liable as surety for him; but he can be made liable as indemnifier under a contract of indemnity with the bank whether included in the guarantee or the subject of a separate document. Unless the bank's form of guarantee includes an indemnity, a specific indemnity should be taken from a surety.

3 Can money deposited in the name of a minor be legally withdrawn before he comes of age? In the event of its being withdrawn, could the customer demand payment a second time on attaining his majority?

Answer: No difficulty is likely to arise in allowing the money to be withdrawn before the minor comes of age; he could not claim the money over again on attaining his majority. In the case of a child, a branch manager would no doubt be very circumspect in allowing withdrawals of substantial sums.

4 Is there any objection to opening a deposit account under the style **'A in trust for B,'** or **'A re B,'** where **B** is a minor?

Answer: No. As far as the bank is concerned withdrawals can be made only by **A** (or in the event of his death by his executors or administrators), even after **B** comes of age.

5 Can a minor sign on his father's overdrawn account, due authority having been given by his father?

Answer: Yes, if the authority covers an overdrawn account.

6 Can a minor legally witness a signature to a document?

Answer: Yes, if he is old enough to appreciate the significance of his act.

7 Should a banker
(*a*) accept from a customer an order to purchase stock or shares in the name of a minor, or
(*b*) send such a transfer to the company concerned for registration, without informing the company that the transferee is a minor?

Answer: (*a*) and (*b*) No. A minor is not legally capable of implementing a contract of purchase, or of accepting the stock or shares when purchased.

A transfer to a minor is voidable at his option, and he cannot compel the company to register him as a shareholder nor, if he has been registered, to keep him on the register when the company discovers that he is under age.

A transfer by a minor can be validly executed only in pursuance of an order of the Court.

There is, however, no objection to a transfer into the joint names of an adult and a minor.

Where stock is standing in the joint names of a minor and an adult, a letter of attorney for the receipt of the dividends may be given by the adult.

The National Debt (Stockholders' Relief) Act, 1892, sec. 3, provides that:
(*a*) where a minor is the sole survivor in an account, or
(*b*) where a minor holds stock jointly with a person under legal disability, or
(*c*) where stock has by mistake been bought in or transferred into the sole name of a minor,
the Bank of England may, at the request in writing of the parent,

guardian, or next friend of the minor, receive the dividends and apply them to the purchase of like stock, and the stock so purchased shall be added to the original investment.

8   Mr. and Mrs. B. are joint account customers, who have deposited for safe custody among their various holdings national savings certificates purchased by them for their son and daughter in the names of the children. The son, on reaching the age of 18, requests the bank to deliver the certificates purchased in his name to him, claiming that he is the true owner. This is followed by a similar request from the daughter, who, you know, is under 18. What should the bank do in each case?

Answer: Although, on the face of it the true owner of the national savings certificates is the person in whose name they were purchased, these are held in safe custody on behalf of Mr. and Mrs. B. whose discharge alone is acceptable to the bank.

ADMINISTRATORS, EXECUTORS AND TRUSTEES

9   On the death of a customer, **X,** should the account of his executors be opened as
Executors of **X** deceased (**A, B** and **C**),
or merely in the joint names of the executors?

Answer: Practice varies, but the designation of the account should always clearly show that it is the account of the executors of **X** deceased.

10   If a testator appoints (say) two executors of his will, but on his death (say) one of those appointed does not join with the other in proving the will, but power is reserved to him in the grant of probate to apply for probate later if he chooses to do so, is the executor to whom such power is reserved entitled to join with the proving executor in administering the estate, and in signing cheques on the executorship account?

Answer: No; a non-proving executor, whether he has renounced probate or whether power has been reserved to him to prove, is not entitled to take any part in the administration of the estate, until, if power was reserved, he exercises it by obtaining a grant of probate in his own favour. (Sec. 8 of the Administration of Estates Act, 1925.)

11   In the case mentioned in Q. 10, if the non-proving executor survives the executor who has proved, does he thereupon become entitled to continue the administration of the testator's estate, if this has not already been completed?

Answer: Not unless he applies for and obtains a grant of probate of the will in his own favour. If he does so, he becomes sole executor of the will for all purposes, and on his death his executors (if any) become entitled to take his place; but until he obtains such a grant the executors of the executor who originally proved the will are the testator's executors, provided they take a grant of the deceased executor's estate.

12   On the death of one out of two or more executors or administrators, does the right to continue the administration of the estate, and to draw cheques on the banking account used for that purpose, pass to the survivor(s)?

Answer: Yes; under sec. 18 (1) of the Trustee Act, 1925, a power or trust given to or imposed on two or more trustees (including, under sec. 68 (17), personal representatives) jointly may be exercised or performed by the survivors or survivor of them for the time being.

If the account is overdrawn, as the liability of executors or administrators for debts incurred by them is joint only, unless they expressly agree to be both jointly and severally liable, the estate of the deceased executor or administrator is discharged from liability. If the executors have accepted joint and several responsibility, the account should be stopped where the banker wishes to preserve the liability of the deceased executor.

13   If a sole, or last surviving (*a*) executor or (*b*) administrator dies before he has completed the administration of the estate, who will be entitled to complete the administration, and to draw cheques on the account used for that purpose?

Answer: (*a*) On the death of a sole, or last surviving, executor, his executors, on proving his will, become the executors of the original testator; but cease to be such, when another executor appointed by the will of the original testator, who did not join in proving the will, afterwards obtains probate of it. (See sec. 7 of the Administration of Estates Act, 1925.)

The 'chain of representation' from the last surviving executor to his executor is broken only by:

(1) an intestacy, or

(2) the failure of a testator to appoint an executor, or

(3) the failure to obtain probate of a will.

If the chain of representation is broken at any stage, leaving the administration of the original testator's estate uncompleted, a grant of administration *de bonis non* (of the unadministered estate) has to be applied for, and until such a grant is obtained, no one has authority to sign on the executorship account, or to deal with any of the assets of the estate.

(*b*) On the death of a sole, or last surviving administrator, the grant of administration lapses, and a fresh grant *de bonis non* must be applied for by some person entitled to do so.

14   Where one of two or more personal representatives (who have obtained a grant of probate or letters of administration) or trustees seeks to withdraw securities or other articles then vested in the personal representatives or trustees can the bank accede to his request?

Answer: Bankers should follow the customary practice of only allowing such a person to withdraw securities or other articles from their custody against written authority of all the personal representatives or trustees. There is no reason, however, why such a person should not have the opportunity of examining at the bank the securities and articles in the bank's custody, under supervision.

15   May one of two or more personal representatives who have obtained a grant of probate or letters of administration

    (*a*) withdraw money standing in the name of the deceased, or

    (*b*) draw cheques on an account opened in their joint names as executors or administrators?

Answer: (*a*) No. In practice prudence demands that no attempt to withdraw monies in the name of the deceased should be allowed unless expressly authorised by all the personal representatives.

(*b*) Where the personal representatives have a joint account the mandate will determine whether or not cheques may be drawn by one only.

16   (*a*) In what circumstances, and (*b*) to whom, should a bank pay away the balance standing to the credit of a deceased customer's account where no grant of probate or administration of the deceased's estate is obtained?

Answer: (*a*) In circumstances where the estate is small and no capital transfer tax is payable and the banker is satisfied that the monies will be distributed in accordance with the unproved will, or if no will, as on intestacy to those entitled. As Parliament has empowered the National and Trustee Savings Banks to pay away sums not exceeding £1,500 without a grant of representation, bankers can in the circumstances pay away a like sum, but they may in suitable instances prudently obtain an indemnity from the payee.

(*b*) Where there is a will, payment will be to the executor or the beneficiary or beneficiaries named in the will, or to a solicitor acting for them; where there is an intestacy, to the following relatives in the order mentioned, or to a solicitor acting for them, namely, the surviving spouse, any child or children, or failing them any grandchildren, parent or surviving parent and brothers and sisters of the whole blood. If the person claiming payment is not in any of these categories, reference should be made to head office.

17   In what circumstances and for what period are executors justified in carrying on their testator's business?

Answer: If the testator's will directs the executors to carry on his business, either for a specified period, as for instance during the life of his widow or the minorities of his children, or at their discretion, or, if it contains a general power to postpone conversion of the estate at their discretion, they will be justified in obeying the direction or in exercising the discretion, as the case may be, but they may be liable to the testator's creditors unless their consent is obtained.

If the executors continue the business with the assent of the creditors, they may employ only the assets which the testator himself employed in it, unless the will permits other portions, or the whole, of the estate to be so employed. The executors will be personally liable for any money they may borrow, or debts they may incur, in carrying on the business, but, unless they are in default to the estate, they will have a right, against the assenting creditors of the testator and the beneficiaries under his will, to be indemnified in respect of their liabilities out of the assets directed or permitted to be employed in the business. Subject to these conditions the creditors of the executors will be entitled to stand in their place in obtaining payment out of the estate, in priority to the testator's creditors and the beneficiaries.

If, however, the will contains no directions to carry on the business or discretionary power to postpone conversion, it is the duty of the executors (or if there is no will, of the administrators) to carry on the business only for such time as is reasonably necessary to enable it to be wound up or sold as a going concern. They may do this even without the consent of the deceased's creditors or beneficiaries; but if without such consent they go beyond the period necessary for winding up or sale, neither they nor their creditors will have any right to indemnity or payment out of the estate.

18   A solicitor asks his broker to sell securities standing in the names of **A** and **B** (who are trustees of **C** deceased) and to credit the proceeds to his 'client' account. What is the practice in a case such as this where the securities are

     (*a*) lodged with the bank;

     (*b*) handed to the bank for the purpose of sale and what are the reasons for any precautions which are taken?

Answer: A solicitor has no authority, apart from that expressly given him, to deal with clients' securities. Normally, therefore, in the case in question the trustees' confirmation would be required both of the sale and of the placing of the proceeds to the credit of the solicitor's client account, whether the securities were already deposited with the bank or handed to it for the express purpose of the sale. Whether or not the confirmation would be called for prior to the sale or when forwarding the sale transfers might depend upon the standing of the solicitor.

19   On the death of a customer having an overdrawn account, should the bank debit his executors or administrators with the amount of the overdraft as soon as the grant of probate or administration is produced?

Answer: Not without the authority of the executors or administrators, who cannot be made personally liable for the deceased's debt without their consent. Even if they have an account in their joint names with a balance sufficient to discharge the debt, there is no right of set-off between that account and the deceased's. The money in the hands of the personal representatives is available for distribution amongst all the creditors of the estate.

Where any debit balance is transferred to the account of the executors or administrators, the bank will lose the benefit of any securities held for the indebtedness.

20   If executors or administrators have two accounts, one used for carrying on the deceased's business, and the other for the receipt of the proceeds of sale of other portions of the estate, is there a right of set-off between them, if one is overdrawn?

Answer: Yes.

21   (*a*) Are executors or administrators personally liable, or is the estate of the deceased liable, for an overdraft created by them on the account in their joint names?

(*b*) Can the bank retain, against such an overdraft, securities deposited by the deceased for securing his liabilities to the bank in his lifetime?

Answer: (*a*) Executors or administrators are personally (but jointly, not severally) liable for money which they borrow, and for other debts which they incur, in the course of administering their testator's or intestate's estate, and their creditors are not creditors of the estate. (*Farhall* v. *Farhall* (1871), L.R. 7 Ch. 123; Leading Cases, 4th Ed., p. 177.)

It is the practice of bankers to obtain an acknowledgement of joint and several liability from joint executors or administrators before permitting overdrafts in their names. This is usually included in the mandate form.

If, however, the liabilities are justifiably incurred, the executors or administrators

    (i) may pledge or charge specific assets of the estate as security for them, and

    (ii) are entitled, if they are not in default to the estate, to be indemnified out of the estate in respect of the liabilities, and the bank is entitled to be subrogated to this right. The bank may thus, by standing in the place of the executors or administrators, indirectly obtain payment from the estate, though they cannot claim directly against the estate for the amounts owing to them.

(*b*) Securities deposited by the deceased cannot be held against the liabilities of the executors or administrators unless recharged by them to secure such liabilities.

If the deceased's account was overdrawn at the time of his death, the bank may continue to hold his securities against his overdraft; but if the executors or administrators take the overdraft into their own names (which they are not obliged to do), it becomes a personal liability of theirs, and ceases to be secured by securities deposited by the deceased, unless these are recharged by them.

It is the practice of some bankers to take from executors or administrators, at the time when an account is opened with them, an authority enabling the banker to retain and apply any credit balance on the deceased's account, and any securities deposited by him, against any overdraft incurred on the account of the executors or administrators.

22 Would it be in order for executors or administrators to authorise any person (not one of themselves) to draw cheques on their banking account?

Answer: In practice, such authority would not be acceptable to the bank. Although sec. 23 of the Trustee Act, 1925, enables personal representatives (i.e., executors or administrators), as well as trustees, instead of acting personally, to employ and pay an agent, whether a solicitor, banker, stockbroker, or other person, to transact any business or do any act required to be transacted or done in the administration of the testator's or intestate's estate, including the receipt and payment of money, it is rarely that personal representatives would be justified in delegating to such an agent the authority to draw cheques on the account opened in their names for the administration of the estate.

An exception might be made if the representatives were also the only beneficiaries, absolutely entitled, under the will or intestacy, and therefore were accountable only to themselves as soon as the debts owing by the deceased were paid, but, apart from this case, it would not be the usual practice of bankers to permit such a delegation.

However, sec. 9 of the Powers of Attorney Act 1971 empowers any personal representative to delegate by power of attorney for a period not exceeding twelve months the exercise or execution of any trusts, powers and discretions vested in him.

23 Has one of several executors or administrators power to stop payment of a cheque drawn by the others?

Answer: Yes.

24 After what period do executors cease to act as such, and become trustees, and how does this change affect the bank conducting the account of the executors?

Answer: When the funeral and testamentary expenses, debts and legacies have been paid, normally the banker is on enquiry as to whether the executors have completed the administration of the estate and are acting as trustees. The passage of time alone is also a warning that the executors may have completed their duties in such capacity and are continuing as trustees of the residue. Unless the estate of the deceased is burdened with properties or unquoted shares which are difficult to realise, the average estate can be wound up in 12-18 months, and any continued operations by the original executors beyond this period should cause enquiry. They may or may not have completed their duties as executors, but prudence demands confirmation of the position.

As trustees, the former executors can no longer delegate their authority, except as permitted under the Powers of Attorney Act 1971 or under the terms of the trust deed if one exists, and a fresh mandate will be required of them.

25 Should a banker accept a cheque drawn by a trustee on the trust account in reduction of his personal overdraft?

Answer: Not unless the trustee is also sole beneficiary of the trust, otherwise the banker is put on notice of a likely breach of trust and if such was the case, the bank would be liable to refund the amount of the cheque to the beneficiaries of the trust (*Gray* v. *Johnston* (1868) L.R. 3H. L1; Leading Cases, 4th Ed., p. 150).

26 Does an account in the name of '**A** re **B**,' or '**A** account **B**' imply that the money in the account is held by **A** on behalf of, or in trust for, **B**?

Should the bank allow withdrawals to be made by **A** without the concurrence of **B,** and can a credit balance be set off against an overdraft on **A**'s private account?

Answer: The mere fact that the account is headed in this way does not, without more, vest the banker with notice of a trust.

The bank is bound to honour the customer's cheques drawn on such an account without the concurrence of the beneficiary, and is not bound to inquire into the propriety or destination of such cheques, unless an obvious breach of trust is being committed; but the credit balance cannot be set off against an overdraft on the customer's private account, if the bank has notice that the customer is not the sole person interested in the money.

27 When trustees have an account, and a new trustee is appointed, whether in place of a deceased or retiring trustee, or as an additional

trustee, should the deed of appointment be produced to the bank?

Answer: It is considered that the deed of appointment should be produced.

Under sec. 40 of the Trustee Act, 1925, a deed appointing a new trustee operates, unless it expressly provides to the contrary, to vest the trust property (with certain exceptions, but not excepting a credit balance of a banking account) in the continuing and new trustees jointly, without any further transfer.

28   Who is entitled to continue the administration of a trust, and to sign on the trust account—

     (*a*) on the death of one of two or more trustees;

     (*b*) on the death of a sole, or last surviving trustee?

Answer: (*a*) the survivors or survivor, under sec. 18 (1) of the Trustee Act, 1925;

     (*b*) until new trustees are appointed, the executors or administrators of the deceased sole, or last surviving, trustee, under sec. 18 (2) of the Act.

29   What statutory powers of delegation are conferred on trustees by the Trustee Act, 1925?

Answer: The statutory powers of delegation are now found in sec. 9 of the Powers of Attorney Act, 1971 which substantially amends the provision of sec. 23 of the Trustee Act, 1925.

A trustee may delegate by power of attorney the exercise or execution of any trustees' powers and discretions vested in him as trustee, provided such delegation is not to a sole remaining trustee (unless such trustee is a trust corporation).

So long as the trustees' discretions and powers are exercised by the trustees, minor administrative acts can properly be performed by agents of the trustees.

Trustees have statutory power to employ and pay an agent whether a solicitor, banker, stockbroker or other person to transact any business or do any act required to be transacted or done, in the execution of the trust. For example, it is in order for trustees to employ estate agents to collect rents from tenants and otherwise to manage tenanted property.

30   Have trustees power to delegate their authority to draw cheques on the trust account to one or more, but less than the whole number, of themselves, as executors may?

Answer: Yes, but only to the extent to which the trust deed so authorises or the Powers of Attorney Act, 1971 so permits (see also Q. 29).

31 Does the rule against delegation by trustees of their powers to one or some of themselves apply to trustees of public or charitable trusts?

Answer: Sec. 34 of the Charities Act, 1960, provides for delegation to not less than two trustees.

JOINT ACCOUNTS

32 If **A** lodges a sum of money at a bank in the names of **A, B** and **C** without instructions, would the banker be liable if he repaid the sum, or any part thereof, on the order of **A**?

Answer: In the absence of instructions from **B** and **C,** he would.

33 **A** and **B** open a joint deposit account and sign a mandate authorising the bank to pay to either. Subsequently **A** transfers an amount from this account to the credit of a new current account in the same two names, to be conducted on the same terms as the deposit account. Is it necessary to have a second mandate signed in connection with the current account, or does the authority already given cover both accounts?

Answer: In practice, most banks are now using a joint account mandate which covers all accounts opened subsequently but where this practice has not been adopted **B**'s confirmation in writing of the terms upon which the current account is opened should be obtained.

34 A joint account is opened, either party having power to sign cheques. A cheque is presented, in the handwriting of and signed by one and altered and duly initialled by the other. Is this acceptable?

Answer: Yes.

35 In the case of a joint account for which the mandate covers operations on the account only when it is in credit, who would be liable if the bank pays a cheque which causes the account to become overdrawn?

Answer: The party or parties who signed the cheque would be liable. In the case of two or more signatories the liability would be joint.

In practice, before allowing the account to become overdrawn a fresh mandate should be taken establishing joint and several liability for overdrafts.

36 A bank receives notice that one of two persons having a joint account with the bank is involved in bankruptcy proceedings. Can the bank safely honour cheques drawn by the other party if it holds an authority to honour cheques of either party on the account?

Answer: No; upon the bankruptcy of a joint account holder, the mandate is immediately determined and the account has to be stopped because a portion of the balance may belong to the trustee in bankruptcy and the bank cannot itself apportion the moneys between the insolvent estate and the solvent party. The account will, of course, be stopped when the bank is aware that a receiving order has been made against one party or upon reliable notice that one of the customers has committed an act of bankruptcy, see sec. 1, Bankruptcy Act, 1914. All cheques presented thereafter drawn by the insolvent party can be returned unpaid marked 'refer to drawer,' but cheques drawn by the solvent party or parties should be returned with a much more explicit answer which leaves no doubt in the mind of the holder that the dishonour is no reflection upon the credit of the drawer. For example, the answer 'joint account customer, **Y,** involved in bankruptcy proceedings' will not damage the credit of **X,** the solvent drawer of the cheque which has to be returned unpaid.

The account has to remain stopped until the balance is withdrawn upon the joint authority of the trustee in bankruptcy or the Official Receiver, acting for the bankrupt estate, and the solvent account holder. Alternatively, the Official Receiver or trustee may expressly authorise the release of the balance to the solvent customer. Where the Official Receiver requests the bank at the outset to disclose the extent of the balance on joint account, the bank should obtain the written authority of the solvent joint customer before revealing the position. Any item held in safe custody in the joint names will likewise be released only upon the joint authority of the Official Receiver or the trustee and the solvent account holder.

37 What procedure should be adopted on the death of one of two or more joint account-holders, (*a*) if the account has a credit balance (*b*) if the account is overdrawn?

Answer: (*a*) The general rule is that, as far as the bank is concerned, the balance of a joint account devolves upon the survivor or survivors.

It follows that there is no need normally to stop a credit joint account upon the death of one party. Cheques drawn solely by the deceased should not be paid without the confirmation of the survivor(s), and when there are two or more survivors a fresh mandate should be obtained from all of them authorising future operations on the account.

(b) Where, as is normal, joint and several responsibility has been established and it is desired to preserve the liability of the deceased's estate, the account should be broken; otherwise, under the rule in *Clayton's Case*, credits paid in after his death will reduce his liability.

In the absence of a mandate whereby all joint account parties contract to be jointly and severally liable to the bank, the liability is joint only and, on the death of one, his estate is discharged from the debt. In such unlikely circumstances, the banker has to rely on the survivors for repayment and the account may be continued unbroken.

38 Is an account in the joint names of husband and wife, if the wife is the survivor, considered to be an exception to the general rule that the credit balance of a joint account is payable to the survivor?

Answer: No: the general rule applies. It may be that, as has been seen in reported cases, the husband's representatives can establish that she has no *equitable* title to the money, but this is not the concern of the bank. The wife has the *legal* title, and the bank can safely pay the balance to her.

39 Two persons, not being partners, open a joint account, which is overdrawn. In the event of one of them failing, is the solvent party responsible for the debt?

Answer: The advance is made to the two jointly and each is liable for the whole debt.

40 A and **B,** who are not partners, have a joint account. The mandate is for 'either to sign'.

(a) **A** draws a cheque leaving the account with a nil balance at the same time instructing the bank to close the account. Should this be done?

(*b*) After the death of **A** a cheque drawn by him is presented for payment. Should it be paid?

Answer: (*a*) Although the mandate entitles **A** to draw, without question, the full amount standing to the credit of the account, it is considered that the account should not be closed without the concurrence of **B**.

(*b*) Not without the instructions of **B**.

41 A father deposits money in the joint names of himself and his son, a boy of fifteen, 'payable to either or the survivor.' At the father's death the son has not yet attained his majority. To whom should the bank pay the money?

Answer: When only a relatively modest sum is involved the normal rules of survivorship can be applied, but, where more substantial amounts arise, legal advice should be taken, bearing in mind the facts in the case of *Young and Another* v. *Sealey* [1949] Ch. 278; Leading Cases, 4th Ed., p. 168.

42 Is any obligation imposed upon bankers, before paying money to a survivor in a joint account, to see that capital transfer tax has been paid?

Answer: No. A banker is not a trustee for his customer, but a debtor to him, and, like any other debtor, may by law safely pay over money due upon a joint account to the survivor in that account.

43 On the sale of stock standing in joint names, can the proceeds be properly credited to the account of one of the stockholders?

Answer: Not without the written instructions of both stockholders, and not even then if they are known by the banker to be trustees.

44 When two or more persons deposit, in their joint names,
  (*a*) bearer securities,
  (*b*) certificates of stocks or shares registered in the joint names,
  (*c*) deeds of properties of which they are joint mortgagees,
  (*d*) deeds of properties conveyed to them jointly,
  (*e*) plate, jewellery, or other chattels,
  (*f*) a locked box, or a sealed parcel,
should the bank, on the death of one of them, allow the survivor or survivors to remove or deal with the articles deposited, without the concurrence of the executors or administrators of the deceased?

Answer: (*a*) to (*d*), Yes, because the legal title passes to the survivor or survivors.

(*e*) and (*f*), In the case of boxes, parcels, plate, jewellery and other chattels it is the practice to require the consent of the deceased's personal representatives.

PARTNERSHIPS

45   An account is opened in the name of a firm entitled 'Samuel & John Smith,' either partner to sign the firm-name. After a time a cheque is presented, signed,

> '*Pro* Samuel & John Smith,
>   Samuel Smith.'

If the banker is satisfied that the signature is that of Samuel Smith, the partner, may he pay the cheque?

Answer: Yes. It is difficult to see what risk a banker would incur by paying a cheque in the circumstances named.

46   If a person, or two or more persons in partnership, trades, or trade, as the 'Moon Foundry Company,' is there any objection to his, or their, signing cheques 'Moon Foundry Company,' without the signature of any individual?

Answer: None, if the bank has been instructed by the owners or partners to pay cheques so signed.

Under sec. 23 of the Bills of Exchange Act,
(1) Where a person signs a bill in a trade or assumed name, he is liable thereon as if he had signed it in his own name.
(2) The signature of the name of a firm is equivalent to the signature by the person so signing of the names of all persons liable as partners in that firm.

47   Is there any objection to opening an account with a firm, one of the partners in which is a minor?

Answer: No; a minor may be an agent, but it will be advisable to obtain an express authority signed by the other partners for the minor to sign cheques, bills and notes on behalf of the firm, if they wish him to do so.

The minor will not be personally liable on such cheques, bills or notes, or for any overdraft or other indebtedness of the firm; and if the firm should become bankrupt, the receiving order will be made against the partners, other than the minor unless the debt incurred is one not falling within the Infants Relief Act, 1874, in which case the minor would be included.

48   Is it the practice of bankers to insist that customers to whom the Registration of Business Names Act, 1916, applies shall register under that Act?

Answer: No, but where the firm name differs from the actual names of the partners, or from the name of the sole proprietor, it is necessary for the customer(s) to register under the Act. Moreover, unless the banker has seen the Certificate of Registration under the Act and has searched the register to obtain confirmation of the names of the partners or proprietors, the banker might be unable to avoid liability for conversion.

49   In what circumstances has a partner in a firm an implied authority to borrow money on behalf of the firm, and to pledge or charge its assets as security for the money borrowed?

Answer: Under sec. 5 of the Partnership Act, 1890, every partner is an agent of the firm and of his fellow partners for the purpose of the firm's business; and his acts, done as a partner for carrying on, in the usual way, business of the kind carried on by the firm, bind the firm and the partners; unless in any particular matter he has in fact no authority to act for the firm, and the person with whom he is dealing either (*a*) knows that he has no authority, or (*b*) does not know or believe him to be a partner.

In order to avoid all question of the authority of the partners, it is the practice of bankers, when opening an account with a firm, or on a change in its constitution, to obtain a mandate, signed by all the partners, stating how bills, notes and cheques are to be signed on behalf of the firm, and authorising the bank to pay and debit bills, notes and cheques so signed to the firm's account, even (if this is the intention) though the account may be overdrawn, or may become overdrawn in consequence of such payment and debit.

If a legal mortgage of freehold or leasehold property belonging to the firm is required, all the partners must join in executing it.

50   Are the partners in a firm both jointly and severally responsible for their firm's overdraft and other liabilities incurred to the bank?

Answer: It is normal banking practice to ask partners to sign an undertaking of joint and several responsibility for the firm's liabilities for, unless this is done, under sec. 9 of the Partnership Act, 1890, every partner is liable jointly with the other partners for debts and obligations of the firm incurred while he is a partner. (See also Q. 49).

51 Can one, of two or more partners in a firm, give a valid mandate or authority for a person not a partner to sign cheques on the firm's account?

Answer: No; the authority of the partner himself to sign cheques is as agent for the firm, and an agent cannot delegate his authority. Such a mandate should therefore be signed by all the partners.

52 Has one partner in a firm authority to stop payment of a cheque drawn on the firm's account by another partner?

Answer: Yes.

53 Can a partner bind his firm by signing on the firm's behalf a guarantee or indemnity for another person's account?

Answer: Not unless it is usual, in a business of the kind carried on by the firm, to give such guarantees or indemnities, or the guarantee or indemnity is necessary for carrying into effect a partnership contract, or is expressly authorised or adopted by the other partners.

54 On the death or retirement of a partner, should the firm's account be broken, if it is (*a*) in credit, or (*b*) overdrawn?

Answer: Under sec. 38 of the Partnership Act, 1890, after the dissolution of a firm the authority of each partner to bind the firm, and the other rights and obligations of the partners, continue for the purpose of winding up the firm's affairs.

(*a*) The continuing partner or partners has or have therefore authority to draw upon the credit balance of the firm's account, which accordingly need not be broken, but the name of the deceased or retiring partner should be struck out of the ledger heading.

(*b*) If it is desired to maintain the liability of the deceased or retired partner for the overdraft (or the liability of a surety), the account should be broken, otherwise credits paid into the account after the death or retirement will, under the rule in *Clayton's Case,* go in reduction of such liability.

If, however, the banker is satisfied with the personal liability of the continuing partner or partners, the account may be continued without a break in this case also.

55   A, B and C are partners. On A's death, B and C continue the partnership account, and, to secure an overdraft which they create on the account, they deposit the deeds of property originally conveyed to A, B and C as partnership property. Is the security valid against the claim of A's executors in respect of his one-third share of the property?

Answer: Yes, the bank's equitable mortgage is valid against the claim of A's executors provided the overdraft has been used for the purpose of winding up the partnership. Otherwise the executors claim would have priority subject to any provisions to the contrary in the partnership deed (if any). It has been held in similar circumstances that the bank was entitled to assume, at all events for a reasonable time, that the account was continued by the surviving partners for the purpose of winding up the firm's affairs.

56   On the retirement of one of the partners in a trading firm, the continuing partners notify the bank that the retired partner will no longer sign on the firm's behalf, and they give the bank a new mandate for the payment of bills, notes and cheques signed in the firm-name by any one of themselves.

Should a bill accepted, or a cheque drawn, on behalf of the firm by the retired partner before his retirement, but presented after, be paid?

Answer: Yes, as the partner was, at the time of the acceptance or drawing, entitled to act as agent for the firm. If the continuing partners do not wish the bill or cheque to be paid, they may stop payment of it.

57   On receiving a balance sheet of a customer who is a sole trader, a banker finds evidence of the existence of a partner of whom he was unaware. Should he take any action with regard to the account?

Answer: The balance of the account should be transferred to a new partnership account with a mandate completed by both partners. It would be advisable to examine the Certificate of Registration under the Business Names Act.

58   What effect has the bankruptcy of a partner on the banking account
of the firm? Is the trustee in the bankruptcy entitled to take part in
the management of the firm's business?

Answer: A partnership is automatically dissolved when a partner
therein is adjudicated bankrupt. The solvent partners are
empowered to continue the business for the purpose of winding-up
and it is their duty to account to the trustee in bankruptcy for the
bankrupt's share in the business. Neither the bankrupt nor his
trustee can interfere in the conduct of the firm and all that the
trustee is concerned with is to obtain an account from the solvent
partners paying over the bankrupt's share in the business.

Although the mandate is determined by the bankruptcy, the
solvent partners may continue to draw cheques and use the account
for the purpose of winding up the business, and where the firm
account is in credit there is no need to stop it. A fresh mandate
should be taken from the solvent partners to confirm their wishes for
the conduct of the account by them whilst they are closing down the
old firm and accounting to the trustee in bankruptcy for the
bankrupt partner's share in the partnership. Cheques drawn by the
bankrupt partner before the commencement of his bankruptcy
proceedings, but presented after the petition or adjudication, should
not be paid without the confirmation of the solvent partners. Any
cheque signed by a partner who, to the sure knowledge of the bank,
has committed one of the acts of bankruptcy should be referred to
his co-partners before payment. In practice, however, the banker
will rarely be fixed with notice of an act of bankruptcy by a partner
in his personal capacity unless, of course, trouble has arisen in
connection with the conduct of his private account.

If the account is overdrawn at the time of a partner's bankruptcy
and the bank wishes to preserve its rights against the insolvent
partner, it must be broken to determine the liability and to avoid the
operation of the rule in *Clayton's Case.* Where the joint and several
liability of the partners has been established for the firm's debts to
the bank, it can claim *pari passu* with the private creditors for the
full amount of the firm debt, less the value of any security deposited
by the bankrupt partner. In the absence of joint and several liability,
the bank's claim against the bankrupt's estate will be deferred until
all his private creditors have been paid in full. In other words,
without joint and several liability there is usually no worthwhile
claim against the bankrupt. Security in the shape of assets of the
firm, or private assets of the solvent partners, is, of course, collateral
for the purpose of any proof against the private estate of the
bankrupt partner.

COMPANIES

59 Where a company mandate by resolution of the Board authorises designated officials to sign on the company's account and changes or additions are made in the officers concerned, what notification or fresh authority is necessary to the bank?

Answer: In the absence of any mandate to the contrary, it is sufficient in the case of the appointment of a new secretary, or other officer, to obtain satisfactory evidence of his appointment, signed by the chairman. This should preferably take the form of a certified copy of the resolution appointing him, but it may be by way of correspondence from the chairman. In the case of the appointment of a new director, a certified copy of the resolution should be obtained.

60 A private company has only two shareholders, who are also the only directors of the company. The articles provide (*a*) that there are to be not less than two directors, (*b*) that the quorum at a board meeting, unless otherwise fixed by the directors, is to be two, and (*c*) that the qualification of a director is to be the holding of at least one share in the company. The resolution of the board authorising the signature of cheques requires them to be signed by two directors.

On the death of one of the two director-shareholders, how can the survivor provide for the valid signature of cheques on the company's account, pending the appointment of personal representatives of the deceased?

Answer: Clause 100 of Table A (1948), if not excluded by the company's articles, enables the surviving director, notwithstanding the vacancy, to act as a director for the purpose of increasing the number of directors to the minimum number required. He should appoint some person to fill the vacancy, and, within two months thereafter, should transfer at least one share in the company to him, or the newly appointed director will automatically vacate his office under sec. 182 of the Act. The two directors will be in a position to sign cheques under the original resolution, or to pass a further resolution, if so desired.

If however Clause 100 of Table A (1948) is excluded, and the company's articles contain no similar provision, the surviving director cannot sign cheques or transact any business, and steps should be taken under sec. 135 of the Companies Act, 1948, for a meeting to be called and a new director appointed.

N.B.—Reference would have to be made to the relevant Table A of any company statutes prior to the Act of 1948.

61 Where the sole directors and secretary of a company who between them hold all the company's shares die in an accident or otherwise simultaneously, what can be done to enable the company to continue trading and use its bank account?

Answer: The personal representatives of the deceased cannot procure the registration of themselves as shareholders without the aid of the Court, as there is no board of directors to approve and effect the registration. Further, the personal representatives not being registered shareholders, cannot appoint new directors. As the company is without direction and incapable of making decisions concerning its business affairs, the personal representatives should immediately, with legal advice, apply to the Court for the registration of themselves as shareholders and such other relief as the Court may provide, possibly including the appointment of directors. Any interim borrowing may need to be secured otherwise than from the company and care should be exercised to ensure that any payment to the debit of the company's account before and subject to the directions of the Court pending the appointment of new directors, is only in respect of the true and just debts of the company.

62 A company's cheque, which should bear the signatures of two directors, countersigned by the secretary, is signed by one director and the secretary with autograph signatures, but the second director uses an impressed stamp, purporting to be a facsimile of his signature. Is such a facsimile valid?

Answer: The facsimile signature is valid only if authorised by the company. Such authority should be obtained covering all cheques bearing the facsimile signatures, by whomsoever affixed.

63 A company incorporated in a foreign country opens an account with a bank in London. Is it necessary for the London bank to inquire whether the company has complied with the requirements of the law of the country in which it is incorporated, or to see that the account is conducted in accordance with those laws?

Answer: The bank should satisfy itself that the persons with whom it is dealing are properly authorised by the law of the foreign country, and by the company's statutes and by-laws, to act for the company. This may conveniently be done by enlisting the aid of a correspondent bank in the country concerned. Such banker's confirmation of the signatures is desirable.

64 A banking account is opened for a company whose articles state that there shall be not less than three directors, but only two are appointed. The mandate empowers any two directors to sign. Is this situation acceptable?

Answer: No. A banker should refuse to open or continue an account for a company the board of which he knows is not properly constituted. Until the company appoints a third director the account should be stopped as far as payments are concerned.

65 Is a cheque in order if signed in the following manner?
               'For the **X** Company Limited

                            Peter Jones,
John Smith, Secretary.   John Smith,   Directors.'

   John Smith is both a director and the secretary of the company, and the bankers are authorised to honour cheques signed by two directors and the secretary.

Answer: The mandate implies that signatures of three different individuals are required. Sec. 179 of the Companies Act, 1948, prohibits a person from acting in a dual capacity where there is a provision or requirement authorising a thing to be done by a director and the secretary, but until the section receives judicial interpretation no opinion is expressed whether it has any application to a bank mandate. The section, however, supports the view that the safe and correct course is to treat the mandate as requiring the signatures of three different individuals.

66 Is a banker safe (*a*) in discounting bills on the endorsement of the secretary of a company, the proceeds being placed to the credit of the company's current account, or (*b*) in transferring sums from the deposit account to the current account of the company, on the signature of the secretary only, without a minute of authority from the directors instructing such transactions, provided the cheques subsequently withdrawing the money from current account are signed in accordance with the directors' resolution authorising operations on that account?

Answer: Unless express authority is contained in the mandate, the only safe course in either case would be to procure a covering authority from the company by resolution of the directors.

67 Does a banker incur any risk in handing a cheque book to the secretary of a company when the order is duly signed by the secretary only? The secretary is authorised to countersign the company's cheques.

Answer: No.

68 Is a resolution of the board necessary before transferring the credit balance of a company's dividend account to its general account, or may the bank act on a cheque signed in accordance with the general instructions given by the company as to signing cheques?

Answer: The bank may act on a cheque signed in accordance with instructions, provided those instructions are so worded as to apply to the dividend account.

69 (a) May John Jones trade as John Jones Limited without being registered as a limited company?
(b) May the Soho Coal Co. Limited (this company being registered as a limited company under the Act), trade also as the Strand Coal Co. Limited, without registering the latter title?

Answer: (a) No. Under sec. 439 of the Companies Act, 1948, a person trading or carrying on business under a name of which 'limited,' or a contraction or imitation of that word, is the last word, shall, unless incorporated with limited liability, be liable to a fine of £5 for every day on which the name has been used.
(b) No. Although a company is not debarred from carrying on business under a name 'which does not consist of its corporate name without any addition' provided registration is effected under the Business Names Act, 1916 (extended to companies by sec. 58 of the Companies Act, 1947), the Registrar will refuse to register a name ending with the word 'limited.'

70 The directors of a company pass a resolution authorising its bankers to honour cheques signed by any two directors and countersigned by the secretary. If cheques are honoured in excess of the credit balance, can the bankers recover from the company the amount of the overdraft?

Answer: Yes, provided the borrowing is for a purpose within the powers of the company as described in its memorandum of association. In practice, the mandate will expressly authorise the payment of cheques signed as indicated whether the account of the company is in credit or overdrawn, but in any event the directors are usually empowered by the articles to borrow for the normal business of the company. Unless there is clear evidence to the contrary or there are circumstances putting him on enquiry the banker is entitled to presume that the directors, acting within the mandate, are drawing for a purpose within the ordinary course of business of the company.

A commercial or trading company has, subject to its memorandum and articles, an implied power to borrow to any extent for the purpose. Moreover, where anyone dealing with a company has satisfied himself that the transaction is not inconsistent with the memorandum and articles, he is not bound to verify, or enquire into, the regularity of any internal proceedings (*Royal British Bank* v. *Turquand* (1856) 6 E. & B. 327, Leading Cases, 4th Ed., p. 185).

71   The borrowing power of a company's directors is limited by its articles of association to a total of £30,000 at any one time. The company has a credit balance with its bankers of £10,000 and at the same time a loan from them of £35,000. Is this borrowing *ultra vires* the directors?

Answer: In the absence of express arrangements to the contrary, the banker may set-off the credit balance against the loan and have regard to the net indebtedness, which is *intra vires*.

72   What protection is afforded the bank by sub-section 1 of section 9 of the European Communities Act, 1972 if it should lend money to a company for a purpose which is 'ultra vires'?

Answer: None, because it is established English banking practice to require production of the memorandum and articles of association of a company customer and the bank is therefore on notice of their contents.

73   A company's articles of association provide that the powers of the directors to borrow money, including loans from the company's bankers, are limited so that the amount outstanding at any one time shall not exceed a certain figure without the consent of the company

in general meeting. What is the best course for a banker to adopt if he wishes to lend to the company in excess of this figure?

Answer: The company should be asked to pass an ordinary resolution in general meeting authorising borrowing by the directors from the bank up to a specified figure and ratifying any previous borrowings in excess of the limit provided by the articles. This procedure is not only simpler and quicker than an alteration of the articles, for which a special resolution is required, but also protects the banker against *ultra vires* excesses over the limit which might have been taken unknown to him due to borrowing from other sources.

74 Under sec. 95 of the Companies Act, 1948, every charge created by a company registered in England on land, wherever situated, or any interest therein is void against the liquidator or any creditor of the company unless the prescribed particulars of the charge are registered within twenty-one days after the date of its creation.

What is the date of the creation of the charge in the following cases?

(*a*) Deeds are deposited under an equitable mortgage on June 29, but no advance is made until July 2.

(*b*) Deeds are deposited under an equitable mortgage to secure any balance which may become due. The advance is made by way of overdraft upon current account, and the balance of the latter is a fluctuating one, sometimes in credit, sometimes overdrawn.

Answer: In both cases the charge is created by the company when the equitable mortgage is executed and delivered, not when the money is advanced. (See *Esberger* v. *Capital and Counties Bank,* [1913] 2 Ch. 366; Leading Cases, 4th Ed., p. 274).

75 (1) Express power being given to the directors in a company's articles of association to create equitable charges upon its landed property, deeds of its property are deposited with its bankers as security for an overdraft upon current account. The deeds are accompanied only by a copy of the resolution of the board, signed by the directors, authorising the deposit. No registration of the deposit as a mortgage or charge is made, either in the books of the company or with the Registrar of Joint Stock Companies. Is this a valid security to the bank?

(2) Would the answer be the same if the articles of association

give power to mortgage but do not expressly mention equitable charges?

Answer: (1) and (2). In each case the charge is valid but would be void against the liquidator and any creditor of the company, unless registered as required by sec. 95 of the Companies Act, 1948.

76   A company has three directors, and two of them have guaranteed its overdraft. The bank afterwards requires additional security, and it is agreed that the company shall issue to the bank a debenture charging the company's assets as security for the overdraft. The articles provide that the quorum at a board meeting is to be two, and that no director shall vote in respect of any contract or matter in which he is interested. Can the proposed debenture be validly issued?

Answer: In *Victors* v. *Lingard,* [1927] 1 Ch. 323 (Leading Cases, 4th Ed., p. 190), where the articles provided that no director should vote in respect of any contract or matter in which he was interested, and all the directors had guaranteed the overdraft, it was held that a resolution to issue debentures to the bank was invalid, on the ground that all the directors were interested in the provision of additional security for the debt for which they had all made themselves personally responsible. No doubt if only some of them had guaranteed the debt, and if a number of disinterested directors, sufficient to constitute a quorum, had voted for the resolution, it would have been valid. In the case put in the question this cannot be done, because there is only one disinterested director, and the quorum is two.

The issue of the debenture might however be validated by a resolution of a general meeting of the company, at which the interested directors, if shareholders, would be entitled to vote as shareholders; and it would be valid without such a resolution if the directors were the *only* shareholders of the company, and if their decision to issue the debenture were unanimous.

77   The bank is asked to lend money to company **A** in order to enable it to purchase the shares of company **B**. Debentures and cross-guarantees are taken by way of security from both companies. The loan is taken up but in the event the borrowing is repaid not from company **A**'s assets but from a sale of the assets of company **B**.

Both companies a few years later are put into liquidation and the bank subsequently receives a claim from the liquidator that the original transaction was in breach of sec. 54 of the Companies Act, 1948. What is the bank's position?

Answer: Sec. 54 of the Companies Act, 1948 provides that it is unlawful for a company directly or indirectly to give any financial assistance by way of loan, guarantee, provision of security or otherwise, for the purpose of, or in connection with, a purchase of, or subscription for shares in the company or its holding company made or to be made by any person.

There are exceptions:

(*a*) for the lending of money by the company in the ordinary course of business.

(*b*) for the provision of money to trustees for the acquisition of shares for employees.

(*c*) for the making of loans to *bona fide* employees (other than directors) to acquire for their own account shares in the company or its holding company.

Contravention of the section is an offence but whilst the criminal penalty imposed is limited to a fine not exceeding £100, nevertheless civil action may be brought following the liquidation of a company which may result in very substantial losses for a bank; for example, the bank which is party to a transaction in breach of sec. 54 may be liable as a constructive trustee insofar as it assisted the directors to misuse the funds under the control of the company, and if the bank should have been put on enquiry by the circumstances, it may be liable to its customer for negligence. Security given to or by the company in respect of financial assistance in contravention of sec. 54 is void.

It may be asked what advice should be given to avoid the possible infringement of this section and the answer must be that company **A,** when it makes its offer to purchase the shares of company **B,** should be able to repay any borrowing which is taken out of its own resources and not look to the assets of company **B.**

78 A bank receives notice that a petition for the winding up of a company customer has been presented. On contacting the managing director the bank is told that the petitioner is a trade creditor with whom they are in dispute over the quality of the goods which he supplied. The creditor has, however, issued a petition alleging indebtedness in a sum exceeding £200 (sec. 223(*a*), Companies Act, 1948); sch. 1, sec. 1, Insolvency Act, 1976). The managing director assures the bank that the company is solvent and that the petition

will be dismissed by the court. He, therefore, asks the bank to continue to run the company's bank account to enable the company's business to be continued.

How should the bank respond to this request?

Answer: The problem here is that whilst, if the facts given are correct, the petition will in all probability be dismissed, there is no certainty that this will happen. Under sec. 229 of the Companies Act, 1948, a winding up order relates back to the time of the presentation of the petition for winding up and from that time any disposition of the company's property is void, unless the court orders otherwise (under sec. 227).

Strictly, therefore, it is necessary to stop the payment of all cheques immediately the bank receives notice of a petition, although cash in respect of essentials, such as wages, may be paid out against the receipt of an authorised official under the ruling in *Mersey Steel Co.* v. *Naylor* [1884] 9 A.C. 434.

The bank's reaction to the customer's request to continue the account must depend upon its faith in the customer and its knowledge of the company's financial strength.

The safest course would be to stop the account and insist upon the company making application to the court for an order under sec. 227 permitting specified cheques to be paid for the major payments needed to keep the business operating, whilst allowing cash to be drawn under the *Mersey Steel Co.* v. *Naylor* ruling enabling the smaller payments to be made in cash. This would take time, of course, and as the order would relate to specific payments only, would make life difficult for the customer.

Alternatively, banks often feel that the strength of the company is such that the risk of a winding up order being granted is slight so that they can allow the account to be continued unbroken, relying in the event of winding up upon the court exercising its discretion under sec. 227 to validate *bona fide* transactions which the bank has entered into in the ordinary course of business for the purpose of enabling the company to continue its business which would be deemed, therefore, to be for the benefit and in the interests of the company.

If the company's account is overdrawn it would be advisable to break the account and open a new account to be operated in credit so as to avoid the Rule in *Clayton's* case operating to the detriment of any security which the bank may hold.

79   What action should the bank take upon the appointment of a
receiver for the debenture holders of a company customer? Is it
protected in its dealings with the balance if it has not received notice
of the appointment?

Answer: The bank should of course discuss the position with the
receiver.

If the debenture contains a floating charge the bank must not, on
receiving notice of the appointment of a receiver for the debenture
holders, without the receiver's consent, pay any cheques drawn on
the company's accounts having credit balances, and must on
demand pay such balances to the receiver, unless they are required
by the bank as set-offs against debit balances on other accounts of
the company. Credit balances cannot be retained by the bank
against contingent liabilities of the company on bills discounted.
(*Bower* v. *Foreign and Colonial Gas Co.* (1874), 22 W.R. 740.)

The position regarding overdrawn accounts will depend upon the
security held by the bank but, unless there are unusual circumstances, it would be normal practice to break overdrawn accounts.
Much depends upon the type and extent of security granted in the
Debenture and legal advice may be required.

It is not considered that the bank is affected by the appointment
of a receiver unless it receives notice, or becomes aware, of the
appointment, which is not required to be advertised, though it must
be notified to the Registrar of Companies. (Sec. 102 of the
Companies Act, 1948.)

80   A company having a credit balance on its current account discounts
bills with its bankers. A receiver and manager is appointed on behalf
of the debenture-holders, and notice of the appointment is given to
the bank. Can the bank hold the credit balance of the company as a
set-off against its contingent liability for the bills discounted?

Answer: No, not unless there is an irrevocable agreement for
set-off with the customer, but if the company went into liquidation
the bank would be obliged to set-off the credit balance against the
company's contingent liability on the bills.

81   A company goes into liquidation, having at the time a debit balance
on current account, and various credit balances on dividend
accounts, made up of unclaimed dividends.

Can these credit balances be applied by the bank in reduction of
the overdraft in case of need?

Answer: Yes. It is not considered that balances on dividend accounts are impressed with a trust in favour of the holders of the dividend warrants.

82 A company declares a dividend and transfers the amount of the dividend from its general current account with its bankers to the credit of a 'Dividend Account.' Before the dividend warrants are all presented for payment:

(a) the company goes into compulsory liquidation; or

(b) a receiver for the debenture-holders is appointed. .

Does the balance of the dividend account belong to the shareholders whose warrants are outstanding, or to the liquidator or receiver as the case may be?

Answer: To the liquidator or receiver.

83 Sec. 322(1) of the Companies Act, 1948, provides that when a company is being wound up, a floating charge on the undertaking or property of the company created within twelve months of the commencement of the winding-up shall, unless it was proved that the company immediately after the creation of the charge was solvent, be invalid, except to the amount of any cash paid to the company at the time of or subsequently to the creation of, and in consideration for, the charge together with interest on that amount at the rate of five per cent. per annum, or such other rate as may for the time being be prescribed by order of the Treasury.

To what extent, therefore, may a bank rely on a floating charge taken as security for the existing indebtedness of a company which goes into liquidation within twelve months of creation of the charge?

Answer: Whether or not a company is solvent when it creates a floating charge is a question of fact depending on whether it can pay its debts as they fall due. The fact that the assets exceed the liabilities is not of itself sufficient to prove solvency.

It follows that when a bank takes a floating charge as security and the company goes into liquidation within twelve months of the date of the charge, the security will usually be available only to cover amounts advanced by the bank in consideration for, or subsequent to, the creation of the floating charge. Whilst a floating charge will be useless to secure a dormant debt incurred before the charge was created, it will be valid to cover any fresh advances granted after the date of the charge, and with an active account the rule in *Clayton's Case* will operate in favour of the bank.

In the case of *In re Thomas Mortimer Ltd.* [1925], (Leading

Cases, 4th Ed., p. 333), it was held in such circumstances that all amounts credited to the account after the date of the charge went in reduction of the original overdraft on the account, whilst all sums withdrawn after due date of the charge were 'cash paid to the company in consideration for the charge' and were validly secured by it. This ruling was reaffirmed in the case of *In re Yeovil Glove Co. Ltd.* ([1962] 3 All E.R., 400; Leading Cases, 4th Ed., p. 331).

84 In what circumstances has money advanced to a company for the payment of wages or salaries priority in the event of (*a*) the company's liquidation, or (*b*) the appointment of a receiver by debenture-holders?

Answer: (*a*) Under sec. 319 of the Companies Act, 1948, money advanced for the payment of the wages or salary of a clerk or servant or the wages of a workman or labourer for four months, prior to the company's liquidation, if the money is so applied, is entitled to priority of payment out of the company's assets *pari passu* with other preferential debts. (The amount so protected has increased from £200 to £800 by the Insolvency Act, 1976).

(*b*) Under sec. 94 of the Act of 1948, a similar priority is granted (and the amount was similarly increased by the Insolvency Act) to advances for the payment of wages and salaries prior to the date of the appointment of a receiver by the holders of a debenture or debentures containing a floating charge, or to the date of possession being taken by or on behalf of such debenture-holders, but only in respect of the assets subject to the floating charge, not of those subject to any fixed charge contained in the debenture(s).

The extent to which a bank may rely on this right to step into the shoes of the wage earners and rank as a preferential creditor in their place, subject to the given limitations on time and amount per person, will depend upon the facts of each case. Where there is only one account used expressly for wage payments, little difficulty will emerge and, even where the bank's advances for wages are made through the ordinary current account of the company, they may have priority so far as such advances are not extinguished by subsequent credits. The position may be complicated in practice by the provisions in secs. 64-69 of the Employment Protection Act, 1975, enabling the Secretary of State, upon an insolvency, to make payment out of the Redundancy Fund in respect of payments due to the employee, including salaries, wages and holiday pay. Any such payments by the Secretary of State will rank as preferential in the same manner as payments by the bank.

85 The question of opening a special wages account is normally recommended for a company customer who is in financial difficulties but what is the bank's position if a company goes into liquidation, or a receiver is appointed under a floating charge, and wages have been paid not from a special account but from the company's ordinary current account?

Answer: Although the practice of opening a special account for wages is to be recommended if it seems likely that a company customer may be wound up, this step is not essential. The banker may claim preferential status for wages advances made through the company's ordinary account—see *Re Primrose* (*Builders*) *Limited* (1950) 1 Ch. 561; Leading Cases, 4th Ed., p. 339.

The risk involved in making the wages advances through the company's ordinary account is that credits paid into the account may have the effect of repaying the preferential wages advances before those advances have ceased to be preferential. The ultimate result will depend, therefore, upon the turnover in the company's ordinary account (i.e. the extent and frequency of payments in and out). A rapid turnover would have the effect of repaying the preferential advances speedily and the benefit of the above-mentioned legislation would be lost.

To calculate a preferential claim where wages have been paid on the company's ordinary account it is necessary to note the debit balance at the date of liquidation (or the appointment of a receiver). Then, starting with the *last* debit entry and working backwards through the account, cast up all the debit entries back to the point where their total equals the final overdraft figure.

Wages cheques paid in the period between that point in the account and the date of liquidation may be claimed as preferential debts, subject to the provisions of sec. 319 of the Companies Act, 1948 and other limitations (see Question 84). It will be readily appreciated that with a substantial turnover, it may not be possible to claim wages advances during the full period of 4 months.

Wages cheques frequently include sums which are not utilised for wages, but are required for national insurance, holiday funds, etc., or for payment of sub-contractors who cannot be classified as employees. These are not preferential debts and the final figure agreed by the liquidator or receiver is therefore unlikely to match the total of payments advanced by the bank.

86 Overdraft facilities were agreed for a limited company on the condition that the sole director, Mr. A, would undertake not to demand repayment of a loan he had made to the company while the bank advance remained outstanding.

A written undertaking was duly given by Mr. A, but, in a subsequent review of the company's accounts, the bank discovered that the loan from Mr. A had been repaid. Mr. A disclaims responsibility. He contends that he had at no time demanded repayment of his loan but that the company had decided to repay it, and that he, on his part, had accepted.

Mr. A holds 99 of the 100 issued shares of the company, his wife holding the remaining one. Can the bank claim therefore that Mr. A, in controlling the affairs of the company, has in effect repaid himself the loan in breach of his undertaking to the bank?

Answer: Mr. A is relying on the well-established principle that the company is a separate legal entity (*Salomon* v. *Salomon & Co. Ltd.* ([1897] A.C. 22) and that the acts of the company are not necessarily the acts of Mr. A as a shareholder. The undertaking he gave does not therefore bind the company in any way.

To protect itself the bank should have required the *company* to join in the undertaking by agreeing not to repay A's loan. The usual *deed of postponement* required in this situation should, ideally, also have referred to present and *future* borrowing.

87 When two or more joint liquidators of a company are appointed, may one, or less than the whole number, of them sign cheques on the banking account opened for the purpose of the liquidation?

Answer: (*a*) In a voluntary winding-up, whether members' or creditors', if two or more liquidators are appointed, their powers may, under sec. 303 (3) of the Companies Act, 1948, be exercised by such one or more of them as may be determined at the time of their appointment, or, in default of such determination, by not less than two.

(*b*) In a winding-up by the Court, sec. 242 (4) of the Act provides that if more than one liquidator is appointed by the court, the court shall declare whether any act authorised or required to be done by them is to be done by all or by any one or more of them.

The liquidator in a winding-up by the court (but not in a voluntary winding-up) must pay all moneys received by him into the Companies Liquidation account at the Bank of England, unless the Department of Trade authorise him to have an account at such other bank as the Committee of Inspection may select (sec. 248 (1)). All payments out of such an account are to be made by cheques payable to order, bearing the name of the company, and signed by the liquidator, by at least one member of the Committee of Inspection, and by such other person, if any, as the Committee may appoint. (Companies (Winding up) Rules, 1949, Rule 170.)

LOCAL AUTHORITIES

88   Should the banking accounts of a local authority be conducted in the name of the authority, or in the name of its treasurer, and how should cheques drawn on behalf of the authority be signed?

Answer: Sec. 151 of the Local Government Act, 1972, stipulates that every local authority shall make arrangements for the proper administration of its financial affairs and shall secure that one of its officers has responsibility for the administration of those affairs.

Arrangements for handling receipts and payments necessarily extend to the operation of the banking account of the local authority, including not only the terms agreed for management but also the number of accounts to be opened, the manner in which they are to be operated, and the name or names in which they are to stand. It is, therefore, incumbent upon the local authority to decide the name of the account and the manner in which cheques may be drawn and to authorise the bank so to act by appropriate mandate embodied in a resolution passed by the council.

The account will normally be opened in the name of the authority, but where a subsidiary account is opened upon the express instructions of the authority in the name of an officer it should be designated as an account of the officer of the council, and not as an account of the individual. For such accounts subsidiary to the local authority's main account it is prudent to arrange that any overdrafts require the express approval of the authority.

The local authority should furnish the bank with a complete mandate by resolution of the council or corporation stating precisely how and by whom cheques are to be signed on each account. The method to be adopted rests with the local authority and the bank's duty is to comply with the mandate given to it.

89   (*a*) Must a local authority have a separate banking account for each of its separate functions and activities, or will one banking account suffice for all?

(*b*) If separate accounts are kept, can a credit balance on one account be set off against a debit balance on another?

Answer: (*a*) The number and nature of separate banking accounts to be maintained by a local authority rests with the officer responsible acting within sec. 151 of the Local Government Act, 1972, but it is usual for separate accounts to be kept for:
  (i) Motor tax receipts,
  (ii) Any trading undertakings carried on under special local Acts or Orders which restrict the application of surplus revenue to certain specified purposes, and
  (iii) The Loan Fund, if it exists.
  (*b*) Where separate banking accounts are kept for purposes other than those mentioned above in (i), (ii) and (iii), a local authority may consent by resolution to a set-off between credit and debit balances on such other accounts. It is usual to operate the accounts of a local authority (other than the exceptions stated above) on a group basis to show daily the net amount due to or from the bank.

90   The accountant of a District Council wishes to open in his own name a petty cash imprest account, into which it is intended that the council shall make periodic transfers of money from their General Rate Fund account.
  Is the authority of the council necessary for opening such an account?

Answer: Yes; the account should preferably be opened in the name of the council itself, styled 'Accountant's Petty Cash Account,' and a resolution should be obtained authorising the accountant to draw on it. The approval of the full-time treasurer or the chief financial officer must be obtained.

91   For what evidence should the bankers of a local authority ask concerning the appointment of a new treasurer, accountant, or other official of the authority, who on appointment is entitled *ex officio* to sign, or to join in signing, cheques on the authority's accounts?

Answer: On the appointment of a new treasurer or chief financial officer, the bankers should obtain a copy of the minute recording the appointment of the new official, duly certified by the chairman and countersigned by the clerk or chief executive officer.
  On the appointment of other officers, written advice signed by the full time treasurer or the chief financial officer will suffice.

SOCIETIES

92   What procedure should be adopted in opening an account with

(a) a Building Society, (b) a Friendly Society, and (c) an Industrial and Provident Society, and what are their borrowing powers respectively?

Answer: In all these cases a copy of the society's rules should be examined, with particular reference to the powers of the directors or committee, and to any provisions regarding the signing of cheques. A resolution opening the account and conferring authority on the persons who, in accordance with the rules, are to sign cheques should be passed by the directors or committee, and a copy of the entry in the minute book, certified by the chairman and the secretary should be supplied to the bank, together with specimen signatures of the authorised persons. In the case of Building Societies, the Certificate of Incorporation should be exhibited and likewise, with Friendly Societies, the Certificate from the Chief Registrar of Friendly Societies.

Subject to any special provisions in the rules, the borrowing powers are as follows:

(a) Under the Building Societies Act, 1962, a Permanent Building Society may borrow, or receive on deposit, up to two-thirds of the amount for the time being secured to the society by mortgages from its members (not including mortgages the payments in respect of which were upwards of twelve months in arrear at the date of the society's last preceding annual statement, or mortgages of properties of which the society had been twelve months in possession at that date). A Terminating Building Society may in its rules adopt either the two-thirds limit mentioned above, or a limit equal to twelve months' subscription on the shares for the time being in force.

An unincorporated Building Society registered under the Act of 1836 has a borrowing power to the extent expressly conferred upon it by its rules, but no further.

(b) A registered Friendly Society is allowed by the Friendly Societies Act, 1974, to hold, and to mortgage, land, and to charge any other property as security if its rules contain an express provision to that effect. But any borrowing allowed by the rules must be strictly necessary to the carrying on of the Society's activities.

(c) An Industrial and Provident Society registered under the Acts of 1893-1968 may borrow money for the purpose of its business if the rules so permit and may charge as security any assets which its rules allow to be charged.

If there are no provisions with regard to borrowing, the society may mortgage any land which it is authorised by its rules to hold (sec. 36). It may create mortgages on land and also issue debentures creating a fixed or floating charge on its property or assets (except personal chattels). Debentures require registration within 14 days of creation at the Central Office of the Registry of Friendly Societies.

93 What is the custom of bankers in opening accounts with un-registered associations such as clubs, societies, etc? Is there any objection to opening an account with such a society and taking the instructions of the committee of management on the drawing of cheques?

Answer: The custom is, after examining the rules of the club or society, to open the account in its name, the treasurer or other official or officials being authorised to sign cheques by resolution of the committee of management, in accordance with the rules.

The practice of opening accounts in the personal name or names of officers of the association was once common but is not now usually accepted. It may, however, be appropriate where a small group of people form a temporary organisation or an informal 'club'. The nature of the account should nevertheless be specified in the title, e.g. J. Smith (Sports Club Account).

94 What should be a banker's attitude when asked to allow an over-draft on the account of an unincorporated body such as a social club etc?

Answer: Voluntary organisations such as clubs and societies which are not incorporated cannot be sued, neither are the individual members who administer the funds personally liable for an over-draft provided that the members of the committee or council deputed to act on the account clearly sign cheques in their represen-tative capacities and have not held themselves out as having authority to overdraw. Such an overdraft is, therefore, not recoverable at law so it is essential that the banker obtains security. A joint and several guarantee by responsible persons is usually obtained (the guarantee must cover the incapacity of the principal debtor) unless other security is available.

If the club owns property it will be vested in trustees who may execute a mortgage under authority expressed by resolution of the governing committee. Care must be taken to ensure that the rules of the club enable the committee to exercise such authority: if in doubt a resolution should be passed at a general meeting of the members.

95 An account is opened under the title of 'Parish Hall, per H. D. Rogers.'

Rogers subsequently desires to give Smith an authority to draw cheques, but the bank objects that he has no power to delegate his authority.

Rogers contends that no official status is appended to his name and that the effect is the same as if the account had been opened under the style of H. D. Rogers *a/c* Parish Hall, in which case he contends that he could have operated as he pleased.

Is the bank right or wrong?

Answer: Having regard to the irregular form of the account, the contention of the bank is correct. The question is really whether the funds are under the sole control of Rogers or whether he is the trustee of trust funds. If enquiry shows that he is not entitled to the funds authority from those managing the Parish Hall should be obtained and preferably the account should be closed and re-opened in the name of the body in which the management of the Parish Hall is vested, with a resolution of that body authorising the proper official or officials to sign on the account.

96 What is the correct form in which the banking account of a Parish Church in England should be opened, and who may sign cheques on such an account?

Answer: The account should be opened in the name of 'The Parochial Church Council of . . . Parish' upon the authority of a resolution of the Council, duly signed by the Chairman, which should embody precise instructions as to operations on the account.

97 A and **B** open an account at Northtown in the name of the Northtown Methodist Chapel Trust, and state that they have been appointed by the rest of the trustees to act as secretary and treasurer respectively.

How should the account be opened, and who should sign?

Answer: The account should be opened in the name of the Northtown Methodist Chapel Trust, and the bank should ascertain the powers of the trustees from the trust deed and have a copy of the resolution authorising certain members of the body to sign cheques in accordance with the powers so conferred.

The rule against delegation by trustees does not apply to the trustees of a charitable or public trust.

98   An account is entitled
         'X Chapel,
             A, *Treasurer.'*
The present treasurer has been told that, in the absence of a
guarantee to secure an overdraft, cheques which overdraw the
account will only be paid on his responsibility.

     A small debit balance now exists, which the treasurer declines to
pay out of his own money.

     Is he liable after being so warned or not?

Answer: The treasurer would not be liable unless it could be
proved that he accepted the conditions stated.

99   With regard to the accounts of units of the Army (Regular or
Territorial), or of the Royal Air Force,

     How should such accounts be opened, and by whom should
cheques drawn on them be signed?

Answer: The accounts of a Regiment, Battery, Battalion, Royal
Air Force Squadron, or other unit should in the first instance be
opened by the Commanding Officer, who should designate the
officers having authority to sign cheques on the accounts, and
should supply specimens of their signatures.

     Subsequent changes should be notified by the Commanding
Officer, or by the Adjutant acting on his behalf.

DEATH

100   What should be considered sufficient evidence of the death of a
customer?

Answer: The sure knowledge of the event or the production of a
death certificate. A letter or confirmation from the deceased's
nearest relatives or solicitors, accountants or other professional
persons acting in the estate will suffice. Announcements in responsible newspapers have generally been an adequate guide, but
mistaken announcements have been noticed.

101   If, on the day on which a banker becomes aware of a customer's
death, cheques drawn by or on behalf of the customer have been
presented for payment in the clearings, or received direct from other
bankers, should these cheques be returned?

Answer: Yes; unless the presenting bankers have already been
informed that the cheques are paid.

102 Should bills accepted by a customer payable at his bank be paid after the bank has received notice of the customer's death?

Answer: No; although sec. 75 of the Bills of Exchange Act mentions only cheques drawn on the bank, the bank's duty and authority to pay bills accepted payable at the bank are also determined by notice of the customer's death.

103 If a customer who has given to his banker an order to buy or sell stocks, shares or bearer securities dies before the settlement day, can the banker, notwithstanding his death, debit his account with the cost, or credit it with the proceeds, as the case may be?

Answer: Yes, since in doing so he is merely completing the contract already entered into by the customer.

104 On the death of the treasurer, secretary or other official of a society or club, who has had authority to draw cheques on the society's or club's account, should cheques signed by him and presented after his death be returned?

Answer: No; the deceased was not the 'customer,' and sec. 75 of the Bills of Exchange Act does not apply.

105 One of the partners in a firm, each of whom signs cheques in the firm-name, dies, and cheques signed in the firm-name by him are presented after his death. Should such cheques be paid or returned?

Answer: Upon the death of a partner, the surviving partners are empowered to continue the business for the purpose of winding-up the firm's affairs (See Question 54). Strictly speaking, cheques drawn by the deceased partner should be returned unpaid marked 'Drawer deceased' unless payment is confirmed by the survivors. In practice, they might be paid without such confirmation, but where the account is in debit the deceased partner's estate cannot be held liable for the amount of cheques paid after his death even though he has signed them. Therefore, when the account is in debit the cheques should be returned unpaid as above, the account should be stopped and proof made in the deceased's estate unless satisfactory arrangements are made with the remaining partners to take over full liability for the debt.

106 If **A** gives his banker a mandate or authority to pay cheques drawn on his account by **B,** should cheques drawn by **B** under the mandate, but presented after **B**'s death, be paid or returned?

Answer: As **A,** who was in effect the drawer of the cheques drawn on his behalf by **B,** is still alive, the cheques should be paid, notwithstanding the death of **B.**

107 Should a banker accept from his customer a mandate or authority to pay cheques drawn on the customer's behalf by his wife, with a provision that the mandate is not to be revoked by the customer's death, but is to continue in force for a period of a month after his death?

Answer: A mandate containing such a provision should not be accepted. Even if accepted it would be determined at once by the customer's death, and no cheques drawn under it could lawfully be paid after notice of that event, unless confirmed by the customer's executors or administrators.

108 If a customer dies, when and upon what authority can the banker release:
(*a*) credit balances in the sole name of the deceased;
(*b*) securities and other articles deposited in the name of the deceased;
(*c*) the will of the deceased?

Answer: Although an executor derives his title and powers from the will itself, which comes into operation immediately the testator dies, probate of the will, or letters of administration where applicable, are required for conclusive proof of the executor's or administrator's power to act.

It follows that:
(*a*) Any balance on the banking account of the deceased should not be withdrawn by the executor(s) or administrator(s) until probate or letters of administration are produced. Instructions can then be given to transfer the balance to the account of the executors or administrators.

The provisions of the Administration of Estates (Small Payments Increase of Limits Order, 1975) permit the disposal of certain property (under £1,500 in each case) to persons entitled without representation. Thus, the bank may agree to pay out, under indemnity, balances below this amount to the persons holding themselves out to be entitled without production of grant of representation.

(*b*) All items held by the bank on behalf of the deceased customer likewise should not be released until a grant of probate or administration is produced. They may, however, be examined by the executors or their approved solicitors to assist in marshalling the assets of the estate for the Inland Revenue Affidavit.

(*c*) The will of the deceased is a necessary exception to the foregoing rules and can be delivered as soon as possible after the testator's death to the executors named in it or to their solicitors.

(See Question 44 for items held in joint names.)

109 Is there any objection to a banker's receiving money for the credit of a customer's account after the customer's death?

Answer: None, unless the banker is aware that the money is an instalment of a pension or annuity that would cease to be payable on the customer's death.

If probate or letters of administration have not been produced, the money received may be credited either to the deceased customer's account, or to a separate account to be dealt with by the executors or administrators after production of the grant.

110 Should a banker continue to receive, after the death of a customer, dividends which have hitherto been paid to the banker and credited to the customer's account under mandates signed

(*a*) by the customer, in respect of dividends on stocks and shares standing in his name;

(*b*) by other persons presumably trustees for the customer, in respect of the dividends on stocks and shares standing in their joint names?

Answer: (*a*) Although mandates for the payment of dividends to a banker are probably determined, like other mandates, by the death of the person who has signed them, it is a common, but not universal, practice for bankers in such circumstances to continue to receive the dividends, crediting them to the account of the deceased, or to a new account to be operated upon by the executors or administrators after production of the grant.

(*b*) The instructions of the stockholders should be sought, and in the meantime dividends received should be credited to an account opened in their joint names.

111 Where interest is payable on credit balances does it cease to be payable on the death of the customer?

Answer: No; the practice in such cases would be to allow interest until the money is withdrawn.

BANKRUPTCY

112 If a banker hears that a customer is insolvent but no receiving order has been made, is he justified in dishonouring cheques issued by that customer? What is a banker's liability if he pays a customer's cheques after he has heard from a reliable source that the customer is in a state of insolvency?

Answer: A mere statement by the customer or by other persons that the customer is 'insolvent' will not alone justify the banker in dishonouring the customer's cheques. The test is whether the banker is fixed with notice that the customer has committed an available act of bankruptcy (see sec. 1, Bankruptcy Act, 1914).

As soon as reliable notice of an act of bankruptcy is received the account should be stopped to ensure that no cheques payable to third parties are paid, as the amount so paid away could be recovered by a trustee in bankruptcy under the doctrine of 'relation back'. The customer may, however, be permitted to withdraw cash over the counter, provided there are adequate funds in the account; if such payments are pursuant to the ordinary course of business or otherwise *bona fide*, they are protected by sec. 46, Bankruptcy Act, 1914. These restrictions upon the operation of the account should be continued for three months from the date of the act of bankruptcy unless notice of a petition is received or a receiving order is made.

113 A customer has, to the knowledge of the bank, committed an act of bankruptcy. His account is overdrawn and there is ample margin of security to cover further drawings. Should the banker allow the customer to draw cheques for cash over the counter?

Answer: No. By virtue of the doctrine of relation back, the securities will be admitted to have belonged to the trustee in bankruptcy from the date of the available act of bankruptcy of which the bank has notice. Thus the bank will not be able to look to the security as cover for such drawings.

114 Is it safe to continue the current account of a customer who has called his creditors together, and arranged with them to accept a composition of less than 100 per cent?

Answer: Even if the notice to the creditors was not an act of bankruptcy, the offer of the composition at the meeting can hardly have failed to amount to a notice of suspension of payment of debts. The account should therefore not be continued, but the balance may be paid to the debtor himself under sec. 46 of the Bankruptcy Act, 1914.

115 A customer writes to his banker: 'I have called a private meeting of my creditors for Wednesday next, and will see you after that.' Is this an act of bankruptcy?

Answer: The question whether a notice to creditors does or does not amount to an act of bankruptcy is often a difficult one.

The essential requirement is notification to creditors generally (not just one or two) of the debtor's intention to suspend payment of his debts.

The banker should obtain a copy of the notice calling the meeting and, if in doubt as to its effect, should seek legal advice immediately.

116 A customer issues a circular calling a meeting of his creditors, and stating that he is unable to meet his business engagements. Does this constitute an act of bankruptcy?

Answer: Yes.

117 A customer writes as follows: 'I am obliged to pull up, so suspend payment from today.' At the time of receipt of this letter there is a credit balance on the account of £200, and bills under discount £110. Before further instructions can be obtained from the customer a cheque and an acceptance are presented. Should the banker refuse payment; if not, can he retain an amount equal to the liability for bills under discount?

Answer: The acceptance should not be paid, nor should the cheque, if it is payable to a third party.

The credit balance, or part of it, cannot be retained as a set-off against the contingent liability on the bills, until a receiving order is made.

118 Should the cheques of a customer who has a credit balance on his account be returned in either of the following cases, on the ground that an act of bankruptcy has been committed; and if so, what answer should be given?

(a) The customer's goods are seized by the sheriff or by the county court bailiff under an execution levied against him.

(b) A judgment creditor has served upon him a bankruptcy notice requiring him to satisfy the judgment within seven days.

Answer: (a) An act of bankruptcy is committed if the execution is levied under process in an action in any court, or in any civil proceeding in the High Court, but not before the goods have been either sold or held by the Sheriff or Bailiff for twenty-one days (except where an inter-pleader summons has been taken out). (Bankruptcy Act, 1914, sec. 1 (1) (e).)

(b) An act of bankruptcy is committed when, but not before, the period of seven days from the date of service of the bankruptcy notice has elapsed without satisfaction of the judgment (sec. 1 (1) (g).) Until then, knowledge of the service of a bankruptcy notice is not notice of an act of bankruptcy. (*Herbert's Trustee* v. *Higgins,* [1926] Ch. 794.)

In either case when the bank has notice that the act of bankruptcy has actually been committed, the customer's cheques payable to third parties should be returned, and the appropriate answer is considered to be 'Refer to drawer.'

119 A customer executes a deed of assignment for the benefit of his creditors. Can his banker safely part with any credit balance to the trustee named in the deed before the expiration of the three months within which a creditor may present a petition?

Answer: Yes, provided the deed has become effective; if the payment were made before the actual date on which a receiving order is made, and without notice of the presentation of a bankruptcy petition, the payment is made to a person claiming by assignment from the debtor, and as such is protected by sec. 46 of the Bankruptcy Act, 1914.

The trustee may open an account in the name of the debtor's estate, but he should not be allowed to draw cheques on the account until three months have elapsed since the execution of the deed, as unless all creditors have assented to the deed, a petition could be based on it. (The three months may be reduced to one month where non-assenting creditors have been served with notice of the deed). Before assenting to the deed or allowing the trustee to deal with the customer's credit balance, the bank would need to peruse its terms carefully and after taking into consideration all prevailing circumstances (e.g. the standing of the trustees) the bank may exceptionally allow the trustee to operate the account before the three month period has elapsed.

120 A customer is insolvent and calls his creditors together. At the meeting it is agreed that he shall assign everything to a trustee on behalf of the creditors. After execution of the deed of assignment, but before all the creditors have assented to the deed of assignment, the debtor commences trading again in another part of the town. Does the bank incur any liability in allowing him to open a new account in such circumstances?

Answer: The bank should not open a new account in the circumstances. Any creditor (or group of creditors for that amount) for £50 or upwards, not having assented to the deed may, at any time within three months, present a bankruptcy petition based on the execution of the deed as an act of bankruptcy, and, if adjudication follows, the title of the trustee in bankruptcy will relate back to the date of execution, or to the date of any earlier act of bankruptcy committed within three months before the presentation of the petition. (Sec. 37 of the Bankruptcy Act, 1914.)

121 A firm in which **A** and **B** are the partners assigns its partnership assets to a trustee for the benefit of the firm's creditors. Can **A**'s bankers safely allow him to continue to draw cheques on the credit balance of his private account?

Answer: As the act of bankruptcy constituted by the execution of the deed of assignment is the act of both partners, the bankers should not, within the period of three months available for the presentation of a petition in bankruptcy founded on it, pay cheques drawn by **A** on his private account in favour of third parties; but (subject to what is said below) it is considered that the bankers would be protected by sec. 46 of the Bankruptcy Act, 1914, in paying cheques drawn by **A** payable to and presented by himself, provided that the bankers have no notice of the presentation of a petition, and that a receiving order has not actually been made.

It is, however, possible that the deed of assignment may expressly include the separate assets of the two partners, as well as their joint assets. In that case the balance of **A**'s account will be payable to the trustee under the deed as **A**'s assignee, but until three months have elapsed, only under the conditions mentioned above.

122 A customer who has an overdraft on his account, and for whom bills not yet due have been discounted, commits an act of bankruptcy of which the bank has notice. Before a bankruptcy petition is presented, the customer offers to take up one of the undue bills by paying cash for it, under rebate of discount for the time unexpired. Can the bank safely accept the money, and deliver the bill to the customer?

Answer: No, the bank should refuse to deliver the bill against payment. If the funds are provided by the acceptor who wishes to accelerate payment of the bill and who has provided the customer with cash to take it up from the bank, the safest course would be for the acceptor to be requested to attend at the bank himself and take up the bill. It is not considered that sec. 46 of the Bankruptcy Act, 1914, would protect the bank so far as the receipt of the cash is concerned because that section has no relevance to a payment *by* a person subsequently adjudged bankrupt.

123 A becomes bankrupt. At the date of the receiving order there is a credit balance of £100 on his current account, and the bank holds bills discounted for him, but not yet due, amounting to £200. There are no other liabilities to the bank, present, future or contingent.

    (*a*) Must the bank pay the credit balance to the trustee in the bankruptcy?

    (*b*) For what amount should the bank prove in the bankruptcy?

Answer: (*a*) The bank is entitled to hold the credit balance as a set-off against the contingent liability of A's estate on the bills discounted.

(*b*) If proof has to be lodged before the bills fall due, or if, when due, they are dishonoured by the acceptors the bank may prove, and may receive dividends upon, the total amount of the bills after deducting the credit balance of the account.

If, however, the bank wishes to vote at a meeting of A's creditors it must, for the purpose of voting, but not of dividend, estimate the value of the liability to it of the acceptors and other parties to the bills prior to A, and must deduct such estimated value from the proof. (Bankruptcy Act, 1914, 1st Schedule, Rule 11.)

If the acceptors or other prior parties to the bills also become bankrupt, the bank may prove against the estate of each for the amount of the bills to which he is a party, deducting any sums received from, or dividends actually declared in the estate of, that or any other party to the bills, but not receiving more than 100p. in the pound. Dividends declared or sums received after proof do not have to be deducted for the purpose of future dividends.

124 If the acceptor of a bill discounted for a customer becomes bankrupt, or goes into liquidation, can the bank insist on the customer's taking up the bill at once?

Answer: No; the customer's liability as drawer or endorser does not become enforceable until the bill is dishonoured at maturity, and he receives notice of the dishonour. (Sec. 55 (2) (*a*) of the Bills of Exchange Act.)

125 A customer, whose account is overdrawn, pays into it a sum of money with an instruction that the money is intended to meet a certain cheque. The banker accepts the money for this purpose, but before the cheque is presented the customer commits an act of bankruptcy, of which the banker is aware. Should the banker pay the cheque when presented, or if not, what should he do with the money?

Answer: The position appears to be as follows:

(*a*) The mandate to apply the money in payment of the cheque is revocable until acted upon, and will be *ipso facto* revoked by the customer's bankruptcy, if that ensues within three months.

(*b*) In that event the revocation will relate back to the time when the act of bankruptcy was committed.

(*c*) If the banker, on the further instruction of the customer, had informed the holder of the cheque (before the act of bankruptcy) that the money was held to his order, this would have constituted an equitable assignment of the money to him, and the payment of the cheque, if made without notice of the presentation of a petition and before the making of a receiving order, would then have been protected by sec. 46 of the Bankruptcy Act, 1914, as a payment to an assignee of the customer.

(*d*) If, however, no such communication was made to the holder of the cheque before the act of bankruptcy the payment of the cheque would not be protected, and accordingly it should not be paid.

(*e*) The repayment of the money to the customer himself at his own request (if no communication has been made to the holder of the cheque) would, it is considered, be protected by sec. 46, if effected without notice of a petition and before the making of a receiving order.

(*f*) If the money is not repaid to the customer, and his bankruptcy ensues, it may be claimed by the trustee in the bankruptcy. If not so claimed, it will go in reduction of the overdraft.

126 Can a banker safely collect a cheque for a customer whom he knows to have committed an act of bankruptcy?

Answer: Yes, provided the proceeds are held in suspense for three months from the act of bankruptcy in order to see whether bankruptcy ensues. If the customer becomes bankrupt within that period, the title of the trustee will relate back to the act of bankruptcy, and the trustee will be deemed to have been the 'true owner' of the cheque collected unless the banker can obtain protection under sec. 46 of the Bankruptcy Act, 1914. (See Question 112.)

127 A customer who is in business saves some money, and wishes his daughter (a minor) to have the benefit of it, while not losing entirely his control of the money. He places it on deposit in the joint names of himself and the daughter. Some years afterwards, through a large bad debt, he is rendered insolvent and becomes bankrupt.

(a) Can the trustee in the bankruptcy claim the money deposited?

(b) If the trustee is not aware of its existence, should the bank inform him?

(c) If the trustee in bankruptcy does not claim the money, should the bank allow the father to withdraw it, before or after his discharge from bankruptcy, during the daughter's minority?

Answer: (a) When a father deposits money in the joint names of himself and a child a legal presumption arises that he intends to make a gift of it to the child, at all events in the case of the child's surviving him; but such a gift is invalidated (i) if the father becomes bankrupt within two years after the gift, or (ii) if he becomes bankrupt within ten years after the gift, and was not, at the time of making it, able to pay all his debts without the aid of the money deposited (sec. 42 (1) of the Bankruptcy Act, 1914). In either of these cases, the trustee will certainly claim the money, and even if the gift is not invalidated he may perhaps claim the money because of the father's contingent interest in it in the event of his surviving his daughter. Should the trustee so claim, it would be necessary for the bank to be protected by an order of the court against possible subsequent claims by the daughter. If the daughter predeceases the father, payment will then be made by the bank to the trustee instead of to the father.

(b) If the trustee is unaware of the joint deposit, the bank should inform him of its existence.

(c) Unless the trustee states definitely that he makes no claim to the money, the bank should not, without his consent, allow the money to be withdrawn until the father obtains his discharge, nor should it be withdrawn until the daughter attains her majority, and then both should sign for it. During her minority, the daughter cannot give a valid authority for payment of the money to the father.

128 A convened a meeting of his creditors and declared himself insolvent and unable to pay each and every one of his creditors, having at the time £66 to the credit of his current account. Prior to the act of bankruptcy, two cheques for £200 and £400 had been simultaneously presented and dishonoured.

  (a) Have the payees of these cheques any claim on the estate prior to that of the general body of creditors?

  (b) Is the credit balance payable to the trustee in A's bankruptcy?

Answer: (a) No, because in England a bill or cheque does not, of itself, operate as an assignment of funds in the hands of the drawee available for the payment thereof (Bills of Exchange Act, sec. 53 (1)). But it is otherwise in Scotland.

  (b) Yes, unless it is required by the bank as a set-off against some liability of A's.

129 Certificates of shares in a company are deposited by a customer with a memorandum of deposit to secure his overdraft from time to time. No notice of the charge is given to the company. On the customer becoming bankrupt, can the banker retain the certificates and enforce his charge against the trustee?

Answer: The memorandum of deposit creates an equitable charge in favour of the bank which takes priority over the trustee in bankruptcy's claim.

130 A banker holds for a customer a life policy on the customer's life and in his favour as part of an arrangement for an overdraft. There is no assignment of the policy to the banker nor any memorandum of deposit. The customer becomes bankrupt and the trustee asks for the delivery of the policy to him. Can the bank retain the policy as security for the overdraft which is in excess of the surrender value and, if so, how can the security be realised?

Answer: The deposit for security creates an equitable mortgage of the policy which can be retained by the bank against the trustee. However, the bank cannot surrender the policy without an assignment and, unless the trustee is willing to redeem this for its surrender value, he must be asked to execute a surrender to the insurance company or a sale to a third party and authorise the payment of the proceeds to the banker. In such circumstances he may reasonably be entitled to charge the banker a small fee for his services.

131 A deposits with his bankers warrants for goods lying in a public warehouse. The warrants are transferred, by endorsement on the back, to the bank, and bear on the face the following: 'This warrant must be presented regularly assigned by endorsement and all charges must be paid before the delivery of the goods can take place,' also, 'Deliver the above-mentioned goods to A or assigns as by endorsement hereon.'

Is it necessary for the bank to give notice to the warehouse-keeper that the warrants are assigned to the bank, and to get such notice acknowledged by him in writing, or does the possession of the warrants, regularly assigned to the bank, secure to the bank the control of the goods in the event of A becoming a bankrupt?

Answer: If the warrants were issued by warehouse-keepers having power, under a private Act of Parliament, to issue transferable documents of title to the goods deposited in their warehouses (as, for instance, the Port of London Authority and the Liverpool Warehousing Company Limited), the transfer of the warrants by endorsement and delivery would be sufficient to transfer the possession of the goods, without any notice to the warehouse-keepers or attornment by them; and it appears that the warrants of some other warehouse-keepers may acquire the attribute of negotiability by mercantile custom. But in other cases, or if mere warehouse certificates or receipts are held, the documents should be sent to the warehouse-keepers with a request to transfer the goods into the bank's name.

132 B deposits security with a bank for the overdraft from time to time of the bank's customer A, but does not undertake any personal liability for the overdraft. Later A, by various means, makes large payments into his account, which reduce and ultimately pay off the overdraft. B thereupon demands the release of his security, and the bank complies. Shortly afterwards A becomes bankrupt, and his repayment of the overdraft is held by the bankruptcy court to have been, under sec. 44 of the Bankruptcy Act, 1914, a fraudulent preference of B as surety for it. The bank accordingly has to refund the money to the trustee in the bankruptcy.

Has the bank any remedy against **B**?

Answer: Yes. Secs. 92 and 115 of the Companies Act, 1947 (unrepealed in the 1948 Act) provide that in the bankruptcy of an individual or a firm, where there has been (within six months before the liquidation or bankruptcy) a fraudulent preference of a person interested in property mortgaged or charged to secure the bankrupt's debt, that person is to be subject to the same liabilities, and to have the same rights, as if he had undertaken to be personally liable as surety for the debt, to the extent of the charge on the property or the value of his interest in it (estimated as at the date of the transaction constituting the fraudulent preference), whichever is the less.

This remedy is made applicable in the case of companies by sec. 321 of the Act of 1948.

133 A bankrupt customer has at the date of the receiving order an overdraft on his current account, against which the bank holds security deposited by the debtor, and also a guarantee by a third party. For what amount should the bank prove in the bankruptcy?

Answer: Under Rule 10 (Second Schedule to the Bankruptcy Act, 1914), a secured creditor (i.e. a creditor holding a mortgage, charge or lien on the property of the debtor, or any part thereof, as security for the debt owing to him) may, if he realises his security, prove for the balance of the debt, after deducting the net amount realised.

Under Rule 11, if the secured creditor surrenders his security to the official receiver or trustee for the general benefit of the creditors, he may prove for his whole debt.

Under Rule 12, if the secured creditor does not either realise or surrender his security, he must deduct the value at which he assesses it from the amount of his debt for the purpose of proof.

A guarantee not being a security upon the property of the debtor, its amount does not have to be deducted.

If the assessed value of the security on the debtor's property is deducted, the valuation may at any time, with the leave of the trustee or of the court, be amended (Rule 14), and if the security is realised after proof, the net amount realised is substituted in the proof for the assessed value (Rule 16), dividends already received being in either case, if necessary, adjusted (Rule 15).

Before realisation the trustee may at any time redeem the security at the assessed value, or if he is dissatisfied with the valuation, he may require the property to be offered for sale. The secured creditor may at any time, by notice in writing, require the trustee to elect whether he will or will not exercise his power of redeeming the security or of requiring it to be realised, and if then the trustee does not within six months signify his election to exercise the power he will not be entitled to exercise it; and the equity of redemption, or any other interest in the property vested in the trustee, will vest in the secured creditor, whose proof will be reduced by the amount of the valuation (Rule 13).

134 Under what conditions can interest on a bankrupt customer's overdraft, accruing after the date of the receiving order, be recovered?

Answer: (*a*) If no security on the property of the debtor is held, no interest after the date of the receiving order can be included in the banker's proof, unless there is a surplus of the bankrupt's estate, after payment in full of all the debts proved in the bankruptcy. Such interest, in that event, is payable at 4 per cent. per annum. (Sec. 33 (8) of the Bankruptcy Act, 1914.)

(*b*) If the banker holds a security on the property of the debtor, and considers its value to be less than the amount of the debt, he will no doubt decide to prove against the estate, deducting, as he must, the estimated value of the security. In that case also, as in (*a*), no interest accruing after the date of the receiving order can be included in the proof. If, however, the security is one which produces income, in the shape of rents, profits or dividends, receivable by the banker without the aid of the trustee in the bankruptcy, as in the case of a legal mortgage of land, or a mortgage of stocks or shares standing in the name of the banker or his nominees, such income may be applied by the banker in or towards payment of accruing interest on the debt. The banker will lose this advantage if the trustee decides to redeem the mortgaged property at the value placed upon it in the proof; but if the trustee does not exercise his right of redemption, or of requiring the property to be offered for sale, within six months after being called upon by the banker to elect whether he will exercise it or not, the banker will become the absolute owner of the mortgaged property, and may deal with it as he pleases.

(*c*) If the banker, holding a mortgage as in (*b*), considers the value of the property to be greater than the debt, he will probably decide to stand aside from the bankruptcy proceedings, and not to lodge a proof. In that event, if the proceeds of the property, when ultimately realised by the banker, justify his estimate by exceeding the capital amount of the debt, the excess may be applied in or towards payment of interest up to the date of repayment, any ultimate surplus being accounted for to the trustee. The same rule will apply if the banker originally estimated the value to be less than the debt, and accordingly lodged a proof for the difference, but the proceeds turn out to be greater; but in this case he must refund to the trustee any dividends that he may have received on the proof.

(d) If the banker holds a guarantee or other third-party security in the usual form, this may be held and applied in or towards the recovery of both principal and interest accruing before or after the date of the receiving order.

135 A customer whose overdraft is secured by his mortgage to the bank of a policy for £100 on his own life, without profits, becomes bankrupt at a time when the surrender value of the policy is £50 and the overdraft £180. No other security is held. In its proof the bank values the policy at £50, and, deducting that sum, proves for £130. Before any dividend is declared, the customer dies, and the bank receives £100 from the insurance company. Must the bank's proof be reduced by deducting £100 instead of £50?

Answer: Yes; Rule 16 of Schedule II to the Bankruptcy Act, 1914, provides that if a creditor after having valued his security subsequently realises it, the net amount realised shall be substituted for the amount of any valuation previously made by the creditor.

136 A and B are partners. The firm, and each partner, all have accounts at the same bank, and A deposits security belonging to himself to secure his own liabilities either alone or jointly. The firm, and therefore each partner, becomes bankrupt, and at the date of the receiving order the firm's account and A's account are overdrawn, but B's account is in credit.

    (a) Must the bank, in proving against the firm's estate, deduct the value of the security deposited by A?

    (b) Can the bank set off B's credit balance against the firm's debt?

Answer: (a) No; a joint creditor holding a security on the separate estate of one of the partners is entitled to prove against the joint estate for the full amount of his debt without giving up or deducting his security.

The test is, whether the security if given up would augment the estate against which proof is sought to be made. (*Re Turner, ex parte West Riding Union Banking Co.* (1881) 19 Ch.D. 105; *Re Rushton, ex parte National Westminster Bank Ltd.* v. *Official Receiver* [1971] 2 A11 ER 937).

The proceeds of the security may be apportioned by the bank in whatever way is most to the bank's advantage. (*Re Foster, ex parte Dickin* (1875), L.R. 20 Eq. 767).

(*b*) In the normal way the mandate taken by a bank when opening a partnership account will establish the joint and several liability of the partners. If this has been done, **B**'s credit balance can be set off against the partnership debt.

If, however, joint and several liability has not been established, the joint debt is a joint responsibility only and **B**'s separate account cannot be set off.

137 Under what conditions may proof be made, in a firm's bankruptcy, against the separate estates of the partners for a debt owing by the firm?

Answer: In the normal way, the mandate taken by a bank when opening a partnership account will establish the joint and several liability of the partners and proof can then be made in the firm's bankruptcy against the separate estates of the partners. In the absence of such a mandate a debt owing by the firm cannot be proved against the separate estates in competition with the separate creditors of each estate.

Sec. 33 (6) of the Bankruptcy Act, 1914, provides that in the case of partners the joint estate shall be applicable in the first instance in payment of their joint debts, and the separate estate of each partner shall be applicable in the first instance in payment of his separate debts. If there is a surplus of the separate estates, it shall be dealt with as part of the joint estate. If there is a surplus of the joint estate, it shall be dealt with as part of the respective separate estates in proportion to the right and interest of each partner in the joint estate.

138 A and **B** are partners in a firm which fails, and, in consequence, **A** and **B** also become bankrupt. At the time of the failure **A** has an overdraft on his private account guaranteed by **B**. Can the bank prove against the assets of the firm as well as against the private estates of **A** and **B,** or is the claim restricted to the latter only?

Answer: **A** and **B** are not jointly liable for **A**'s debt, but each is separately liable for it. Consequently the debt cannot be proved against the joint estate in competition with the joint creditors. (See sec. 33 (6) of the Bankruptcy Act, 1914.)

139 The account of a firm is secured by (*a*) property mortgaged by a partner to secure his own liabilities either alone or jointly, and (*b*) a guarantee by a person not a member of the firm.

In the event of the firm's bankruptcy, for what amount should the bank prove against the firm's estate, and in what order should the securities be realised and applied in reduction of the debt?

Answer: Since (*a*) a joint creditor holding a security on the separate estate of one of the partners is entitled to prove against the joint estate for the full amount of his debt without giving up or deducting his security; and since (*b*) under a guarantee in the usual banker's form for securing the whole liabilities of the person or firm guaranteed, with a limitation on the amount recoverable from the guarantor, the bank may prove for and receive dividends on the whole debt; the bank should prove against the firm's estate for the whole amount of the firm's debt, without deducting either the value of the partner's security or the amount of the guarantee.

The security and guarantee may be realised in any order convenient to the bank, and money recovered under them should be held in suspense until a final dividend in the firm's bankruptcy is received.

140 A bank is holder of a bill for £100, the drawer and acceptor of which have failed. The bank has proved against the drawer and received a dividend, amount £50, and the bill has been endorsed to that effect. Must the bank when proving against the acceptor deduct the amount of the dividend received from the drawer and claim only for the balance?

Answer: He must, if the proof against the estate of the acceptor is made after the declaration of the dividend on the drawer's estate; otherwise proof can be made against both estates for the full amount of the bill.

141 A bank holds a bill for £100, the drawer and acceptor of which have failed. No dividend has been declared. The bank proves against both parties for the full amount. In due course a dividend of £20 is paid from the estate of one of the parties, and the bill is endorsed to that effect. Shortly after, a similar dividend is declared from the estate of the remaining party. Will the trustee of the latter pay dividend on the full amount proved for, when he sees from the endorsement on the bill that the bank has already received a dividend of £20?

Answer: He will, as proof against both parties was made in the first instance.

142 A customer leaves at the bank bills endorsed by him with a view to their being discounted if inquiries to be made as to the solvency of the acceptors prove satisfactory. Pending such inquiries the bank makes small temporary advances to the customer on the security of the bills, and before any of the bills are actually discounted, the customer becomes bankrupt. Must the amount of the bills be deducted from the bank's proof in respect of the advances made to the customer?

Answer: Bills deposited 'pending discount' need not be valued and deducted. The bank can prove for the full amount due and recover from the other parties to the bills, provided that not more than 100p. in the pound is received.

If after proof against the customer's estate any of the bills held as collateral security are paid, the amounts received must be deducted from the proof for the purpose of future dividends. (*Re Bentley, ex parte Brunskill* (1835) 4 D. & C.442.)

143 A files his petition owing his banker at the time £100 on unsecured overdraft and with a further liability to the banker of £200 on two unmatured bills discounted for him. The banker proves for the £300 and receives a total dividend of 50p. in the £.
How must this dividend be applied?

Answer: The banker is entitled to recover from the acceptors on the bills in full. In respect of the unsecured overdraft the banker will receive 50p. in the £. Anything more than 100p. in the £ which the banker receives on the bills must be refunded to A's estate.

144 A guarantor for a customer's account becomes bankrupt, and, as the account guaranteed happens to be in credit at the time when the receiving order is made against the guarantor, the bank does not prove against his estate. Can the guarantee be relied upon for any overdraft incurred by the customer after the guarantor has obtained his discharge from bankruptcy?

Answer: Sec. 28 (2) of the Bankruptcy Act, 1914, provides that, with certain exceptions immaterial to this question, an order of discharge shall release the bankrupt from all debts provable in bankruptcy.

It is considered accordingly that the guarantor would be discharged from liability in the case put in the question.

145 A customer whose account is overdrawn executes a deed of arrangement for the benefit of his creditors. Can the bank claim interest on the balance from the date of the deed until the claim is sent in to the trustee; or does the case come under the bankruptcy rule which prohibits a claim for interest accruing after the date of the receiving order?

Answer: Such a deed is an act of bankruptcy. Assuming no bankruptcy proceedings follow, the payment of interest is dependent upon the terms of the deed, and a deed of arrangement usually provides that the debtor's estate shall be divided amongst the creditors in the same manner as if the estate had been administered in bankruptcy.

If bankruptcy ensues, proof for interest can be made only to the date of the receiving order, unless there is a surplus. (Sec. 33 (8) of the Bankruptcy Act, 1914.)

146 A customer has entered into a deed of arrangement by executing an assignment of his property to a trustee for the benefit of his creditors generally. The balance of his account has been stopped and transferred to the trustee. The bank is approached to allow drawings on the trustee's account immediately the deeds and assents to it are registered. Should the bank agree?

Answer: As the execution of the deed constitutes an act of bankruptcy, no payments should, strictly speaking, be made from the trustee's account until three months after execution of the deed, as during this period it is available for the foundation of a petition, unless summary notice has been issued, when payments could be made after one month. If, however, the whole body of creditors has assented to the deed, there seems little likelihood of a petition being presented, and therefore it would appear safe to honour cheques payable to third parties on the trustee's account. Deeds usually provide for payment in full up to £10 to £20. It should be noted that the trustee has no statutory power to borrow.

147 **A,** who has an overdraft on his account, gives equitable mortgages on lands, cottages and shares as security. A makes an assignment to a trustee for the benefit of his creditors. The bank offers to surrender all securities to the trustee on his paying them off, which the trustee refuses to do. Up to what date can the trustee claim the rents of the lands and cottages, and dividends on the shares?

Answer: The trustee is entitled to claim the rents and dividends until the bankers obtain the appointment of a receiver, or otherwise exercise their rights as mortgagees.

148 An undischarged bankrupt presents for payment an open cheque drawn in his favour by a customer of the bank. The trustee has not intervened; what is the banker's position towards his customer and towards the trustee,

    (*a*) where he does not know of the bankruptcy;

    (*b*) where he knows of the bankruptcy?

Answer: (*a*) If the banker does not know of the bankruptcy, he pays the cheque to the holder in good faith and without notice of the holder's defective title, and he thus obtains a good discharge under sec. 59 of the Bills of Exchange Act, and can debit his customer. Although the trustee is the 'true owner' of the cheque, he cannot sue the banker for conversion of it after it has been paid in due course.

(*b*) If the banker is aware of the bankruptcy, he has notice that the trustee is, *prima facie,* the true owner of the cheque and that the payee's title to it may therefore be defective. Payment of the cheque should not therefore be made without enquiry of the trustee in view of the risk to the banker involved in making payment which might not be regarded as in due course under sec. 59. If the payee will not leave the cheque for the requisite enquiry to be made, the cheque, before being handed back to the payee, should be marked in such a way as to protect the credit of the drawer by the use of some such words as 'Title of payee requires confirmation.' If the banker is satisfied that the cheque was received by the bankrupt in the capacity of a trustee it is considered that it may safely be paid as the trustee in bankruptcy would not in such circumstances have any interest in the money.

149 Does a banker run any risk in collecting for a customer a cheque payable to a third party who is known by the banker to be an undischarged bankrupt?

Answer: Yes; unless the bank is collecting for a customer of undoubted standing to whom he would have recourse. If the cheque had in fact belonged to the trustee, the circumstances in which the customer obtained it might not be such as to divest the trustee of his title.

150 Can an undischarged bankrupt act as agent? Would a banker be justified in honouring his signature on behalf of the drawer of a cheque?

Answer: An undischarged bankrupt may act as agent, and the banker would not incur any special risk in the circumstances. An undischarged bankrupt may not, however, act as a director of a limited company. (See Q. 154.)

151 (*a*) What risk does a bank run by opening a current account for a man known to be an undischarged bankrupt?

(*b*) Does a bank incur any liability by allowing a person known to be a nominee of an undischarged bankrupt, to open and work a current account, and to draw against cheques payable to, and endorsed by, the bankrupt?

Answer: (*a*) Sec. 47 (2) of the Bankruptcy Act, 1914, provides that where a banker has ascertained that a person having an account with him is an undischarged bankrupt, then, unless the banker is satisfied that the account is on behalf of some other person, it shall be his duty forthwith to inform the trustee in the bankruptcy or the Department of Trade of the existence of the account, and thereafter he shall not make any payments out of the account, except under an order of the Court or in accordance with instructions from the trustee in bankruptcy, unless by the expiration of one month from the date of giving the information no instructions have been received from the trustee.

(*b*) If the bank is satisfied that the person in whose name the account stands is in fact only a nominee of an undischarged bankrupt, the account must be considered to be virtually that of the bankrupt, and the bank's duty is as quoted in (*a*) above.

Even, however, if the account-holder were not a mere nominee, but an independent customer, the bank could not safely collect for him cheques payable to the bankrupt. (See also Q. 149.)

152 Would a banker be justified in opening an account for the wife of an undischarged bankrupt, if she were apparently carrying on the business formerly worked by her husband?

Answer: It would be contrary to practice, but if satisfied by the trustee that the business had been regularly transferred, such an account might be opened.

153 A bank has for some time been operating an account in the sole name of Mrs. Brown when it becomes aware that her husband is an undischarged bankrupt. The bank knows that its customer has allowed the account to be used by her husband, since not only are his pay cheques collected for the credit of the account but other credits have been collected apparently on his behalf: the wife has also executed an authority enabling her husband to operate on the account.

Bearing in mind the provisions of sec. 47 of the Bankruptcy Act, 1914, is the bank under any obligation to stop the account and report it to the husband's trustee in bankruptcy or to the Department of Trade?

Answer: Sec. 47 (2) of the Bankruptcy Act, 1914, requires a banker to report to the trustee in bankruptcy or the Board of Trade (now the Department of Trade) any person having an account with him who is an undischarged bankrupt.

It is submitted that the terms of this section should be strictly construed, and that, as in the present instance the account is not in the name of the bankrupt, the bank is under no obligation to report it as required by the section.

Despite this, however, if the bank should allow the account to continue to be operated in this manner with notice of the husband's bankruptcy, it would clearly lay itself open to a charge of conversion at the suit of the trustee in bankruptcy, as it is now on notice that such credits as are received for the account from the husband's resources are within the disposition and control of the trustee. The bank can, therefore, only allow the account to operate in this manner at its peril. It should accordingly seek an interview with Mrs. Brown and advise her that she must no longer allow her husband to use her bank account for his own purposes. She should be told that, unless she is prepared to undertake in future to conduct it in a regular fashion and not as a vehicle to enable her husband to evade the laws of bankruptcy, the bank will have no alternative but to close the account. She should further be advised that, if it is necessary for her husband to operate a bank account, then he should approach his trustee in bankruptcy with a view to obtaining an express consent to open an account in the bankrupt's own name.

Alternatively, it may well be that the trustee in bankruptcy would agree to the husband's pay cheques being collected for the wife's account. In this event, there would be no objection to the husband using his wife's account to this limited extent.

154 Would a bank be justified in accepting a mandate from a limited company customer stating that a person known by the bank to be an undischarged bankrupt has been appointed a director and is authorised to sign cheques, etc., on behalf of the company.

Answer: The bank should make enquiries before accepting such a mandate to ensure that the undischarged bankrupt has been given leave to act as a director by the Court by which he was adjudged bankrupt. Sec. 187 of the Companies Act, 1948, imposes penalties on an undischarged bankrupt who acts as a director. In any case, if the company's articles include the provisions of article 88 of Table 'A' of the Companies Act, 1948, the appointment will be ineffective.

MENTAL DISORDER

155 Your customers, Mr. and Mrs. Brown, have a joint account on which either can sign. Mr. Brown has substantial private means. For some time past his conduct, which has always been somewhat eccentric, has seemed increasingly irrational; you have observed this yourself, and your staff have frequently commented on his strange conduct in the branch.

Mrs. Brown now calls to tell you that her husband has entered a mental hospital. She wishes to continue as far as possible her normal way of life.

What action, if any, should you take?

Answer: The answer to this question depends on the answer to another: is Mr. Brown incapable of understanding the effects of his purported contracts? His entry into a mental hospital is not in itself conclusive evidence—nor, of course, is your own observation. The medical superintendent of the hospital should be asked for his opinion before a decision is reached.

The variety of circumstances in which mental incapacity can arise, and the lack of legal guidelines in the whole area, make it impossible to lay down general rules, and when situations of this kind arise you will be well advised to seek guidance from your head office. It can be said, however, that it is normally necessary to stop the account when mental incapacity is established—and this is so even though the account is a joint account: the mandate 'either to sign' will not now entitle Mrs. Brown to operate the account.

You will naturally want to help her as much as possible, and subject to head office approval you will probably be able to allow her, if necessary, to overdraw on an account opened in her own name, to the extent of the normal operation of the joint account. If the incapacity is likely to be more than temporary she should be urged to ask the Court of Protection, under the Mental Health Act of 1959, to appoint a receiver: only thus can either her own financial position, or that of the bank, be regularised.

156 On the death of a mental patient, of whose estate a receiver has been appointed by the Master of the Court of Protection, what steps are necessary?

Answer: The death of the patient determines the jurisdiction of the Court of Protection and the powers of the receiver and the receiver is discharged without any formal order, see sec. 105 (2) of the Mental Health Act, 1959. Thus the account should be stopped and the balance paid over to the executors or administrators on production of grant of probate or letters of administration.

157 On the death of a receiver appointed by the Court of Protection what steps are necessary?

Answer: When a receiver dies, application for a new appointment should be made and this will normally be by a close relative of the patient. It should be noted however that if the receiver is the Official Solicitor, there is the inference that no close relative or friend was willing to act and in such event the next holder of the office of the Official Solicitor will be the receiver without further appointment.

THE CUSTOMER'S ACCOUNT

MANDATES, POWERS OF ATTORNEY

158 Will a mandate given by a customer to his banker to pay cheques drawn on his account by a third party, or a mandate given by customers having a joint account to pay cheques drawn by either, apply only to the account then in existence, or will it apply also to any other, say a deposit, account that he or they may open in future?

Answer: This depends on the terms of the mandate. Bankers' printed forms of authority or mandate are frequently expressed to apply to 'any account now open or to be opened in my name,' or 'in our joint names,' as the case may be. If such a form is intended to apply to only one account, amendment will be necessary.

159   A customer informs his banker that he has authorised a third party to draw, accept, and make cheques, bills and notes on his behalf, and generally to act for him in all matters relating to his account.

Does such an authority justify the banker in delivering to the third party securities or other articles deposited with him by the customer?

Answer: No; the delivery of securities or other articles deposited by the principal is not covered by the authority given.

160   If **A** gives his bank an authority to pay cheques drawn on his account by **B,** will **A** be responsible to the bank for an overdraft on the account created by **B**?

Answer: No; unless the authority expressly included the payment of cheques overdrawing the account, or unless **A** has himself arranged the overdraft with the bank, or has by his conduct approved or adopted it.

161   Can a customer of a banker authorise a minor to sign cheques on his behalf, and is a banker justified in paying cheques so signed?

Answer: There is nothing which incapacitates a minor from being an agent, and accordingly such an authority may be accepted.

162   On depositing money in his own name, **A** wishes to give the bank an authority to pay the balance, if any, of the account at the time of his death to **B.** Should such an authority be accepted?

Answer: An authority is a mandate, and, like any other mandate, is revoked by the death of the person who gives it. On the death of **A** the right to any balance remaining on the account standing in his name would pass to his executors or administrators, and the money could not lawfully be paid to **B** without their consent. The authority should therefore not be accepted.

163   If two or more persons have an account in their joint names, whether as partners or not, should an authority signed by one of them, for the payment of cheques drawn on behalf of the account-holders by an agent, be accepted?

Answer: No; such an authority should be signed by all the account-holders.

164   John Smith opens an account in the name of John Smith, trading as Smith Brothers. He authorises the bank to honour the signature of his brother (who is not a partner), and who is also to sign 'Smith Brothers.' instead of *per pro*. Is this strictly in order?

Answer: It is in order as between John Smith and his banker, but it could involve the brother, so signing, in personal responsibility to the creditors of the firm.

165   Is it contrary to law or banking practice for bankers to pay cheques drawn by one firm *per pro* another, the firm signing being duly authorised agents of the other?

Answer: No.

166   **A** instructs his bankers not to pay any cheque drawn by him in future unless it is countersigned by **B.**
Can **A** revoke this instruction at any time without **B**'s consent?

Answer: Yes; such a mandate, like any other mandate, is revocable at any time by the person who has given it.

167   A customer writes to his banker cancelling an authority given to a third party to draw cheques on his behalf and account. Subsequently a cheque is presented for payment signed by the agent and dated some days before the letter cancelling his authority.
In the absence of any instructions in the letter of cancellation, and prior reference to the customer being impossible, what course should the banker pursue?

Answer: The cheque should not be paid.

168   A power of attorney contains several clauses conferring various specific powers on the attorney, but a specific power to draw cheques on the donor's banking account, or to borrow money on his behalf, is not among them.
In the final clause, however, the attorney is empowered 'generally to act in relation to my estate and affairs as fully and effectually in all respects as I myself could do.'
Should the donor's banker, in reliance on the final clause, allow the attorney to draw on the donor's account, and, if necessary, to overdraw the account?

Answer: No; 'general' words in a power of attorney (such as those of the final clause in the present instance), unless their generality is expressly stated not to be limited to the specific powers already conferred do not give the attorney general powers, but give him only such powers as may be necessary for carrying into effect the purposes of the specific powers set out in the previous clauses.

169 Where a power of attorney is expressed to be irrevocable to what extent may the bank rely upon the power in dealing with the attorney?

Answer: The provisions of sec. 127 of the Law of Property Act, 1925, which gave validity to an irrevocable power of attorney for a period not exceeding one year were repealed by the Powers of Attorney Act, 1971. The 1971 Act only enables powers of attorney to be irrevocable when they are given to secure the proprietary interest of a donee of the power or the performance of an obligation owed to the donee. However, the relevant Sections (4 and 5) of the Act are difficult to apply and branches are recommended to consult head office.

170 A customer who has given an authority for his wife to sign cheques on his account executes a power of attorney in favour of another person, conferring, amongst other powers, a power to operate on the account.
    Does the power revoke the authority?

Answer: Not necessarily, but in order to avoid misunderstanding it would be advisable for the customer's express instructions to be obtained.

171 Has a company any right to demand a copy, certified by a notary, of a power of attorney lodged with them for registration?

Answer: It is reasonable and customary to ask for a copy of a power to be lodged with the original, but not for a notarially certified copy unless executed abroad.

DEPOSITS

172 Is money placed on deposit account transferable by the depositor to another person?

Answer: Money deposited is money lent by the depositor to the bank, and the debt owing by the bank is assignable, like any other debt or 'chose in action,' under sec. 136 of the Law of Property Act, 1925. This is so, even if the deposit receipt or passbook is marked 'not transferable.'

The assignee, on producing the assignment, and where applicable producing also the deposit receipt or pass-book, can demand payment of the deposit and can give the bank a good discharge for it, without further signature by the assignor.

Endorsement and delivery of a deposit receipt, although expressed to be 'not transferable,' by the depositor to another person with the intention of transferring the deposit, but without any written assignment, was held in *Re Griffin,* [1899] 1 Ch. 408, to operate as an equitable assignment of the deposit; but in such a case, as the legal title is not assigned, the signature of the depositor, as well as that of the equitable assignee, should be demanded when the money is withdrawn.

173 A brings in for the credit of his account a deposit receipt in the name of, and purporting to be endorsed by, **B.** Should the receipt be accepted for **A**'s credit, and if it is accepted, what will be the bank's position if **A** is afterwards discovered to have acquired it by fraud?

Answer: As **B**'s endorsement and delivery of the receipt to **A** amounted at most to an equitable assignment of the money, the receipt should not be accepted for **A**'s credit without **B**'s written instructions. Failing such instructions, the bank can have no better title to the money than **A** had, and if he has obtained it by fraud the bank may have to refund it to **B.**

174 If a depositor represents that he has lost his receipt or passbook, can the deposit safely be repaid to him?

Answer: Yes. In practice, however, an indemnity is called for, at all events in the case of a missing receipt, though it is doubtful whether this can be insisted upon.

175 **X** transfers money from his account to a deposit account in the name of **A.** Later, **X** asks to have the money retransferred to him, stating that the transfer to **A** was made in error, and has not been disclosed to **A.** Should the bank retransfer the money to **X** without **A**'s consent?

Answer: If the bank is satisfied that the credit has in fact not been disclosed to **A**, the re-transfer to **X** without **A**'s consent may be permitted if made on the same day. If there is any doubt about **A**'s knowledge, an indemnity may be considered desirable.

If **X**'s request is received later than the same day the position may now be more doubtful. In the past it has been considered that the fact that **A** does not know of the transfer justifies re-transfer at any time; but in *Momm and Others* v. *Barclays Bank International Ltd.* 1976 3 All E.R. 585; (Leading Cases, 4th Ed., p. 65) it was held (albeit in circumstances different from those in the question) that the bank was not entitled to reverse entries between two customers' accounts on the morning following the transfer, even though the transfer had not been communicated to the transferee.

176 Is a banker justified in returning the cheque of a customer who has money on a deposit account, on the ground that the current account upon which the cheque was drawn has an insufficient credit balance to meet the cheque, or is already overdrawn?

Answer: A banker might be legally justified in refusing cheques drawn against the current account, more especially if the deposit were subject to notice of withdrawal, but it would not be customary for him to do so. In practice he would honour the cheque relying on his lien or set off against the deposit account.

177 May a deposit account be opened in the name of a firm, or should it be opened in the joint names of the individual partners?

Answer: There is no objection to opening a deposit account in a firm-name. If this is done withdrawals may, in the absence of instructions to the contrary, be made by any partner signing the firm-name.

178 Money is deposited in the joint names of **A** and **B** without any authority or arrangement for payment to either. If **B** afterwards presents the deposit receipt bearing **A**'s endorsement, can the bank safely pay the amount to him?

Answer: No; unless **A**, in addition to endorsing the receipt, has given a written authority to pay to **B**.

179 What signature should a married woman use in withdrawing money deposited by her before marriage in her maiden name?

Answer: If the bank is satisfied as to her identity, there is no reason why she should not sign her married name.

180 Money standing in the name of **A** is claimed by **X**, who states that **A** has stolen it from him, and who warns the bank not to repay it to **A**. Can the bank safely disregard the warning?

Answer: The bank is responsible to **A** alone for money standing in his name, and cannot refuse to repay it to him, unless **X** obtains an order of a Court to the contrary.

181 Is a deposit for a fixed term expiring on a Sunday repayable on the Friday or the Monday?

Answer: On the succeeding business day.

182 Is the interest on a joint deposit payable to either party?

Answer: Not without the express authority of all the depositors. An authority for the payment of the principal to either is considered to include the interest.

183 When a deposit is subject to notice of withdrawal, is it the practice of bankers to stop the allowance of interest on the day on which notice of withdrawal is given, or on the day on which the notice expires?

Answer: On the day of the expiration of the notice. Notice is often waived and it is a common practice for the banker to deduct from the interest which has already accrued in favour of the customer an amount equal to that which would have accrued during the period for which notice should have been given.

184 If one of the terms of a deposit is that interest shall vary with Base rate, and if Base rate goes up on, say, the 7th of a month, from what day should the higher rate be allowed on the deposit?

Answer: From and including the 7th. Interest should continue to be allowed at the new rate up to, but not including, the date of the next change in Base rate, or the date of withdrawal of the deposit.

NEGOTIABLE INSTRUMENTS
BILLS OF EXCHANGE

(Reference to 'Uniform Rules for Collections' (see Appendix B) will provide the answer to many questions on this subject.

185 Does the instruction 'Documents on acceptance' (abbreviated 'D/A') or 'Documents on payment' (abbreviated 'D/P') written on a bill, or on a slip attached to it, make the bill a 'conditional order' under sec. 3 of the Bills of Exchange Act, and is the instruction binding on any holder into whose hands the bill may come?

Answer: It is considered that such an instruction is merely a memorandum, not rendering the bill a conditional order, and that it is binding on all holders who take the bill and documents. Precise information should be obtained in the remittance letter.

186 A banker receives for collection a foreign bill at 90 days' sight with documents attached. No instructions are given regarding the surrender of documents.
(1) Is the banker justified in assuming that surrender of documents on acceptance is implied?
or(2) Is such surrender left to the banker's discretion?
(3) Is the banker liable if, without the drawer's permission, he surrenders documents on the assumption of either (1) or (2)?

Answer: (1) and (2) No. (3) Yes, the remittance letter should state whether the documents are to be released against acceptance or against payment (Uniform Rules for Collections—Article 10).*
    In the absence of such instructions the documents will be released only against payment, but in practice steps would already have been taken to refer back to the remitter.

187 'Four months after date pay to my order the sum of . . . pounds for value to be received.' As the words 'to be' inserted here are unusual, would a bank be safe in discounting such an acceptance while having to rely on the acceptor for payment?

Answer: The words inserted may perhaps be intended to imply that value has not yet been given by the drawer to the drawee, but is to be given at some time before the bill becomes due. If this is intended the instrument is clearly a conditional order, not a bill of exchange. It should therefore not be discounted in its present form.

*See Appendix B

188   **A,** in London, wishes to draw a bill at three months' date on **B,** in Capetown, payable to drawer's order, for a sterling amount, which he intends shall be converted into Rands at a rate of exchange which will include interest for the term of the bill and the cost of collecting it in Capetown. **A** will then be able to sell the bill in London for the full sterling amount. How should the bill be drawn?

Answer: Under sec. 9 (1) of the Bills of Exchange Act the sum payable by a bill may be required to be paid according to an indicated rate of exchange, or according to a rate of exchange to be ascertained as directed by the bill. **A** might, therefore, name the rate at which the bill is to be paid in the bill itself, but the usual practice is to draw the bill payable 'with exchange as per endorsement.' The rate is then indicated in an endorsement, usually in that of the bank to which **A** negotiates the bill.

This method of drawing should not, however, be adopted unless the drawee has agreed to it beforehand, because it casts upon him a burden which, except by agreement, he may be unwilling to bear.

189   A bill drawn in sterling on Gibraltar, and expressed to be payable 'by bankers' cheque on London,' is sent by a London bank to an agent in Gibraltar for collection, and payment is received less exchange and the agent's charges.

How should such a bill be drawn in order that the full sterling amount, without any deduction, may be received by the London bank?

Answer: The bill should contain the words 'payable at the collecting bank's selling rate for sight drafts on London, together with all costs of collection including stamps,' or some similar clause; but as the effect of this will be to cast the loss in exchange and the expenses of collection on the drawee, his consent to bear them should be obtained beforehand.

190   May a bill expressed in foreign currency be drawn in such a manner as to secure a fixed rate of exchange?

Answer: Yes; under sec. 9 (1) (*d*) of the Bills of Exchange Act a bill may be drawn payable at an indicated rate of exchange.

191   The words 'payable in London' are sometimes added at the bottom of a bill beneath the name and address of the drawee, instead of being written in the body of the bill. Are these words an integral portion of the bill, as they are often in such a position that they could be cut off without the bill appearing to be mutilated? It is no

uncommon thing for the word 'London' to be struck out and the name of another place inserted without the alteration being initialled or otherwise authorised by the parties to the bill.

Answer: The words 'payable in London' are, in such a case, considered an integral part of the bill, and an alteration in the place of payment is one of those mentioned in sec. 64 (2) of the Bills of Exchange Act as being 'material alterations,' and as therefore avoiding the bill under sub-sec. (1) of that section, unless assented to by all parties liable on the bill. But if the words 'payable in London,' instead of being altered, were cut off the bill without the bill appearing to be mutilated, as suggested in the question, the bill would be valid and enforceable according to its original tenor in the hands of a holder in due course. See the proviso to sec. 64 (1), and see sec. 29 for the definition of a 'holder in due course.'

192 A lithographed form of bill bearing 'London' at the top, but neither address nor date, is accepted by the drawee. The intended drawer then signs the bill as such, and substitutes 'Lausanne' for 'London.' Has the alteration avoided the bill under sec. 64 of the Bills of Exchange Act?

Answer: In *Foster* v. *Driscoll,* [1929] 1 K.B. 470, this was held not to be an alteration of an existing instrument (as the alteration had been made before the drawer signed the bill), and the bill was held to be a good foreign bill; but in *Koch* v. *Dicks,* [1933] 1 K.B. 307; (Leading Cases, 4th Ed., p. 29) it was held that an alteration of the place where a bill purports to be drawn, after completion, making it a foreign bill, is a material alteration if it alters the rights and liabilities of the parties.

193 A series of bills, instead of being drawn at three, six, nine, and twelve months' date, are all drawn at three months, but are dated forward at intervals of three months.
     Are such bills legal? And can money be raised upon them?

Answer: Such bills are not illegal (Bills of Exchange Act, sec. 13 (2)), but bankers would not discount or lend upon them before the date upon which they appear to have been drawn.

194 Can a bill of exchange be drawn for any period, say five, seven, or ten years, or is there a limit of time?

Answer: There is no limit of time.

195 Can a bill of exchange, other than a cheque, be made not negotiable,

(*a*) by being so drawn,

or(*b*) by being so accepted,

or(*c*) by being so endorsed?

Answer: (*a*) Under sec. 8 (1) of the Bills of Exchange Act, when a bill contains words prohibiting transfer, or indicating an intention that it should not be transferable, it is valid as between the parties thereto, but is not negotiable. In *Hibernian Bank* v. *Gysin & Hanson,* [1938] 2 K.B. 384, and on appeal, [1939] 1 K.B. 483, a bill was drawn payable to the payee 'only,' and the words 'not negotiable' were written across it. The latter words (apart from the effect of 'only') were held to make the bill not transferable. bill not transferable.

For the effect of 'not negotiable' when added to the crossing of a cheque, see sec. 81 of the Act. This special meaning of the words applies to cheques only.

(*b*) A bill negotiable in its origin may, it appears, become not negotiable, i.e. not transferable, by being accepted by the drawee payable to the payee only. *Meyer* v. *Decroix,* [1891] A.C. 520, in which, however, the words 'in favour of the payee only' were written above the acceptance, and were held not to be part of it. to be part of it.

Presumably the words 'not negotiable' if forming part of the acceptance, would also render the bill not negotiable, i.e. not transferable.

In either of these cases the acceptance would be a qualified acceptance under sec. 19.

(*c*) A bill negotiable in its origin may be restrictively endorsed, e.g. 'pay **A** only,' under sec. 35. Such an endorsement gives the endorsee no power to transfer his rights as endorsee.

196 A bill drawn by **A** payable to his own order is specially endorsed by him to the order of the **X** bank 'for the credit of **A**.'

Can the bill be further negotiated after being endorsed by the **X** bank?

Answer: The endorsement in favour of the **X** bank for the credit of **A** is a restrictive endorsement under sec. 35 of the Bills of Exchange Act, and the **X** bank accordingly takes the bill merely as agent for **A,** with power to receive payment of it at maturity, or to sue the acceptor, but without power to negotiate it further.

197   The second of exchange of a foreign draft, drawn after date and bearing the reference:

'First accepted with the Blanktown Bank,
Blanktown,'

is forwarded by a London bank to their agent at that place, with a request to pick up the first, and an instruction to note in case of non-delivery.

On presenting the second of exchange to the Blanktown Bank they give the answer:

'Have not had time to obtain acceptance of the first, having received it only today, please call tomorrow.'

Is it the duty of the presenters to have the second of exchange noted on the day of presentation, or can they, without incurring any liability, hold it over until the following day?

Answer: Under sec. 42 of the Bills of Exchange Act a drawee is entitled to 'the customary time' within which to accept or refuse acceptance. The customary time is until the close of business on the day following presentation for acceptance. Noting must be made on the day of dishonour or the day following, and a bill is not dishonoured by non-acceptance until acceptance is refused or cannot be obtained. In the circumstances described the question of noting the second of exchange does not arise until the following day.

198   It is the custom of London bankers to keep bills left for acceptance until twelve o'clock on the following day. Do they do this simply as a matter of convenience, or would they be liable to their customer or correspondent if they returned a bill accepted on the same day it was left for acceptance, and if the advice to accept was cancelled before twelve o'clock the following day?

Answer: There may be a practice with some London banks, as a matter of convenience, not to give up bills accepted until twelve o'clock on the following day, but there is no general custom to do so. The banker is at liberty to accept at once if he pleases.

199   Bills drawn abroad after sight upon third parties in this country are sent to a bank to be presented for acceptance. How long may the bank hold them over before noting or protesting for non-acceptance?

Answer: Till the business day following the day of dishonour.

200   A bill is drawn on a person in Liverpool, payable in London at sight. Can the holder in Liverpool demand immediate payment, or can the drawee insist on having the bill left with him for acceptance payable in London?

Answer: Sec. 39 (2) of the Bills of Exchange Act provides that where a bill is drawn payable elsewhere than at the residence or place of business of the drawee, it must be presented for acceptance before it can be presented for payment. Under sec. 42 the drawee can insist upon having the bill left with him for 'the customary time,' which in practice is twenty-four hours.

201 Bills for collection, payable locally, and due two or three days from the date of receipt, are received unaccepted from correspondents. What is a collecting banker's duty in regard to presentation of the above for acceptance?

Answer: It is not generally considered incumbent on the banker to present bills specially for acceptance when received only two or three days from the due date.

202 A country branch receives from a customer a bill drawn on a foreign bank, at ten days' date, payable at the foreign bank's agency in London. The bill having but a few days to run, the country branch retains it till maturity, without sending it abroad for acceptance. In the interim the drawer fails and the bill is returned protested. Is the bank liable to its customer for the amount of the dishonoured bill?

Answer: The bank, as agent for its customer, would be liable to its principal for any loss resulting from its omission to present for acceptance. The bill, being drawn payable elsewhere than at the residence or place of business of the drawee, must, in accordance with English law (Bills of Exchange Act, sec. 39 (2)), be presented for acceptance before it is presented for payment. Delay before presenting it for payment caused by presenting the bill for acceptance is excused.

203 **A,** residing in France, sends a first of exchange, drawn in that country on an English house, to **B,** his London banker, to have the bill accepted. The bill on being presented by **B** to the drawees, is lost in the hands of the latter.

A wants to hold **B** responsible for all damages resulting from the loss of the bill. Is he justified in doing so?

Answer: If there has been no carelessness on the part of **B** in presenting the bill for acceptance, he cannot be held responsible for

its loss, and the bill can be replaced by obtaining a duplicate from
the drawer. (See Bills of Exchange Act, sec. 69, but the conditions of
obtaining a duplicate from the drawer in France would be determinable by French law.)

204 A Dutch firm draws on a London house at ten days' date. The draft
is remitted to London bankers who do not present it till the day it is
due. Can the drawees require the bill to be left for acceptance till the
following day?

Answer: No. (Bills of Exchange Act, sec. 39 (3).)

205 A banker in London receives from a country customer for presentation for acceptance, a bill drawn abroad upon the London office of
a foreign firm. The bill is duly lodged at the office of the drawees
and called for on the following day, when the presenting banker is
informed that the bill has been forwarded to the drawees' chief office
at Paris for acceptance, on the ground that the representatives of the
firm in London have no power to accept. Was the firm in London
within its rights in so acting, and, if not, what course should the
presenting banker adopt?

Answer: The firm had no right to send the bill out of the country
without the holder's consent. The presenting banker should protest
for non-delivery and should give notice of dishonour to his customer.
(See Bills of Exchange Act, secs. 42, 48 and 51 (2).)

206 A banker abroad remits to his agent in this country a bill drawn at
fifteen days' sight; the agent sends the bill by post to the drawee for
acceptance. The bill is returned accepted, but instead of being
sighted from November 6, the day it was delivered for acceptance, it
is accepted from the 8th, this being two days beyond the correct
date. Does the agent incur any liability by receiving the bill with the
acceptance so dated, or what should he do?

Answer: It is usual to require the acceptance to bear the date of
presentment and not the date of its return to the holder, and the
latter is probably entitled to this as a matter of right. It would be
safer for the agent to have the bill noted or protested for incorrect
acceptance, and to give notice of the fact to his principal abroad.

207 A three months' bill is drawn on Messrs. White and Co., and
accepted by 'B. White.'

Is the bill enforceable against the acceptor as though his name had appeared as drawee?

Answer: If B. White is a partner in the firm of White and Co., he is liable as acceptor but if he had signed in the firm-name all the partners would have been liable (Bills of Exchange Act, sec. 23 (2)). The acceptance as it stands is a qualified acceptance (sec. 19 (2) (*e*)), unless B. White is the sole proprietor of the business, and the holder of the bill should refuse to take it without the consent of the drawer and endorsers (sec. 44).

208 A bill drawn on a drawee in London is accepted payable at a bank in Newcastle. Is the acceptance in order, or can the holder insist upon the drawee accepting payable in London?

Answer: Such an acceptance is in order, and the holder cannot insist on the drawee accepting payable in London. Under sec. 19 (2) (*c*) of the Bills of Exchange Act an acceptance to pay at a particular place is a general, not a qualified, acceptance, unless it expressly states that the bill is to be paid there only, and not elsewhere.

209 By the Bills of Exchange Act, sec. 19 (2) (*c*), an acceptance of a bill 'payable at the . . . bank only' is a qualified acceptance. What responsibility or risk would a holder incur by taking such an acceptance? Would he lose any right against previous endorsers, and what effect would it have on his claim if the bank at which the bill is accepted payable were to fail before the bill became due?

Answer: The acceptance described is a qualified acceptance, and the holder, by being content with such an acceptance, thereby releases the drawer and endorsers, unless he immediately gives notice to them, and receives their direct or implied assent thereto. (See Bills of Exchange Act, sec. 44.) Whether all or any of the other parties give their assent to the qualified acceptance or not, the holder must, when the bill falls due, present it for payment at the bank where it is domiciled. If it is dishonoured he will have recourse, on giving them notice of dishonour, against all the parties to the bill who assented to the acceptance but not against those who did not assent.

210 (*a*) In the case of a bill accepted on the back, is the acceptor's signature sufficient without the word 'accepted,' or some other word or words to distinguish the acceptor's signature from an endorsement?

(*b*) When a bill has been accepted on the back, should not the fact be notified prominently on the face of the document?

Answer: (*a*) A drawee's signature anywhere on the bill constitutes an acceptance. (See Bills of Exchange Act, sec. 17 (2) (*a*))

(*b*) It is usual to do so.

211 A bill drawn on A. Jones is accepted by him, 'A. Jones, No. 2 a/c.' Is this a qualified acceptance?

Answer: No; a qualified acceptance is one which in express terms varies the effect of the bill as drawn. (Sec. 19 (2) of the Bills of Exchange Act.) If the bill is domiciled at the drawee's bank, the words 'No. 2 a/c' must be considered to be merely an indication of the account to which the bill, when paid, is to be charged.

212 A bill of exchange drawn abroad upon a drawee in London, accepted payable in London, is unpaid at maturity. By arrangement with the holder the drawee reaccepts the bill for a further period of three months.

Such a reacceptance is recognised in the country in which the bill was drawn.

Would not such reacceptance of the bill nullify the right of action on the original acceptance?

Answer: It would not free the acceptor from his liability on the bill, but the drawer and endorsers would be discharged unless they assented to the extension of the period of the bill.

213 From what date should a bank in London accept a 90 days' sight draft drawn under a confirmed documentary credit in the following circumstances?

The credit is issued by an Australian bank in favour of XYZ Limited, London and is available by drafts at 90 days' sight on the London office of the Australian bank, accompanied by shipping documents representing cost and freight. Shipment by container is authorised and the document of movement will therefore be a combined transport document.

At the time the beneficiary wishes to despatch his goods, the staff of the forwarding agent are on strike, and so there is a considerable delay in shipment. The beneficiary, however, draws under the credit and the draft is presented for acceptance clean in London and returned with answer 'Requires shipping documents'. A month later, the strike is settled and the goods are shipped, and so the draft is re-presented with shipping documents attached, in accordance with the terms of the credit.

Should the draft be accepted as of the original date of presentation and noting for non-acceptance, or only as of date when the draft was re-presented, accompanied by documents as specified in the credit?

Answer: Sec. 18 (3) of the Bills of Exchange Act provides that when a bill payable after sight is dishonoured by non-acceptance, and the drawee subsequently accepts it, the holder, in the absence of any different agreement, is entitled to have the bill accepted as of the date of first presentment to the drawee for acceptance.

Special notice should therefore be taken of the words 'in the absence of any different agreement'. In this case there is such an agreement, inasmuch as the credit terms require that the draft be accompanied by shipping documents. The acceptor will therefore be under no liability to accept until the documents come forward. For this reason, on re-presentation the drawee need only accept as of the date of re-presentation with documents attached.

214 A foreign bank issues a documentary letter of credit authorising drafts to be drawn on a London bank at 30 days after sight. On January 2 a draft drawn under the credit is presented for acceptance, but acceptance is declined on the ground that no instructions have been received from the foreign correspondent. Three days later the necessary instructions are received and the bill and documents are re-presented. On what day is it the practice to date the acceptance—on the day of the original or of the second presentation?

Answer: Sec. 18 (3) of the Bills of Exchange Act provides that when a bill payable after sight is dishonoured by non-acceptance, and the drawee subsequently accepts it, the holder, in the absence of any different agreement, is entitled to have the bill accepted as of the date of first presentment to the drawee for acceptance.

In the circumstances set forth in the question the holder is entitled to have the acceptance dated on January 2, and it is the practice so to date the acceptance.

215 An acceptance drawn three months after date is dated September 30. The word 'September' has been struck out, and 'October' substituted. Should this alteration be initialled or confirmed?

Answer: Such alteration must be confirmed by all parties to the bill other than endorsers subsequent to the alteration. (Bills of Exchange Act, sec. 64 (1).)

216 A & Co. accept a bill as follows:
       'Sighted December 20.
       Accepted December 21.
              A & Co.'
  Is the due date taken from the sighted date or the accepted date?

Answer: Sec. 14 (3) of the Bills of Exchange Act states that where a bill is payable at a fixed period after sight, the time begins to run from the date of the acceptance if the bill be accepted. The practice, however, in a case such as the above, is to calculate the due date from the sighted date of the bill.

217 A bill is drawn:
       'Pay to our order the sum of . . . pounds for value received.'
       When is the bill due?

Answer: Sec. 10 (1) (*b*) of the Bills of Exchange Act states that a bill in which no time for payment is expressed is payable on demand.

218 A bill falls due for payment on May 10 which is a Saturday. When is the bill payable?

Answer: If a bill falls due for payment on a non-business day, it is payable on the succeeding business day. The bill in question would therefore be payable on Monday, May 12.

219 A bill is drawn in France upon an English town, payable 'middle of November.' Upon what day must payment be demanded? What is the custom in England with regard to such terms? How are the months with 31 days, and how is February, treated?

Answer: Bills so dated are not now common, but it has been the custom in England to consider them as maturing on the 15th, whatever the month may be. However, in the case of a substantial amount it would be advisable to contact one's principal.

220 Bank X receives for collection from its branch at Z, on June 11, a bill falling due on the 12th, and accepted payable at bank X. On the same day (June 11) X receives from its customer an advice to pay the bill 'on presentation.' The bill is correctly described as due on June

12. May **X** debit its customer on the 11th, i.e. as soon as it receives both bill and advice?

Answer: No, as the bill is not due until the 12th, and is payable at bank **X**.

221   John Smith accepts a bill payable at his banker's, **B**. The drawer pays it into his account at the same bank. The day before the bill is due, **B** (evidently in mistake) returns the acceptance to the drawer marked 'no advice,' and debits his account with it. Can John Smith sustain a claim for damages against **B** for dishonouring his acceptance a day before it was due?

Answer: No, a bill cannot be dishonoured before it is due.

222   On or before November 28 **A** accepts **B**'s draft dated December 11, payable four months after date. Would this be a valid security in the hands of a holder in due course, who took it before December 11, in case of the death or bankruptcy of **A** before that date?

Answer: The Bills of Exchange Act enacts (sec. 13 (2)) that a bill is not invalid by reason only that it is post-dated. The bill in question is a good bill, and consequently a valid security in the hands of the holder in due course, although he took it before December 11.

223   If a bill payable at a fixed period after date is issued undated, or if the acceptance of a bill payable at a fixed period after sight is undated, is:
   (*a*) a banker into whose hands the bill comes for collection,
or(*b*) a banker at whose office the bill is accepted payable,
a 'holder' of the bill who may, under sec. 12 of the Bills of Exchange Act, insert the true date of issue or acceptance; or may he do so as a 'person in possession of the bill' under sec. 20?

Answer: 'Holder' means the payee or endorsee of a bill who is in possession of it, or the bearer thereof; and 'bearer' means the person in possession of a bill which is payable to bearer (sec. 2), i.e. which is expressed to be so payable, or on which the only or last endorsement is an endorsement in blank (sec. 8 (3)).
   (*a*) The collecting banker is a 'bearer' of the bill, and is therefore a 'holder' to whom sec. 12 applies; but in practice he would not usually take upon himself to insert what he supposed to be the true date of issue or acceptance without communicating with the person from whom he received the bill for collection.

(*b*) The banker at whose office the bill is payable is not, it is considered, even the 'bearer' of it in the sense intended by sec. 2. He accordingly cannot insert the date under sec. 12.

For completion under sec. 20, authority, express or implied, is necessary. If the date omitted is that of acceptance, the banker would usually endeavour to obtain the authority of his customer, the acceptor, to insert it, or would ask the customer to insert it himself.

224 A country branch of a bank advised its London office to pay **A**'s acceptance, but the holder of the bill did not present it for payment. After it had been outstanding at the London office for some time, the country branch, at the request of **A**, cancelled the advice and repaid him the money.

Has the holder of the bill any claim against the London office, or the branch, for parting with the money?

Answer: The holder of the bill could have no claim against anyone but the acceptor.

225 If the acceptor of a bill of exchange is a surety on the bill, which is for the drawer's accommodation, is it necessary to present the bill at maturity and, if it is unpaid, must notice of dishonour be served on him?

Answer: Sec. 46 (2) (*c*) of the Bills of Exchange Act provides that presentment for payment is dispensed with, as regards the drawer of a bill, where, as in the present case, the acceptor is not bound, as between himself and the drawer, to pay the bill, and the drawer has no reason to believe that the bill would be paid if presented; but if there are any endorsers (other than the drawer, if the bill is payable to his order), the bill must be presented for payment at maturity, or they will be discharged from liability. (Sec. 45.)

As regards the acceptor, it is unnecessary to present the bill for payment in order to render him liable, if the bill is accepted generally (sec. 52 (1)); nor is it necessary to give notice of dishonour to him (sec. 52 (3)).

226 A bill is drawn abroad at sight upon a merchant in England, whose address (number of street and town) is given. Is it necessary that, before noting or protesting, the notary should make a personal presentation to the drawee, or is presentation at the given address sufficient?

Answer: Presentation at the given address is sufficient. (Bills of Exchange Act, sec. 45 (4) (*b*), which states that where no place of payment is specified a bill is presented at the proper place if presented at the address of the drawee given in the bill.)

227 The holder of a bill payable to his order dies intestate without having endorsed it. Before the intending administrator can obtain a grant of administration the bill becomes payable. What steps should the intending administrator take in order to claim against the previous parties to the bill?

Answer: The bill should be presented without endorsement at maturity, and on dishonour should be noted, or, in case of a foreign bill, protested, notice being given to the parties thereto; at the same time intimation should be given to them that as soon as an administrator of the estate of the deceased has been appointed, the bill will immediately be re-presented. If these precautions are taken and due diligence is observed in giving notice of the dishonour of the bill, in procuring administration and in afterwards presenting the bill, the remedies against the parties will be preserved. Sec. 46 (1) of the Bills of Exchange Act provides that delay in making presentment for payment is excused when the delay is caused by circumstances beyond the control of the holder, and not imputable to his default, misconduct or negligence. When the cause of delay ceases to operate, presentment must be made with reasonable diligence.

228 A bill drawn in London on a drawee at Southtown, is accepted 'payable at the **X** Bank' simply.
  (1) Should the holder take it for granted that the head office in London is meant, or ought he to present it at the branch at Southtown on maturity?
  (2) In the event of there being no branch of the bank in Southtown, would the holder be justified in having the bill noted there at maturity?

Answer: (1) The bill should be presented at the branch at Southtown, unless stated in the body of the bill to be payable in London or another town. (2) Before noting, the bill should be presented at the head office of the bank.

229 A bill drawn at Bristol on a drawee at Leicester, and expressed to be payable at Bristol, is accepted by the drawee payable at a bank in London. Where should it be presented for payment at maturity?

Answer: This is a qualified acceptance varying the effect of the bill as drawn, and the drawer, and the endorsers, if any, were discharged when it was taken, unless they then assented to it. In order to charge any such parties who may have assented, the bill must be presented for payment at the bank in London. (Bills of Exchange Act, secs. 19 (2), 44 and 45 (4).)

230   May a banker in a country town, where there is no notary, retain bills sent for collection for one day after due date before returning them to his correspondents, as is done by London banks in the case of unpaid bills which are noted?

Answer: It is quite usual and correct (see Bills of Exchange Act, sec. 49 (12)) for bankers to retain in their hands bills that have been remitted to them for collection until the day after maturity, whether noted or not.

231   A bill is received for collection by a banker through the post two days after maturity. Has he the right to hold it over one day, or should he return it, if unpaid, the same day it is received?

Answer: Though in practice bankers would not generally hold it over, they have the legal right to do so.

232   Ought a banker, to whom a bill of exchange is sent for collection by a customer, by another banker in this country, or by a correspondent abroad, to accept payment of part of the amount of the bill?

Answer: Under the continental codes a holder cannot refuse part payment, but this is not English law. Provided, however, that no further time is allowed to the acceptor or security taken from him, so as to discharge the other parties to the bill, it is considered that part payment may properly be accepted. In *Gould* v. *Robson* [1807], 8 East 576, Lord Ellenborough said: 'As to the taking part payment, no person can object to it, because it is in aid of all others who are liable upon the bill.' Such a payment operates as a discharge *pro tanto.*

The bill should not be given up, and, if a foreign bill, it should be noted or protested, not later than the day after partial dishonour, for the unpaid balance. The principal's instructions as to further action should be obtained.

233 When a bill is presented for payment, whether to the drawee's banker or (rarely) to the drawee himself, is the presenting banker safe in accepting in payment a cheque or draft drawn on another bank?

Answer: Payment should normally be accepted only in cash or by bankers payment or bankers draft (care being taken with any name which is not well known), or by cheque which can be cleared either specially or in the Town clearing, the same day. Pending such same-day clearance, the relative bill should not be treated as paid or be given up. The object must be to receive cash or equivalent, or to treat the bill as dishonoured and to preserve recourse against all parties thereto. Recourse would be lost if for example the bill were delivered up against uncleared effects which were later dishonoured.

234 A banker receives a draft drawn on a West End firm for collection on behalf of a customer.

The amount of the draft is placed to the customer's credit on the day it is received, but it is not actually presented for payment until the following morning.

The drawees pay by cheque on a clearing banker and the walk clerk surrenders the original draft. The clearing cheque is presented without delay, but at 5.30 p.m. it is returned unpaid, the drawers having failed in the afternoon.

What is the position of the collecting banker towards his customer in consequence of having accepted the clearing cheque? Would his position be affected in any way if the credit entry on the customer's account had not been made?

Answer: The collecting banker, by surrendering the original draft, has deprived the holder of his recourse on the drawer and any endorsers, and so he is liable to his customer. The omission of the credit entry would make no difference in this respect.

235 A country bank receives a demand draft for collection with instructions to give up the attached shipping documents on payment.

The bill is presented to the drawees on the day of receipt, and they ask for time to consider.

Are the drawees entitled, either by law or custom, to a reasonable time, say 24 hours, to decide whether they will pay?

Answer: The draft must be paid or refused on demand. If it is unpaid at the close of business on the day of presentation, and is drawn abroad, it should be noted or protested not later than the day after. (Bills of Exchange Act, sec. 51 (4), as amended by the Bills of Exchange (Time of Noting) Act, 1917.)

236 A banker having been requested by a customer to collect for him a bill payable abroad, sends the bill to his agent in the place where the bill is payable. The agent duly collects the amount, but fails to remit it to the banker in England, and ultimately becomes insolvent.

Who loses the money, the banker or the customer?

Answer: Since 1967, British banks have, as far as their U.K. branches are concerned, adopted Uniform Rules for Collections, of which art. 16 provides that where branches utilise the services of another bank they do so for the account of/at the risk of the customer. In practice banks may also obtain their principal's signature to an instruction form which may contain a clause relieving them from all liability except that arising from their own fault or negligence and stating that the collection is subject to Uniform Rules for Collections.

237 When a bill which has been credited to a customer's account is dishonoured on presentation for payment at maturity, within what time must the banker give notice of dishonour to the customer, and to the drawer and prior endorsers, if any, in order to preserve his right to proceed against all or any of them for the amount of the bill?

Answer: Under sec. 49 (12) of the Bills of Exchange Act,
   (*a*) where the person giving and the person to receive notice reside in the same place, the notice must be given or sent off in time to reach the latter not later than the day after the dishonour of the bill;
   (*b*) where the person giving and the person to receive notice reside in different places, the notice must be sent off not later than the day after the dishonour of the bill, if there is a post at a convenient hour on that day, but if not then by the next post thereafter.

In such a case the banker should not debit the customer's account, but should charge the bill to a suspense ('Overdue Bills') account.

If, however, the customer has a sufficient credit balance, or the banker is content to rely entirely on his liability, the customer's account will usually be debited, and the bill returned to him. Such return will have the same effect as giving him notice of dishonour (sec. 49 (6)), and the banker's rights against the prior parties will thereby be transferred to him. If the banker has given notice of dishonour to the prior parties, such notice will be available for the customer's protection (sec. 49 (3)); if he has not, the customer has the same time for doing so (but counting from the receipt of notice, or of the bill, by himself) as the banker would have had (sec. 49 (14)).

It is not necessary to give notice of dishonour to the acceptor of a bill in order to maintain his liability (sec. 52 (3)).

238 Is a banker obliged to give notice of dishonour of a bill which has been left with him for collection, in the same way as if it had been discounted; and does the fact of the customer's account being in credit or overdrawn affect the banker's responsibility?

Answer: Notice must be given in the same way as if the banker had discounted the bill or had made an advance upon it. The usual course is for the bill to be returned the day after dishonour, which is equivalent to notice. (See Bills of Exchange Act, sec. 49 (6).)

239 A bill remitted from abroad is presented for acceptance to the drawee in London, who refuses acceptance, giving an answer which conveys the inference that funds may be available in a day or two. Should the holder cable the remitter before presenting the bill to the 'case of need,' whose address is also in London?

Answer: There is no general duty upon the holder to cable the dishonour of the bill. It is entirely a matter of arrangement between the parties.

240 If a bill or cheque which has been credited to a customer's account is dishonoured, and the banker wishes to debit the account with it, is he entitled to do so without the customer's authority?

Answer: Yes. The right to debit a customer's account with unpaid bills or cheques was recognised long ago by Lord Lindley in *Capital & Counties Bank* v. *Gordon* [1903] A.C. 240, Leading Cases, 4th Ed., p. 84.

Where insufficient cleared funds are available in the account to meet an unpaid cheque or bill and the banker wishes to proceed against other parties to the cheque or bill, it should preferably be retained by the bank in suspense to preserve all rights beyond question.

241 A banker is the holder for value of a bill of exchange, the acceptor of which executes a deed of assignment for the benefit of his creditors. The banker assents to the deed, and receives a dividend, thereby releasing the acceptor from liability for the balance of the amount of the bill.

(a) If this release is given without the consent of the drawer of the bill, is he and his estate (if he becomes bankrupt) discharged from all liability on the bill?

(b) Is the drawer (or his estate) discharged if, when the bill falls due and is dishonoured, the banker omits to give notice of dishonour to him or to his trustee in bankruptcy?

Answer: (a) If the deed of assignment contains the usual clause expressly reserving the rights of the assenting creditors against sureties for their debts, the drawer, who is, as regards the acceptor, in the position of a surety to the holder of the bill, is not discharged by the release of the acceptor.

(b) Omission to give notice of dishonour either to the drawer or to his trustee in bankruptcy discharges him or his estate from liability (secs. 48 and 49 (10) of the Bills of Exchange Act), unless there are special circumstances dispensing with such notice (sec. 50). The fact that the drawer has reason to believe that the bill will, on present-ment, be dishonoured, does not dispense with notice.

It is assumed that the bill was not accepted by the acceptor for the accommodation of the drawer; if it were, the drawer would be in the position of principal debtor, and the acceptor in that of surety. The release of the acceptor would not then in any circumstances discharge the drawer, and notice of dishonour to him would not be necessary. (Sec. 50 (2) (c) (4).)

242 A bill drawn by **A** is addressed to **B** 'at the **X** Bank, London,' and is accepted by **B** without stating where it is to be payable. If **B** is a customer of the **X** Bank, should that bank pay the bill at maturity without special instructions from him?

Answer: It is considered that **B**'s acceptance indicates that the bill is payable at the bank named in the address, and that it may accordingly be paid without special instructions.

243 What is the position of bankers in regard to the payment of bills domiciled with them, with and without advice?

Answer: Where there is express or implied agreement for

domiciled bills to be paid, whether with or without advice, that agreement may not be departed from by the bank without reasonable notice. What amounts to such an agreement is a question of fact. Apart from agreement, the fact of making an acceptance payable at the acceptor's bank amounts to an authority to the banker to pay it.

244 The X bank receives for collection from the Y bank a bill accepted payable at the bank by a person who is not a customer. Must the X bank accept the amount, if tendered by the acceptor or by any other person, or are they justified, if they prefer, in refusing it, and returning the bill unpaid to the Y bank?

Answer: London bankers invariably refuse to pay bills domiciled with them by parties who are not customers at either their London office or their country branches, and they consequently decline to accept money from the acceptors of such bills for the purpose of meeting them when due, and would, in the case referred to, return the bill unpaid.

245 A bill is sent for collection to the bank at which it is domiciled. On the day of maturity the acceptor has no funds to meet it, but a person who does not state that he acts on the acceptor's behalf offers to take it up for cash. Should the bank allow him to do so without the acceptor's consent?

Answer: No, because, under sec. 59 (1) of the Bills of Exchange Act, payment made otherwise than by or on behalf of the acceptor would not discharge the bill.

246 An inland bill drawn on W. J. Mulhen and Co., is accepted 'W. J. Mulhen,' payable at W. J. Mulhen's bankers. Is a banker justified in charging such a bill to the account of W. J. Mulhen, or should the discrepancy in the name of drawee and acceptor be rectified by the acceptor before the bill is debited to his account?

Answer: The banker is justified in charging the bill to the account of his customer by whom it is accepted. The discrepancy between the tenor and the acceptance of the bill is a matter which affects the holder, not the banker with whom it is domiciled.

247 Is a banker justified in returning an acceptance presented by a bank clerk in order that the name of his bank should be stamped on the back thereof?

Answer: It is the custom to stamp acceptances with the name of the presenting bank, but the banker is not justified in dishonouring an acceptance because it is not so stamped.

248 A bill becomes due on a Saturday or Sunday. Are the bankers with whom it is domiciled justified in holding it over until the Monday before returning it?

Answer: If the bill is duly presented on the Friday either at the counter or through the clearing, it must be returned 'not yet due'; but if sent by post direct it may be held over till the Monday.

249 If a bill due on May 9th is presented for payment on May 10th, would such a presentation be judged bad?

Answer: Yes. In *Hamilton Finance Co. Ltd.* v. *Coverley Westray Walbaum and Tosetti and Portland Finance Co. Ltd.* (1969) 1 Lloyd's Rep. 53 the necessity of adhering rigidly to sec. 45 of the Bills of Exchange Act was illustrated. A bill due on Saturday, 1st January, 1966, was sent for collection the previous day but not received until 4th January. The delay could not be explained away by New Year postal delays and the presentation was considered to be bad.

Banks frequently act as agents for collection on behalf of their customers and must use all reasonable care to secure acceptance and due payment of bills lodged with them. Failure to do so renders an agent liable to his principal. Bills which are domiciled at a bank should be sent out by the presenting bank in sufficient time to reach the bank at which they are payable on the due date.

250 A bill is due to be presented for payment on Monday, 4 May, but is delayed through a strike of postal workers. What is the presenting bank's position?

Answer: Sec. 46 (1) of the Bills of Exchange Act applies and the delay in making presentation for payment is excused since the delay is caused by circumstances beyond the control of the presenting bank, and cannot be imputed to its default, misconduct or negligence.

251 If a bill of exchange is crossed '& Co.' does this prevent a holder from demanding payment over the counter?

Answer: Secs. 76 to 82 of the Bills of Exchange Act apply only to cheques. Unless the bill is drawn on a banker, payable on demand, and therefore a cheque, under sec. 73, the holder may demand payment of it over the counter.

252 A bill is presented through the Clearing House with the crossing stamps of two clearing bankers on the back of it. Should the banker pay or return with answer 'crossed by two banks'?

Answer: The provisions of the Bills of Exchange Act as to 'crossing' do not apply to bills of exchange other than cheques; the banker therefore could not return the bill in question with the answer 'Crossed by two banks.'

253 A bank abroad remits to its London agent bills for acceptance and collection, with instructions that documents are to be surrendered on acceptance; in some cases after they have been accepted and the documents surrendered, the drawees wish to retire the bills under discount. Is the collecting banker compelled to allow this, or may he demand payment in full in exchange for the acceptance? If discount must be allowed, at what rate should it be deducted?

Answer: The collecting banker is under no obligation to the acceptor to allow him to retire the bill under discount. If such retirement were permitted, the rate would be a matter of arrangement.

254 A bill, due June 18, held by a bank, is dishonoured. On the 21st the acceptor hands to the bank a cheque for the amount with the request that it be held with the bill until the 23rd; would the bank jeopardise its position with regard to the drawer and endorsers by taking such a cheque without previously obtaining their sanction?

Answer: It is assumed that the bank, as holder of the dishonoured bill, gave notice of its dishonour within the time allowed (see sec. 49 (12) of the Bills of Exchange Act) to the drawer and endorsers, otherwise they would have been discharged from liability. If such notice was given, the bill may be held over without discharging them, but if the taking of the cheque amounted to a binding agreement by the bank to give time, even two days, to the acceptor for payment, it appears that the drawer and endorsers would be thereby discharged, unless the bank expressly reserved its rights against them.

255 (a) An inland bill is cancelled in error, and is returned unpaid

with the answer: 'refer to acceptor; cancelled in error.' Does the bank returning the bill incur any risk by having cancelled it?

(b) If the bill has foreign endorsements, is the presenting bank justified in taking it back marked 'cancelled in error'?

Answer: (a) No; under sec. 63 (3) of the Bills of Exchange Act a cancellation made unintentionally, or under a mistake, or without the authority of the holder, is inoperative.

(b) By a custom of the Clearing House, if bills bear foreign endorsements they are only accepted as 'Returns' under protest if they are marked 'cancelled in error,' inasmuch as in certain foreign countries the return of cancelled documents is illegal. In such a case the cancelling banker would probably be liable to the holder for the special damage sustained by the cancellation of the bill or cheque if the holder could prove that the banker was guilty of want of due care.

256 A banker is asked on behalf of a customer to present an accepted bill domiciled at the **X** Bank for payment on behalf of a customer. On the due date the acceptor telephones the bank and says that there is no money available at the **X** Bank, but the bill will be paid if presented at the **Y** Bank. What should the banker do? What course should the banker take if his customer gives him similar instructions?

Answer: The banker should take his customer's instructions. If his customer instructs him to present at the **Y** bank instead of the **X** bank he should remind the customer of the possible danger of not making formal presentation at the **X** bank. This is because failure to present in accordance with the terms of the bill releases the drawers and endorsers. In *Yeoman Credit* v. *Gregory* ([1963] 1 All E.R. 245) the endorser escaped liability because the banker presented the bill at the acceptor's request at a bank different from that on which it was accepted payable. The bill was unpaid on presentation at the **X** Bank, when the bill was again dishonoured. This second presentation was of no avail for preserving the endorser's liability.

257 By sec. 24 of the Bills of Exchange Act, when a signature on a bill is forged it is inoperative, and a subsequent holder does not acquire any right to the bill and cannot give a valid discharge for it when paid. By sec. 38, a holder in due course has a complete title, and can give a discharge for a bill in spite of any possible defect of title on the part of a previous holder. How is this apparent inconsistency to be explained?

Answer: There is no inconsistency between secs. 24 and 38. There is a distinction between 'defects of title' and absolute want of title. Sec. 29 shows what is meant by defects of title—a defective title can be made good by negotiation to a holder in due course, but a person who holds under a forgery has no title at all, as, for instance, a person claiming under a forged endorsement. As soon as the endorsement is shown to be forged it becomes wholly inoperative, and must be regarded as not written. The person who claims under it is not a holder as defined by sec. 2—he is a mere wrongful possessor, and not being a 'holder,' he cannot be a 'holder in due course.' The bill has never been negotiated to him (sec. 29), for by sec. 31, a bill to order is negotiated by the endorsement of the holder, but in the case of forgery the holder has not endorsed it. A forgery is not the 'endorsement of the holder' and the person who claims under it is not an endorsee. No person can be a holder unless he makes title through genuine signatures—estoppel, of course, excepted.

It must not be forgotten that 'holder' is a technical term quite distinct from 'possessor.'

258 Is a banker protected in having paid a bill drawn upon and purporting to be accepted by a customer payable at his bank, if it is afterwards discovered that

(*a*) the acceptor's, or

(*b*) an endorser's

signature is a forgery?

Can the banker, on discovering the forgery, recover the amount of the bill from the person to whom he has paid it, if that person received the money in good faith and without knowledge of the forgery?

Answer: There is no statutory protection in respect of the forgery of the acceptor's signature. Nor is there where an endorser's signature is forged, unless the endorser is a fictitious or non-existent person, in which case the bill may be treated as payable to bearer.

In case (*a*), where it is the customer's signature that is forged, Sir John Paget, though he rejected the view that a banker, as regards third parties is bound to know his customer's signature, thought that 'a Court would be astute to debar a banker from recovering money he had paid to an innocent person on a forgery of his own customer's signature.'

In case (b) the banker's position will depend upon how long it has taken to discover the forgery, and whether the person who received payment has been prejudiced by delay. Thus if the forgery is discovered and notified promptly, repayment can normally be claimed; if a much longer time has passed the possibility of repayment will depend on the circumstances of the particular case. In *National Westminster Bank Ltd.* v. *Barclays Bank International and Another*, 1975 Q.B. 654; (Leading Cases, 4th Ed., p. 79) it was held that detriment to the person receiving money paid in mistake is not in itself a bar to recovery of the money.

259 In what circumstances can a real, existing person be, as against the acceptor of a bill drawn payable to him, a 'fictitious or non-existing person' within the meaning of sec. 7 (3) of the Bills of Exchange Act, which provides that where the payee of a bill is a fictitious or non-existing person, the bill may be treated as payable to bearer?

Answer: If the payee's name was inserted, whether by the drawer or by some fraudulent person, 'by way of pretence only, and with no intention that he should ever obtain or have anything to do with the bill' the payee is a 'fictitious person' and the bill is payable to bearer (*Bank of England* v. *Vagliano,* [1891] A.C. 107, Leading Cases, 4th Ed., p. 31).

But where the drawer of a cheque is induced by fraudulent misrepresentation to name a real person as payee, and intends that that person shall be the payee, the cheque cannot be treated as payable to bearer. (*Vinden* v. *Hughes,* [1905] 1 K.B. 795; Leading Cases, 4th Ed., p. 34; *North and South Wales Bank* v. *Macbeth,* [1908] A.C. 137, Leading Cases, 4th Ed., p. 33).

260 The payee of a bill drawn on and accepted by a bank gives notice to the bank that he has lost the bill, and that if it should purport to bear his endorsement such endorsement would be a forgery. At due date the bill is presented by a person who states that he is a holder in due course, and who is able to satisfy the bank of his good faith. Should the bank pay, and, if so, has the payee any recourse?

Answer: The banker, having notice of the probable forgery of the payee's endorsement, should not pay without confirmation of the endorsement.

261 Is the payment of a Bill affected by the exchange control regulations of this country?

Answer: In *Contract and Trading Co. (Southern) Ltd.* v. *Barbey* (1960) A.C. 244, the appellant company dishonoured three bills of exchange on presentation totalling £8,700, after earlier acceptance of them. The company's defence against the Swiss respondents was that the exchange control consent to the payment of the bills had not been obtained as required by the Exchange Control Act, 1947. The House of Lords rejected this contention while admitting that the debt could not be paid without exchange control consent. As the 1947 Act controlled only the immediate destination of the money, funds could, however, be paid into the court, discharging the debtor, and then held until exchange control clearance had been obtained before making payment to the foreign creditor.

262 Is the holder, in England, of a bill drawn, unstamped, in a country in which such a bill is subject, by the law of the country, to stamp duty, prejudiced in any way by the absence of a stamp?

Answer: Not so far as proceedings against any party to the bill in this country are concerned (sec. 72 (1) (*a*) of the Bills of Exchange Act). The absence of a stamp may prevent the holder from recovering against persons who have become parties to the bill in the country of origin.

PROTEST

263 (*a*) What is the object of noting a bill?

(*b*) Is noting or, in the case of foreign bills, protesting, necessary or optional?

(*c*) Can a bill be validly noted or protested if presented for payment after the due date?

Answer: The object of noting is to have proof of due presentation and of dishonour.

(*a*) and (*b*) Protest, or noting and subsequent protest, is necessary in the case of foreign bills, in order to preserve recourse against the drawer and endorsers (sec. 51 (2) of the Bills of Exchange Act).

In case of inland bills noting is optional, unless the holder wishes to present to a 'case of need' (secs. 51 (1) and 65).

(*c*) When a bill is noted or protested, it may be noted on the day of its dishonour, and must be noted not later than the next succeeding business day (sec. 51 (4) as amended by the Bills of Exchange (Time of Noting) Act, 1917). When the bill has been duly noted the protest can be extended at any time afterwards.

A bill must be presented for payment on the due date, or the drawer and endorsers are discharged (sec. 45 (1), unless delay in presenting is caused by circumstances beyond the control of the holder (sec. 46 (1)).

264 In the event of the holder of a dishonoured foreign bill payable in England neglecting both to protest and to present to the 'case of need,' does he lose recourse against the previous endorsers?

Answer: Yes; he must protest the bill in order to charge prior endorsers (Bills of Exchange Act, sec. 51 (2)), and it may possibly be necessary, in some cases, to present to the 'case of need' in order to charge a foreign endorser in his own country, though in England it is in the holder's option whether he resort to the 'case of need' or not (sec. 15).

265 A bill drawn abroad, stamped on its face 'sans frais,' is received by a banker for collection. Attached to it is a docket, stating that in case of non-payment, it is to be 'noted only.' The bill is unpaid, but the collecting bank does not note. Does any liability for the omission rest with the banker?

Answer: The collecting bank should attend to the instructions of the sender of the bill as stated on the docket attached, and would be liable for any damage resulting from his omission to do so.

266 (*a*) In the absence of specific instructions, is it usual to have a dishonoured foreign bill protested?

(*b*) When such a bill has been protested, or noted under English law, for non-acceptance, must it be protested (or noted) again if dishonoured by non-payment?

Answer: (*a*) 'Uniform Rules for Collections', Art. 17,* states that, in the absence of specific instructions, 'the banks concerned with the collection have no obligation to have the commercial paper protested (or subjected to legal process in lieu thereof) for non-payment or non-acceptance'. Normally specific instructions are taken, but if not it is usual, nevertheless, to protest the bill before returning it. In England, to save expense, it may be noted only, and the protest may be subsequently extended if desired.

(*b*) Further protest may be necessary to charge a foreign drawer or endorser in his own country although under English law, further

*See Appendix B

noting or protest is not necessary (sec. 51 (2) and (3) of the Bills of Exchange Act). Even so in the absence of definite instructions, it is prudent to note such a bill for non-payment. The protest may subsequently be extended if desired.

267 A London banker receives from another banker for collection a foreign bill. On the back of this bill, against the last endorsement, which is that of the customer, is stamped 'Ohne Kosten,' and written alongside, 'No charges.' A ticket is also attached to the front of the bill stating that 'No notarial charges are to be incurred,' but the ticket is neither initialled nor signed.

Is the collecting banker justified on such instructions in not having the bill noted? In other words, is it necessary that signed instructions should be given, or are such instructions sufficient?

Answer: Such indications are usually considered sufficient.

268 The drawer of a foreign bill payable to 'self or order,' adds to his endorsement the words 'sans frais.' Subsequently several endorsements are added to the bill, and ultimately it is returned unpaid with protest charges.

(1) Can these protest expenses be recovered from the drawer?

(2) If, by his stipulation for 'no charges' the drawer cannot be called upon to pay them, are the subsequent endorsers equally freed from liability in respect of any protest expenses?

Answer: If endorsers choose to take the drawer's endorsement with the words 'sans frais' attached, they cannot come upon the drawer for either return commission expenses or protest charges. They are not themselves free from liability for such charges unless they have so stipulated in their endorsements.

269 Can an inland bill be legally noted and a foreign bill protested immediately after its dishonour—say at 11.30 a.m. or should this action be deferred until later in the day.

Answer: Notice of dishonour can be given at once. The bills can also be noted and protested at once, but the usual course is to wait until the end of the business day, or the following morning.

270 By noting or protesting an inland bill is the necessity of sending notice of dishonour to the parties obviated?

Answer: No.

271 A bill payable on demand, drawn abroad, with documents attached, is presented for payment and the drawees request the bill to be held over until the arrival of the ship. Should the collecting bankers have the bill protested for non-payment?

Answer: As the bill is drawn abroad, the collecting banker would appear to be bound by the Bills of Exchange Act, 1882, sec. 51 (2), to note or protest, and to advise a non-payment of the bill. There is, however, some doubt whether this sub-section does, in fact, relate to sight bills.

In any case it appears to be the practice in the City of London not to note or protest sight bills when payment is refused on the grounds that the carrying vessel has not arrived. The procedure customarily followed is merely for non-payment to be advised at once to the principal (normally a correspondent bank) unless, of course, other specific instructions had already been received. The bill is usually retained and presented again on the arrival of the ship.

272 Does a foreign bill drawn after date, and bearing the words 'Presentable at maturity' at the top left corner, require to be noted, if acceptance is refused with the answer that the bill is payable without acceptance?

Answer: The words 'presentable at maturity' do not imply that the bill is not to be presented for acceptance, and it would in practice be presented for that purpose.

The refusal of acceptance, even for the reason quoted, obliges the holder, under sec. 42 of the Bills of Exchange Act, to treat the bill as dishonoured by non-acceptance. He must therefore have it noted, whether the protest is extended or not (sec. 51 (2) and (4)), and must give notice of dishonour to the drawer and endorsers (sec. 48).

273 Can the drawer of a dishonoured foreign bill demand the cost of protest from the acceptor?

Answer: Yes; if he has been charged with such cost. (Bills of Exchange Act, sec. 57 (1) (c)).

274 Can a householder's protest be made by any responsible person, whether strictly a 'householder' or not?

Answer: Sec. 94 of the Bills of Exchange Act provides that where a dishonoured bill is authorised or required to be protested, and the services of a notary cannot be obtained at the place where the bill is dishonoured, any householder or substantial resident of the place may make a householder's protest in the presence of two witnesses. The form given in Schedule I of the Act may be used with necessary modifications, and the person making the protest must first present the bill himself, though it is not necessary that the witnesses shall accompany him when he presents it.

275 What is the object of protesting a bill 'for better security,' and for the purpose of making such a protest, should the bill be presented at the bank at which it has been accepted payable, or at the place of business or residence of the acceptor?

Answer: Under sec. 51 (5) of the Bills of Exchange Act, where the acceptor of a bill becomes bankrupt or insolvent or suspends payment before it matures, the holder may cause the bill to be protested for better security against the drawer and endorsers. The only effect of such a protest in England is that the bill may be accepted for honour under sec. 65 (1), but under some continental codes security can be demanded from the drawer and endorsers.

The bill should be presented at the place of business or residence of the acceptor, claiming better security.

276 When a bill drawn abroad on a person carrying on business or residing in London, and accepted by him payable at a London bank, is dishonoured with the answer 'refer to acceptor,' and is noted or protested, can the notary legally demand two notarial fees, for presenting at the bank and also at the acceptor's place of business or residence?

Answer: It is a well-recognised custom of notaries, in the case of bills having foreign endorsements, to which such an answer is given, to present at the acceptor's place of business or residence, if within a reasonable distance, and to charge for so doing, which, in such a case, they can probably legally do. The object is to give the acceptor a further opportunity of meeting the bill, but, according to English law, such second presentment is unnecessary. (Bills of Exchange Act, sec. 45 (4) (*a*).)

277 A cheque drawn in England on an English bank, but bearing a foreign endorsement, is presented for payment through the clearing and is returned unpaid. The London agents of the foreign holders say that it should have been protested. Was it the duty of the drawee bank to protest it before returning it?

Answer: As the cheque was not drawn abroad, protest was not necessary under sec. 51 (2) of the Bills of Exchange Act.

278 When the original of a bill cannot be obtained or recovered, is noting or protesting a copy of the bill legally of any avail?

Answer: Sec. 51 (8) of the Bills of Exchange Act provides that where a bill is lost or destroyed, or is wrongly detained from the person entitled to hold it, protest may be made on a copy or written particulars thereof.

DRAFTS

279 Can bankers in England or Wales lawfully issue drafts, or draw cheques on themselves, payable to bearer on demand?

Answer: No; under sec. 11 of the Bank Charter Act, 1844, it is unlawful for a banker or banking company, other than the Bank of England, to draw, accept, make or issue in England or Wales any bill of exchange or promissory note which is expressed to be, or in legal effect is, payable to bearer on demand.

280 A draft issued by a bank at a customer's request, payable to a third party, is afterwards returned to the bank by the customer, without the payee's endorsement, on a representation made by the customer that the draft has not been delivered to the payee, and that the purpose for which it was obtained has been abandoned. The amount of the draft is then recredited to the customer's account.
   Is the bank liable to the payee for the amount of the draft
   (*a*) if the draft has in fact not been delivered to him, or
   (*b*) if it has been in his hands, but has been lost or stolen, without having been endorsed by him?

Answer: (*a*) Since, under sec. 21 of the Bills of Exchange Act, every contract on a bill (including a cheque) is incomplete and revocable until delivery of the instrument in order to give effect thereto, the bank may cancel the draft, if it has not been delivered to the payee, without incurring any liability to him.

   (*b*) Where the draft had been delivered to the payee and the bank, without his consent, applied the amount to the account of its customer, the bank might be liable for conversion.

   When asked by a customer to cancel any draft previously issued to that customer, the bank should always ensure by prudent enquiry that the circumstances permit such action, or it should be satisfied that the financial standing of the customer justifies the acceptance of any risk involved.

281 The 'first of exchange' of a draft payable at sight, drawn on the X bank by a foreign agent, and purporting to be endorsed by the payee, is presented and paid. Afterwards the payee in person presents the 'second of exchange,' and demands payment, representing that the first has been lost without his endorsement.

   If the X bank refuses payment of the second of exchange, has the payee a right of recourse against the drawer of the draft?

   Answer: No. Under sec. 10 (1) of the Bills of Exchange Act, a bill expressed to be payable at sight is payable on demand. The X bank, if it paid the first of exchange in good faith and in the ordinary course of business, is therefore protected by sec. 60 of the Act, even though the payee's endorsement was forged; and, one part of the bill having thus been discharged by payment in due course, the whole bill is discharged. (Sec. 71 (6).)

   The payee's only recourse is against the bank or other person to whom the first of exchange was paid.

BILLS OF EXCHANGE—DOCUMENTARY

(Reference to Uniform Customs and Practice for Documentary Credits (1974 Revision) will supply the answer to many queries on this subject. See Appendix A.)

282 What is the practice of London bankers in paying or accepting documentary bills without production of all the parts of the bill of lading?

   Answer: In the absence of special instructions, the practice is to require the full set or a proper indemnity.

283 If a bill is expressed to be drawn against specific goods, but the documents are not attached to it, and the goods are in the hands of the drawee, who has accepted the bill, has the holder of the bill any charge on the goods if the bill is dishonoured?

   Answer: No. To this rule the special case in which both drawer and drawee are insolvent is an exception. *Ex parte Waring,* (1815) 19 Vesey Inn 345.

284   A bank accepts a bill drawn under a letter of credit, and receives the documents that were attached to it. In the event of the insolvency of the customer at whose request the letter of credit was issued, is the bank responsible for the goods to the holder of the bill?

Answer: No.

285   Does a bank, in presenting a documentary bill for acceptance or payment, guarantee the authenticity of the documents attached to it, or the existence of the goods therein mentioned?

Answer: No. (See Art. 9, Uniform Customs and Practice for Documentary Credits (1974 Revision.))*

286   If, when a bill of exchange with documents attached is negotiated to a bank, the bill of lading is specially endorsed to the bank, does the bank, when further negotiating the bill of exchange, incur any liability in respect of the goods by endorsing the bill of lading, without adding the words 'without recourse'?

Answer: Under sec. 1 of the Bills of Lading Act, 1855, the endorsee of a bill of lading *to whom the property in the goods passes* is subject to the same liabilities in respect of the goods as if the contract contained in the bill of lading had been made with himself; but in *Burdick* v. *Sewell* (1884) 10 A.C. 74, it was held that the endorsement and delivery of a bill of lading does not necessarily pass the whole property in the goods so as to transfer to the endorsee all liabilities in respect of them. If the intention is to give a pledge by way of security, the general property in the goods remains in the endorser, and only a special property passes to the endorsee. The general property passes only when the pledgee does something to assert ownership, e.g. by taking actual or constructive delivery of the goods.

The words 'without recourse' therefore do not appear to affect the endorser's liability in any way, and should not be added to the endorsement. Some shipping companies insist that the words 'without recourse' be removed from any endorsement.

287   A bill drawn abroad on a person in England, having documents attached to be given up on payment, is sent for collection to an English bank, and is accepted by the drawee. Before the maturity of the bill, the drawer abroad, believing the acceptor to be in

*See Appendix A

difficulties, wishes to regain possession of the goods, and instructs the bank in England to return the bill and documents to him. Can the bank safely do so, or is it responsible for the documents to the acceptor?

Answer: As the bank is, it is assumed, merely agent for collection, it will be justified in obeying the orders of its principal by returning the bill and documents to him; but, as between the principal and the acceptor, it would appear that the latter has acquired a right to, or a lien upon, the goods by accepting the bill.

288 A bank holds an accepted bill with shipping documents attached, to be delivered against payment. Some time before maturity the acceptor offers part payment of the bill and asks that a proportionate part of the goods shall be released. What is the usual practice when such a request is made?

Answer: Sometimes the instructions accompanying a documentary bill authorise the holder to release part of the goods in exchange for payment of a proportionate part of the amount; but in the absence of such instructions no such release can safely be made.

289 What is the practice of banks in England and Wales allowing rebate on documentary bills in cases where the bills fall due on a Sunday? Is rebate allowed up to Friday only, or up to Sunday?

Answer: The practice is the same both in calculating interest on bills discounted and in calculating rebate, viz. to charge and allow interest up to the nominal due date of the bill, making no allowance for the fact that such date may be a non-business day.

DISCOUNTING

290 A sends to his bankers for discount a bill drawn 'per pro **A, B**,' duly accepted by the drawee, and endorsed by **A** himself. As far as the bankers are aware, **B** has no general authority to sign on **A**'s behalf. Should the bankers raise any objection to the manner in which the bill is drawn?

Answer: Under sec. 54 (2) (*a*) of the Bills of Exchange Act the acceptor of a bill is precluded from denying to a holder in due course the genuineness of the drawer's signature, and under sec. 55 (2) (*b*) the endorser of a bill is precluded from denying to a holder in due course the genuineness and regularity in all respects of the drawer's signature. No objection need therefore be raised, and any defect of authority on the part of **B** must be considered to have been cured by A's personal endorsement.

291 Your customer presents a banker's draft drawn on a foreign centre in a foreign currency and asks you to purchase the draft from him. He states that he feels that the currency is not very stable and for this reason he requires sterling payment as soon as possible. On enquiry you find that the bank is not prepared to purchase the draft but will collect it on behalf of the customer, who agrees.

How do you advise your customer and in what way can you expedite payment of the draft?

Answer: The usual collection instructions should be taken from the customer with a note specifically stating that payment is to be reimbursed by telegraphic transfer. The request for telegraphic transfer will not hasten payment of the draft but it will expedite transfer of the funds after it has been paid. The draft should, of course, be scrutinised to ensure that it is in order, and that it has been endorsed by the customer if this is necessary.

In view of his comments on the stability of the currency, the customer should also be advised that it is always important to consider taking out a forward contract with the bank to protect him from any fluctuations in exchange rates.

292 An inward 60 day sight documentary collection on your customer is received at your branch and the accompanying instructions from the bank abroad state that the bill is to be 'avalised' by the drawee's bankers. What does the term 'avalised' mean?

Answer: It is the intention of the remitter that the drawee's bankers guarantee payment of the bill as a condition upon release of the documents. A banker who endorses a bill 'endorsement pour aval' is guaranteeing the person who has asked for the endorsement and as such would be contingently liable in the event of non-payment of the bill.

An 'aval' is not at the present time recognised under English law although it is widely used on the Continent. The nearest English equivalent of a 'pour aval' is an endorsement on a bill as under sec. 56 of the Bills of Exchange Act, 1882, 'where a person signs a bill otherwise than as drawer or acceptor he thereby incurs the liabilities of an endorser to a holder in due course'. Before guaranteeing or 'avalising' the bill the bank must be satisfied with the customer's standing, his intentions and ability to meet the bill at maturity. As security, an indemnity should be taken from the customer to cover any claims made against the bank in the event of non-payment of the bill.

293 Should a banker discount a bill drawn payable to the payee 'only'?

Answer: No; the word 'only' indicates an intention that the bill shall not be transferable. (See sec. 8 (1) of the Bills of Exchange Act.)

294 The drawer of a bill, after it has been accepted, fraudulently alters the amount of it to a larger amount, utilising for this purpose blanks which he had left in the bill when drawing it. He then discounts it with his banker for the larger amount. When the bill falls due, what amount can the banker recover from (*a*) the acceptor and (*b*) the drawer, respectively?

Answer: The alteration is clearly a 'material alteration' under sec. 64 (1) of the Bills of Exchange Act, and as such avoids the bill except against the person who himself made it, and any subsequent endorsers; but the sub-sec. provides that if, as presumably in this case, the alteration is not apparent, a holder in due course may avail himself of the bill as if it had not been altered, and may enforce payment of it according to its original tenor. (*a*) The banker may therefore recover the original amount from the acceptor. (See *Scholfield* v. *Londesborough,* [1896] A.C. 514, (Leading Cases, 4th Ed., p. 46), in which, in similar circumstances, it was held that the acceptor, in accepting a bill containing blanks, was not guilty of such negligence as to make himself liable for the larger amount.)

(*b*) The banker can recover the larger amount, or the balance of it, from the drawer, against whom the bill is not in any respect avoided.

295 A is the drawer of a bill payable to his own order, which he endorses and negotiates. It is afterwards negotiated back to him, and he then discounts the bill at his bankers, who insist upon his re-endorsing it. At maturity the bill is dishonoured. Can the bankers enforce payment against any intervening party to whom **A** was previously liable, notwithstanding that **A** is barred from doing so by sec. 37 of the Bills of Exchange Act?

Answer: Yes; the bankers, as holders in due course, may recover from any of the parties whose names appear on the bill. The disability imposed by sec. 37 on **A** is merely personal to him, and is intended to prevent 'circuity of action'; for if **A** could sue an intervening party, that party could sue him in turn as drawer.

296 The drawer of a discounted bill which has been remitted for collection, requests his bankers, four days before the due date, to withdraw the bill, and gives them authority to debit his account. Before the bill is received back cheques are presented and paid which exhaust his balance.

Has the bank still recourse against the acceptor, or, supposing the drawer has informed him that the bank has consented to withdraw the bill, can he repudiate liability?

Answer: The usual practice when a discounted bill is retired by the drawer is to obtain from him a cheque, or other authority, to debit the account at once, without waiting for the return of the bill. In the case mentioned, however, the bank still has recourse against the acceptor, who could not repudiate liability in the circumstances suggested.

297 A customer closes his current account, and has at the time bills under discount. The bank requests him to take these up, which he refuses to do. Can the bank compel him to do so?

Answer: No; the bank has no recourse against its ex-customer unless the bills are dishonoured at maturity, and notice of dishonour is given to him.

298 At maturity a discounted bill is paid in part only, and a new bill is drawn and accepted for the balance, but the banker retains the old bill. If when the new bill falls due it is dishonoured, can the bank recover from the parties to the old bill?

Answer: Apart from any special arrangement, the new bill operated only as conditional payment of the balance of the old one, and on its dishonour the remedies on the old bill are revived, provided that in allowing the additional time to the acceptor the banker acted with the consent of any endorsers of the old bill who were in the position of sureties to him for its payment, or that he expressly reserved his rights against them; otherwise they would be discharged.

299 A discounted bill is dishonoured at maturity and the credit balance of the customer's account is insufficient to cover it. As there is no arrangement for an overdraft, the banker debits the bill to a suspense account, and sends notice of dishonour to the customer. Can he appropriate the customer's credit balance as a set-off against his liability on the bill?

Answer: As the banker could, on returning the bill to the customer, have debited his account with the whole amount of it, had the balance been sufficient, it is considered that the existing balance can be appropriated as a set-off *pro tanto;* but the dishonour of cheques drawn before the notice of dishonour of the bill reached the customer should be avoided if possible.

300 A bank discounts for a customer, **A,** a bill drawn by him and accepted by **B,** a customer of another branch of the same bank. At maturity the bill is dishonoured 'orders not to pay.' Can the bank, if unable to debit **A,** ignore **B**'s instruction not to pay the bill, and debit **B**'s account with it, if his balance is sufficient to meet it?

Answer: The bank as holder in due course of the bill is entitled to recover the amount of it from **B,** who is the person primarily liable on it, and, notwithstanding his instruction not to pay it, the bank may, after giving reasonable notice to him, hold a sufficient part of his credit balance as a set-off against his liability. Care should be taken to provide for outstanding cheques. (See *Buckingham* v. *London and Midland Bank* (1895), 12 T.L.R. 70, Leading Cases, 4th Ed., p. 197, and *Prosperity Ltd.* v. *Lloyds Bank* (1923), 39 T.L.R. 372, Leading Cases, 4th Ed., p. 303).

DOCUMENTARY CREDITS

*(Reference to Uniform Customs and Practice for Documentary Credits (1974 Revision) will supply the answer to many queries on this subject—*See Appendix A.

301 A London credit is opened stipulating that goods shall be shipped under a c.i.f. contract and calling for the production, *inter alia*, of a clean bill of lading. Bills of lading are tendered bearing an addition of one of the following clauses:

   (*a*) 'Sorting charge if any to be borne by consignees.'
   'Harbour improvement rate of .... per ton, payable by consignees.'

(b) 'Terminal charges at destination to be added and collected from consignees.'
Can either of these bills of lading be accepted as clean bills?

Answer: A clean bill of lading is one 'which bears no superimposed clause or notation which expressly declares a defective condition of the goods and/or the packaging.' (Uniform Customs and Practice for Documentary Credits—1974 Revision, Article 18).* Neither of these clauses 'expressly declares a defective condition of the goods and/or the packaging,' and the bills of lading are, therefore, clean. In the first case, payment should be refused, not because the bill of lading is not clean, but because sorting is part of the cost and should be included in cost. In the second case payment cannot be refused, for terminal charges at destination are always for the account of the consignees in a 'C.I.F. . . . Port' contract; for example, landing charges are always borne by consignees if the contract is C.I.F. at a specified port.

302 If a banker, at the request of a customer, issues an irrevocable letter of credit undertaking to honour drafts accompanied by documents purporting to relate to goods described in a certain manner, is the banker under any obligation to honour a draft accompanied by documents describing the relative goods in a manner appearing to him to differ materially from the description contained in the customer's request and in the letter of credit?

Answer: 'The description of the goods in the commercial invoice must correspond with the description in the credit. In the remaining documents the goods may be described in general terms not inconsistent with the description of the goods in the credit.' (Uniform Customs and Practice for Documentary Credits—1974 Revision, Article 32(c)).*
A banker acts at his peril if he departs from the precise terms of his customer's mandate, reproduced in the letter of credit.

303 Bank A issues a traveller's letter of credit in favour of X for £500. X cashes several cheques under the credit, including a cheque for £100, cashed at Bank B. This cheque, through Bank B's inadvertence, is not endorsed on the letter of credit. X then calls at Bank C and draws the ostensible balance shown on the letter of credit, £150. On presentation at Bank A the cheque for £150 is dishonoured, as the balance available is only £50.

*See Appendix A

(a) Was Bank **A** right in refusing payment of the draft presented by Bank **C**?

(b) If not, can Bank **A** recover from Bank **B** the £100 paid by the latter?

Answer: (a) Assuming Bank **C** to have acted in good faith and in accordance with the instructions contained in the letter, Bank **A** could not withhold payment of the draft. It is the usual practice, when issuing travellers' letters of credit, to instruct the correspondent making the final payment to attach the letter of credit to the draft. If this was done in the case referred to, Bank **A** would not, in ordinary circumstances, have declined payment.

(b) Probably they can.

304 If a customer on whose behalf his bankers have opened an irrevocable credit with a foreign bank, undertaking to honour bills drawn in accordance with its terms, (a) instructs the bankers, while the credit is still in force, to honour no further bills drawn under it, or (b) becomes insolvent, should the bankers cancel, or attempt to cancel, the credit?

Answer: (a) and (b) No. An irrevocable credit can neither be amended nor cancelled without the agreement of all parties thereto. (Uniform Customs and Practice for Documentary Credits—1974 Revision, Article 3).*

305 A confirmed documentary credit provides that insurance is to be effected by the shippers. If one of the documents attached to a bill presented for acceptance under the credit is an insurance policy of doubtful value, or if the insurers are known to have actually defaulted before the bill is presented, should the drawee bank refuse to accept the bill?

Answer: No; the bank's obligation is to accept the bill if the documents attached to it 'appear on their face to be in accordance with the terms and conditions of the credit.' (Uniform Customs and Practice for Documentary Credits—1974 Revision, Article 8).* If the customer on whose behalf the credit was opened desires to have insurance of a particular kind, this must be specified in the credit. 'All instructions to issue, confirm or advise a credit must state precisely the documents against which payment, acceptance or negotiation is to be made.' (Article 14.)

*See Appendix A

306 Can a banker who has opened a revocable credit, not containing any undertaking to honour bills drawn under it, cancel the credit at any time?

Answer: A revocable credit may be amended at any moment without prior notice to the beneficiary. However, the recipient bank or branch is entitled to reimbursement when it has acted upon the credit prior to receipt of notice of amendment or cancellation (Uniform Customs and Practice for Documentary Credits—1974 Revision, Article 2.)*

307 If the terms of a documentary credit permit the drawing of bills 'without recourse on drawer', does this provision affect the contract between the buyer and the seller of the goods, or does it affect only the rights of the parties to the bills?

Answer: Such a provision authorises the negotiating bank to negotiate bills having the words 'without recourse' added to the drawer's signature. The addition has no effect on the contract of sale, but it relieves the drawer of personal liability on the bills. (See sec. 16 (1) of the Bills of Exchange Act.)

308 A merchanting customer requests his bank to establish an irrevocable documentary credit in favour of his overseas supplier in payment for a shipment of goods. The merchant has already arranged an onward sale of these goods to an overseas buyer in another country and informs his bank that payment in his favour is covered by an irrevocable credit. In support of his request for an outward credit, the customer suggests to the bank that the credit established in his favour should be used as security for the transaction. What considerations should his bank bear in mind?

Answer: This arrangement is known as a 'back to back' documentary credit which involves the establishment of an outward credit against the backing of an inward credit. When documents are presented in due course under the outward credit and assuming they are found to be in order, the bank will be obliged to debit the customer's account. The customer will then be required to produce the necessary documents under the inward credit and if, upon examination, there are discrepancies which prevent the bank making a non-recourse payment to him, the documents can only be held to the order of the bank's customer, subject to any lien of the

*See Appendix A

bank, whilst efforts are made to obtain agreement from the ultimate buyer for payment to be made notwithstanding the discrepancies in the documents. In this event, the inward credit has not constituted good security.

The bank should therefore consider establishing an outward credit on this basis only when the financial status and integrity of their customer is such that they would be prepared to establish the credit on an unsecured basis or when the security presently held on behalf of the customer is considered adequate to cover this new or additional liability.

309 A customer hands to his bank a bill of exchange drawn on his overseas buyer together with supporting documents. Because of a dispute regarding the amount of freight included in the invoice, the bill and documents are released to the overseas buyer for less than the bill amount. The customer claims the difference from his bank as his instructions have not been complied with. Is the bank liable?

Answer: A legal action by the customer against his bankers may well result in the bankers being held responsible through the action of the agent, the overseas banking correspondent, who presented the bill for payment. In practice, however, when collecting documentary bills, banks disclaim responsibility in writing for any losses which are not directly due to the negligence or default of their own officials.

310 A banker collecting a documentary bill on behalf of a customer receives instructions that all charges are to be for the account of the drawee of the bill. The documents are released to the drawee against payment of the bill amount, charges being refused. The customer claims that the correspondent bank had no authority to release the documents without payment of all charges. Was the correspondent bank correct in its action?

Answer: In accordance with Article 22 of Uniform Rules for Collections*, charges, if refused, may be waived unless there is a specific instruction to the effect that charges may not be waived.

311 Documents under a letter of credit advised by a UK bank on behalf of an issuing bank overseas are presented in order to the UK bank. The overseas issuing bank has not arranged for sufficient funds to be available with the advising bank to meet the drawing under its letter

*See Appendix B

of credit and the advising bank refuses payment to the beneficiary. The beneficiary insists that payment be made as the documents are in order. Is the advising bank correct in refusing to make payment?

Answer: Unless the advising bank has confirmed the credit, there is no contractual relationship between itself and the beneficiary of the credit and in these circumstances it would be in order in refusing payment.

312   Documents are presented under a letter of credit to a UK bank. The documents relate to a shipment from London to Antwerp and presentation of the documents is made two weeks after the date of the bill of lading. Neither the last date of permitted shipment nor the expiry date has been reached and the documents are in order but the bank refuses payment, as it considers that there has been an undue delay in presentation of the documents and that the relative goods will already have reached the port of destination. Is the bank correct in its attitude?

Answer: Under the 1974 Revision of Uniform Customs and Practice, Article 41, (see Appendix A) documents may be presented within 21 days of the date of the bill of lading, unless the credit stipulates to the contrary, and, therefore, the bank would be incorrect in refusing to make payment against documents for this reason.

313   A payment is made by a bank to the beneficiary of a letter of credit as the documents are regarded by the bank as being in order. The documents are subsequently mailed to the bank overseas which issued the credit, and some two months after the documents have been mailed, a letter is received from the issuing bank stating that payment has been refused by the opener of the letter of credit because it is claimed there is a discrepancy in the documents. The issuing bank requests the paying bank to reimburse it for the amount of the drawing. Is it correct in so doing?

Answer: No, this would not be correct. The advising bank would resist such a claim on the grounds that it had not been advised within a reasonable time. (Articles 8(d) and 8(e) of Uniform Customs and Practice refer).

314   A UK bank receives a bill of exchange drawn at 90 days sight together with documents. The overseas bank's instructions are that the documents should be delivered to the drawees against their

acceptance with the UK bank adding its aval. What action should the UK bank take?

Answer: The action described as 'adding your aval' or avalising as it is sometimes known, is the act of the bank adding its name to an accepted bill and guaranteeing its payment on its maturity date.

It is not the general practice of UK clearing banks so to do, but it is a common practice in certain continental countries. When confronted with such a situation, the branch manager would be well advised to refer back to his overseas principal, pointing out it was not the practice so to do, and request their further instructions. There is no specific provision for avalising in the Bills of Exchange Act, though sec. 56 relates to endorsement.

It would be dangerous for the bank simply to release the documents against the customer's acceptance alone since, if the bill were subsequently dishonoured by non-payment, the overseas principal could claim that its original instructions had not been complied with and seek recompense for any loss sustained.

PROMISSORY NOTES

315 Is a sterling certificate of deposit which is payable to bearer invalid by reason of being issued payable on demand rather than on a specific maturity date?

Answer: Such a document would constitute a bank note and would as such be illegal. Sterling certificates of deposit, which were first issued in 1968, can only be issued by banks who hold specific exchange control permission to issue such certificates and must be held by authorised depositaries. The document certifies that a certain sum of money has been deposited with the bank, to be repaid with interest at a specified rate. The undertaking to pay by the bank is conditional on the surrender of the certificate on the maturity date through an authorised depositary, who should deliver it to the bank which is the paying agent.

316 Is a promissory note invalid by reason of the omission of the name of a payee, the terms of the note being simply 'I promise to pay the sum of'?

Answer: Such a document is not a promissory note, as it does not come within the definition set forth in sec. 83 (1) of the Bills of Exchange Act, which states that a promissory note must be made payable to, or to the order of, a specified person or to bearer.

317 Would the following be considered to be correctly drawn?
'One month after date I promise to pay to **X** the sum of . . .
pounds for value received.

John Jones.
Wm. Smith.'

Answer: This is in effect a joint and several promissory note. (See
Bills of Exchange Act, sec. 85 (2).)

318 Is the maker of a note drawn in the following form legally liable?
'Three months after date we jointly and severally promise to
pay to **X,** or order, the sum of . . . pounds for value received.

John Brown.'

Answer: It was decided in *Owen* v. *Van Uster* (1850), 10 C.B. 318,
that where a bill of exchange was drawn upon four persons but was
accepted by one only, that one was liable on the bill.

In this case, the maker would appear to be liable on the note to a
holder in due course.

319 Is a promissory note drawn at two months' notice a valid document
under the Bills of Exchange Act? If so, would a written notice
through the post be sufficient, and would the note mature from the
date of posting?

Answer: In *Price* v. *Taylor* (1860), 5 H. & N. 540, it was held that
an order to pay two months after demand in writing was a valid bill
of exchange, and in the present instance 'notice' is apparently
equivalent to 'demand.' It is, therefore, considered that the note is
payable at 'a determinable future time' within the meaning of sec.
83 (1) of the Bills of Exchange Act.

The note would mature from the date at which the notice was
received by the maker, not from the date of posting.

320 A promissory note specifies in the body of the note that the sum is
payable by three equal instalments, at, say, three months, seven
months, and eleven months after date. Is such a document a valid
promissory note?

Answer: Yes. (Bills of Exchange Act, sec. 9 (1) (*b*), applied to
promissory notes by sec. 89.)

321 If the maker of a promissory note omits to state his address on the
note, would the addition of the address by a holder of the note be a

material alteration, avoiding it under sec. 64 of the Bills of Exchange Act?

Answer: Under sec. 3 (4) (*c*) a bill is not invalid by reason that it does not specify the place where it is drawn, and this section applies also to promissory notes. It is therefore considered that the addition, by way of memorandum, of the address of the maker of a note is not a material alteration. But the addition of a place for payment without the maker's consent would be a material alteration. (*Calvert v. Baker* (1838), 4 M. & W. 417).

322 A man named Thomas James Jones, who ordinarily writes his name Thomas Jones only, signs a promissory note in the latter form. Is the note valid?

Answer: Yes. Sec. 23 of the Bills of Exchange Act states that where a person signs a bill (or note) in an assumed name he is liable thereon as if he had signed it in his own name.

323 A joint and several promissory note, payable to the order of, and endorsed by, the payee, is discounted for him by a banker, and is unpaid at maturity. Will it be sufficient for the banker to send notice of dishonour to the endorser of the note, or must he, to protect his right of recourse against all the parties, send notice to all the signatories?

Answer: Notice of dishonour must be sent to the endorser, or recourse against him will be lost. (Bills of Exchange Act, sec. 48.) The makers of a promissory note are deemed to correspond with the acceptors of a bill (sec. 89 (2)), and it is not necessary to send notice of dishonour to them in order to preserve their liability (sec. 52 (3)).

324 A promissory note is endorsed by the payee, and is negotiated to a holder in due course. When the note is presented for payment it is discovered that the maker's signature is a forgery.
    (*a*) Can the holder recover from the endorser, whether the latter is or is not aware of the forgery?
    (*b*) Is the case altered if the holder omits to present the note on the due date?

Answer: (*a*) If the holder gives notice of dishonour within the time allowed (see Bills of Exchange Act, sec. 49 (12)), he can recover from the endorser, who by his endorsement has engaged that on due presentment the note shall be paid, and that if it be dishonoured he will compensate the holder or a subsequent endorser who is compelled to pay it, provided that the requisite proceedings on dishonour be duly taken; and who is moreover precluded from denying to his immediate or a subsequent endorsee that the note was at the time of his endorsement a valid and subsisting note. (Sec. 55 (2), applied to promissory notes by sec. 89.)

(b) According to sec. 87 (1) of the Bills of Exchange Act, 1882, where a promissory note is in the body of it made payable at a particular place it must be presented for payment at that place in order to render the maker liable; in any other case, presentment for payment is not necessary in order to render the maker liable. It follows that omission to present the note on the due date will not affect the rights of the holder unless the note is made payable at a particular place.

325 Is a banker protected by the Bills of Exchange Act, if he pays a promissory note, payable on demand, domiciled at the bank, which bears a forged endorsement?

Answer: No.

CHEQUES—THE PAYING BANKER

326 Is a banker legally justified in returning at once to his customer **A** a cheque drawn on himself by his customer **B**, and paid into **A**'s credit, there not being at the moment sufficient funds on **B**'s account to meet it?

Answer: Yes.

327 A customer has a credit balance of £100, and there are presented for payment on the same day
　　(a) a cheque for £50 in the clearing, and a cheque for £70 at the counter;
　　　　or
　　(b) cheques for £50 and £70, both in the same clearing;
　　　　or
　　(c) two cheques, each for £70, both in the same clearing.
　　Which cheque should the banker pay, if he is not prepared to allow his customer an overdraft?

Answer: The banker is at liberty legally to dishonour whichever cheque in any of these instances he may elect. In practice, an effort will usually be made to limit the damage to the customer's credit as far as can be judged from the amounts and named payees of the cheques in question, without, of course, any responsibility whatsoever to refer to the drawer customer or to make special enquiries. The normal course is to pay cheques strictly in the order in which they are presented, but the banker has complete freedom to decide which cheque may be paid when two or more are presented at the same time.

328   Should a bank refuse payment of a cheque because the body of the cheque is not filled in in the drawer's own handwriting? The signature is correct.

Answer: No.

329   A demand draft, drawn abroad on London and uncrossed, is presented for payment. Can the drawees, before paying, require the person presenting it to identify himself? Does it make any difference whether the drawees are or are not bankers?

Answer: If the drawees are bankers, they are protected by sec. 60 of the Bills of Exchange Act (or, if the draft is drawn on them by their head office or a branch, by sec. 19 of the Stamp Act, 1853) in paying the draft to the person presenting it without identification, if the endorsement appears to be in order.

   If the drawees are not bankers, they have no statutory protection in paying the draft, and may consider identification to be desirable.

330   A customer has £25 to his credit at his bankers. A cheque is presented for £30 and is returned marked 'refer to drawer.' The next day a cheque for £20 is presented. Is the banker right in paying it, or does the holder of the previous cheque hold a lien on the £25?

Answer: Under sec. 53 (1) of the Bills of Exchange Act a bill or cheque does not, in England, operate as an assignment of funds in the hands of the drawee available for the payment thereof, but the case is different in Scotland. The banker acts correctly, therefore, in paying the cheque for £20, notwithstanding the previous dishonour of the cheque for £30.

331   In the event of the loss by the payee of
     (a) an open cheque drawn on the **X** bank; or
     (b) an open draft on demand drawn by a branch of the **X** bank
        on its head office, or on another branch;
   the payee's endorsement having been forged by the finder, to whom

the amount of the cheque or draft is paid by the **X** bank, who has to bear the loss?

Answer: (*a*) If the cheque is paid in good faith and in the ordinary course of business, the **X** bank is protected by sec. 60 of the Bills of Exchange Act, and the loss must fall on the payee.

(*b*) As the draft is payable on demand and purports to be endorsed by the person to whom it is drawn payable, the **X** bank is protected by sec. 19 of the Stamp Act, 1853.

332   Is a banker ever justified in questioning payment of an open cheque duly endorsed and in order, which is presented across the counter.

Answer: Yes. If there is any doubt as to the *bona fides* of the transaction, the banker would be justified in making enquiries.

333   An open cheque payable to **A**. & Co. was duly endorsed by them and presented for payment by their clerk. The bank refused to cash it unless the clerk was identified.

Were they justified in so doing, the cheque being in order and uncrossed?

Answer: No.

334   A cheque is payable to 'John Brown only,' without the addition of the words 'or order.'

(1) Should the banker on whom such a cheque is drawn require the identification of the payee if the cheque is presented over the counter by an unknown person?

(2) If crossed, can such a cheque be safely paid to another banker?

Answer: (1) Yes, it should be paid to no one but John Brown in person.

(2) Yes, as the responsibility would be on the collecting banker.

CROSSED CHEQUES

335   A cheque has written across its face the name of a bank, without the parallel transverse lines. Does this constitute a crossing within the meaning of the Act?

Answer: Yes; it is a special crossing. (See Bills of Exchange Act, sec. 76 (2).)

336 Is a perforated crossing a legal crossing within the meaning of the Act, or must it be written or printed on the face of the cheque?

Answer: Crossing a cheque by perforation is considered to come within the words of the Bills of Exchange Act, sec. 76 (1).

337 If a banker's draft payable on demand is marked in the following manner, does the marking constitute a general crossing under the Bills of Exchange Act?

Under Ten Pounds.

Answer: The Bills of Exchange Act (sec. 76 (1) (*b*)) provides that 'two parallel transverse lines simply' shall constitute a crossing, hence the draft referred to is crossed within the meaning of the Act, notwithstanding the words written between the transverse lines.

338 A cheque is presented having lines × thus across it.
Does this constitute a crossing, or does it cancel and annul the cheque?

Answer: Such a mark does not come within the definition of a crossing contained in the Bills of Exchange Act, sec. 76, and the banker would be justified in asking for information as to whether it was intended for a cancellation.

339 (*a*) Would a bank's stamp on the back of a cheque answer the same purpose as on the face and constitute a crossing? (*b*) In the case of one bank's stamp on the face and another bank's stamp on the back of a cheque, would it be crossed by two banks?

Answer: (*a*) and (*b*) No. (Bills of Exchange Act, sec. 76 (2).) In case (*b*), however, the paying banker might think an explanation necessary.

340 Is the crossing of a demand draft, drawn abroad, payable in the United Kingdom, valid? And can it, for the purposes of crossing, be treated exactly as a cheque?

Answer: Yes, if drawn on a banker.

341 A cheque drawn on a country branch of a bank in favour of a payee in Germany, crossed 'Suddeutsche Bank' between two parallel lines, is presented for payment by a London bank, who have added their crossing stamp. Should the drawee bank return the cheque with the answer 'crossed by two banks'?

Answer: It is considered that the drawee bank would be justified in assuming that the London bank were acting as agents for collection on behalf of the German bank.

342 If the cheque (see Q. 341) bore on its face the name of a foreign bank not carrying on business in the United Kingdom, *without* parallel transverse lines or other indication of a crossing, could it safely be treated as an uncrossed cheque, and be paid across the counter to a stranger?

Answer: Whether or not a foreign bank not carrying on business in this country is a 'banker' within the meaning of sec. 76 of the Bills of Exchange Act, it would be prudent not to pay the cheque to anyone except a bank in this country who may be presumed to be acting as agents for collection on behalf of the foreign bank.

343 A cheque crossed generally is presented for payment at the counter of the drawee banker by the payee, who is personally known to him. Can he safely pay the cheque?

Answer: Normal banking practice would be to insist upon the cheque being presented through a banker or paid into the payee's bank account through the drawee banker, who would then be acting as agent for collection for the payee's own banker. However, since the banker personally knows the payee it is not considered that he would be at risk because he is paying to the true owner to whom alone he would be liable under the terms of the Bills of Exchange Act, 1882, sec. 79 (2).

It should not however be overlooked that the payee may possibly have acquired the cheque by fraud, in which case the drawer would not have 'received the benefit of the payment.'

CROSSED CHEQUE—PAYMENT

344 A crossed cheque is drawn payable to the order of self and endorsed by the drawer **A.** He however writes on the cheque 'Pay cash. **A.**'
   (*a*) Is the instrument thereby rendered an open cheque, or must it still be presented through a banker?
   (*b*) Does the banker run any risk in paying the cheque across the counter to a stranger, provided the endorsement is in order?

Answer: (*a*) Yes: such a cheque is treated as an open cheque. But the Committee of London Clearing Bankers, in 1912, passed the following resolution:
'That no opening of cheques be recognised unless the full signature of the drawer be appended to the alteration, and then only when presented for payment by the drawer or by his known agent.'
Cheques that have been opened should be considered strictly within the ruling so laid down. The full signature of the drawer, rather than merely his initials, is required against the alteration; and, as to
(*b*) the cheque should not be paid to a stranger.

345 Is the crossing of a cheque (whether general or special) set aside by the fact of the cheque having been returned unpaid, and if such a cheque were subsequently paid over the counter, would the banker so paying incur any risk?

Answer: The crossing is not superseded, and the banker on whom the cheque is drawn would pay it over the counter at his own risk.

346 A cheque is received by a branch bank through the clearing, and not being provided for is returned unpaid, but is re-presented direct by the bankers of the payee. As the cheque was originally crossed by the latter to their London agents, are not the drawees justified in refusing payment, even though funds may then have been provided to meet it?

Answer: Sec. 80 of the Bills of Exchange Act provides that where the banker on whom a crossed cheque is drawn, in good faith and without negligence pays it . . . if crossed specially, to the banker to whom it is crossed, *or* his agent for collection being a banker, the banker paying the cheque . . . shall be entitled to the same rights and be placed in the same position as if payment of the cheque had been made to the true owner thereof; hence, in the case in question, the banker on whom the cheque is drawn would be justified in paying it on re-presentation direct by the payee's banker without the latter again passing it through his agent for collection.

347 A cheque crossed in writing, 'X Bank, Fleet Street,' bears the stamp 'X Bank, Oxford Street,' and is dishonoured with the answer—
'Crossed two bankers.'
Is this a correct answer?

Answer: No; as these are only branches of the same bank.

348 A cheque is presented crossed in the drawer's own handwriting specially to a certain person's account at a certain bank. It is also crossed with the private crossing stamp of another customer of the same bank specially to his own account. How should the drawee bank treat this cheque?

Answer: The drawee bank would be justified in paying the cheque to the bank named in the crossings, without regard to the crossings to account.

349 A cheque crossed generally and drawn upon a London clearing banker is presented for payment through the Clearing House without the stamp of the presenting banker.
(*a*) Should the drawee banker return the cheque to the Clearing House for the purpose of finding out the name of the presenting banker and having the crossing stamp affixed?
(*b*) Could the drawer of the cheque, finding the crossed cheque to be without the name of the presenting banker, refuse to allow his account to be debited?

Answer: (*a*) Apart from the obligation imposed by the rules of the Clearing House, there is nothing to require a presenting banker to impress his stamp on a cheque, though it is obviously desirable that he should do so. The omission does not justify the drawee banker in refusing to pay the cheque, but he may return it when paid to the Clearing House to have the omission rectified.

(*b*) No. As far as he is concerned, the cheque may be presented by any banker.

350 A cheque crossed specially to the **X** bank is presented in a clearing without the crossing stamp of that bank. In view of the liability to the true owner of a cheque crossed specially which the drawee banker may incur under sec. 79 of the Bills of Exchange Act if he pays the cheque otherwise than to the banker to whom it is crossed (or to his agent for collection, being a banker), should he refuse payment of the cheque until the omission to cross-stamp it is rectified?

Answer: Apart from the Clearing House rule referred to in the answer to the last question, the **X** bank is under no obligation to cross the cheque, which already bears its name.

351 A cheque payable to the **X** bank or bearer is presented across the counter. Can the drawees refuse to pay on the ground that the cheque must be presented by or through the **X** bank? Could the drawees refuse supposing the cheque was presented through the Clearing House with the crossing of some other bank which was not the **X** bank's agent? Would the answer be different in the case of a dividend warrant?

Answer: A banker would not, without inquiry, pay a cheque or dividend warrant, other than to the **X** bank in the circumstances mentioned.

352 If a bank receives without comment, for the credit of a customer's account, a cheque drawn by another customer of the same bank and branch,
    (1) is the customer whose account is credited justified in assuming, without inquiry, that the cheque is paid, and in drawing against it at once?
    (2) if the customer is not justified in this assumption, and the cheque is afterwards dishonoured, within what time must he be notified of the dishonour?

Answer: (1) The customer is not justified in assuming that the cheque is paid unless he is so informed, or in drawing against it, unless there is an arrangement between himself and the bank that he may draw against uncleared cheques.
(2) In accordance with sec. 49 (12) of the Bills of Exchange Act, the bank has until the following day in which to give notice of dishonour, and, under sec. 49 (6), such notice may be given by the return of the cheque itself; but in practice the cheque is usually returned, if unpaid, at the close of the day on which it was paid in.

PAYMENT UNDER ADVICE

353 A bank in this country is requested by a customer to remit to an agent in a foreign town a sum of money to be held at the disposal of a person who is resident there, but is not personally known to the foreign bank. What precautions should be taken in making such a remittance?

Answer: The foreign bank should be instructed to pay on identification.

354 The protection of sec. 60 of the Bills of Exchange Act available to the paying banker is limited to the banker on whom the cheque is drawn. In every business day cheques are cashed by arrangement at branches other than that upon which the cheque is drawn. Sometimes another bank may be instructed to act as agent in encashing a customer's cheques. In all cases the other branch or agent bank is provided with specimen signatures of the drawer of the cheques and details of any mandate, together with precise instructions as to the powers of encashment. If a cheque is presented by a thief and paid against a forged endorsement, will the paying banker obtain the protection of sec. 60 of the Act?

Answer: If the cheque is paid in accordance with the instructions received from the drawee branch, payment is clearly made in the ordinary course of business because the practice of encashment in such manner by another branch, or bank, under special instruction is well established. Although branches of a bank are regarded as separate from each other in many legal respects, a cheque drawn upon a branch of a bank is drawn on the bank for the purpose of sec. 60 and any branch acting for the actual drawee branch will have the same protection.

Another bank appointed to act as agent for the drawee bank would not however secure the protection of sec. 60 because it cannot be regarded as the banker on whom the cheque is drawn. The other bank becomes the holder of the cheque if the endorsement is regular and, if it is not, may incur liability for conversion. The agent bank would be entitled to be indemnified by its principal provided it had not been negligent.

355 Should a bank cancel the cheques which it pays under the open credit?

Answer: It is not the usual practice of bankers to cancel cheques paid by them under a credit opened by another bank, but such cheques are often stamped on the face 'paid by order.'

356 Bank **A** in London, requests Bank **B** in London to telegraph instructions to an overseas branch of Bank **B** to cash Bank **A**'s customer's cheque. The branch overseas, when cashing the cheque, take all usual care to establish the identification of the holder, but it afterwards transpires that they cashed the cheque for a wrongful holder. Is Bank **A** or Bank **B** responsible for the loss?

Answer: Bank **B** would expect to be indemnified by Bank **A**, assuming that it (Bank **B**) had exercised proper care.

357 A has a banking account at Northtown, upon which office all his cheques are drawn. The Northtown Bank have a sub-branch at Southtown, attended one day a week by Northtown Bank officials.

Is presentation of A's cheques at the Southtown sub-branch on the day it is open, equivalent to presentation at the Northtown office, or is the Southtown sub-branch in order in refusing payment of cheques so presented to them on the ground that they are drawn on the Northtown Bank, and in requesting that they should be presented there?

Answer: The presentation and cashing of cheques at sub-branches, in the circumstances stated, is usually a matter of special arrangement. In the absence of this, the sub-branch are entitled to refuse payment of cheques drawn on the branch.

358 A cheque is presented for payment after the drawer's account has been transferred to another branch of the same bank.

What is the correct answer on such a cheque?

Answer: If no arrangement was made for the payment of outstanding cheques at the time the account was transferred, the cheque should be returned with the answer 'drawer's account transferred to———branch.'

The address of the branch on which the cheque is drawn should not be altered, as any alteration of the place of payment, without the consent of all parties liable on the cheque, avoids the cheque (Bills of Exchange Act, sec. 64.)

359 A customer, whose account is kept at the X branch of a bank, often pays in credits at the Y branch.

(*a*) Before dishonouring the customer's cheque for want of funds, is the X branch bound to inquire, by telephone or otherwise, whether funds have been paid in at the Y branch?

(*b*) Would the bank be liable for damages if, at the time the customer's cheque was dishonoured, he had paid in at the Y branch for the credit of his account at the X branch?

Answer: (*a*) and (*b*) No.

360 A opens an account at the B sub-branch of a bank, but cheques are drawn on and cleared through the C branch, from which the sub-branch is worked. A pays in at the sub-branch at 10 a.m. money sufficient to meet outstanding cheques, but at 3 p.m., before the

sub-branch clerk returns to the branch, cheques are specially presented and payment is refused.
Is the bank liable for damages for returning the cheques?

Answer: No. Money is not available immediately it is paid in. Even in the case of notes or coin, a sufficient period must be allowed to elapse before drawing against it to enable the bank to carry out the necessary bookkeeping operations.

COUNTERMAND OF PAYMENT

361 How long does a customer's order, countermanding payment of a cheque drawn by him, remain in force? Can the banker limit his liability, in the event of his inadvertently paying the cheque, to a period of, say, three months?

Answer: For ever. There is no way in which a banker can limit his liability except by express agreement with his customer.

362 Can a banker evade the consequences incurred by his paying a 'stopped' cheque, if he gives the customer notice when receiving the 'stop' that he will not hold himself responsible for any loss that may be incurred if it be paid inadvertently?

Answer: No.

363 A cashes for a woman an open cheque drawn by a pawnbroker for £5, which the woman says is the balance of £20 received by her from the pawnbroker for a ring taken in pledge, he not having sufficient cash with him, and his bank being closed. On presentation of the cheque it is returned 'payment stopped,' and the pawnbroker informs A that he refuses to pay it, because the ring in respect of which he issued it was stolen and is claimed by the police. The woman is missing. Can A sue the pawnbroker?

Answer: Yes, as the cheque was not crossed 'not negotiable.'

364 A gives B a post-dated cheque, and the latter, before the date of the cheque, negotiates it in payment of a debt to C, who takes it without notice of any dispute between A and B. A stops payment of the cheque, B not having fulfilled his contract. Does the fact of the cheque being post-dated when negotiated prevent C acquiring a good title with full recourse against A?

Answer: No; under sec. 13 (2) of the Bills of Exchange Act a bill or cheque is not invalid by reason only that it is post-dated, and in the circumstances **C** is a holder in due course under sec. 29, and can sue **A**.

365   An open cheque payable to order is lost without having been endorsed by the payee, and the finder forges the payee's endorsement and negotiates the cheque for value to a person who takes it in good faith. If payment of the cheque is stopped, can the person who gave value for it sue the drawer?

Answer: No; because no one can be a holder of a bill or cheque under a forged endorsement. (See sec. 24 of the Bills of Exchange Act.)

If the cheque had been drawn payable to bearer, the person in possession of it would have been holder in due course, and could have sued the drawer; and if, though payable to order, it had been endorsed by the payee before being lost, the holder could have sued either the drawer or the endorser provided that the cheque was not crossed 'not negotiable.'

366   **X** bank asks **Y** bank by telephone 'May we pay against **A**'s cheque on yourselves £50?' and receives a reply, 'Yes, if in order.'

What is the position of the **Y** bank if, during the interval before the cheque is presented, **A** (*a*) stops payment of the cheque, (*b*) dies, (*c*) becomes bankrupt, or (*d*) withdraws his balance?

Answer: In view of the form of the reply, in all four cases (*a*) to (*d*) the **Y** bank is bound to pay the cheque, if it is in order when presented, and in cases (*a*), (*b*) and (*c*) the customer's account cannot be debited. In case (*d*) the payment of the cheque of course creates an overdraft, for which the customer can be sued.

If **Y** bank had, as prudently they should, worded the reply 'If in our hands and in order, it would be paid' they would have avoided any commitment to pay, the answer merely stating that at the time of the enquiry the cheque would be paid.

367   If a customer to whom his bank has issued a draft drawn by one of its offices on another wishes to have payment of the draft stopped, should the bank comply with his request?

Answer: A bank should not attempt to stop payment of its own draft, which is equivalent, under sec. 5 (2) of the Bills of Exchange Act, to the bank's promissory note. Unless the draft is crossed 'not negotiable,' payment of it can be enforced by a holder in due course, even if, without his knowledge, the draft is tainted with fraud or illegality since it left the customer's hands. No one, however, can be a holder under a forged endorsement, and if the customer can satisfy the bank that the draft has been lost or stolen, without having been endorsed by the payee, it may, if presented bearing an endorsement purporting to be the payee's, be returned with the answer 'Draft stated to have been lost. Payee's endorsement requires verification.'

368　Is the position of a banker when asked by another banker to stop payment of a sight draft, which the latter has drawn upon him, similar to that in which he is placed when a customer instructs him to stop payment of a cheque? Would the drawee banker be protected by the instruction from the drawer to stop payment, or should he require the drawer's indemnity?

Answer:　The drawee banker's position would be similar, and he need not require any indemnity.

369　A cheque is presented by **A** bank by post to **B** bank stating that **A** bank will telephone for fate at 11 o'clock. This they do and are told that the cheque is paid. At 11.30 the drawer of the cheque calls at **B** bank and asks that payment be stopped. **B** bank then telephones to **A** bank that it is unable to pay, and returns the cheque with 'orders not to pay.' Can **A** bank refuse to accept notice of non-payment after receiving advice of payment?

Answer:　Yes. **B** bank should not have accepted the order to stop payment after having communicated to **A** bank that it had paid the cheque.

370　An open cheque is presented for payment, but before the money has passed from the banker to the person presenting it, an order is received from the drawer stopping its payment. The holder is then informed that the drawer has stopped payment, but he insists on payment on the ground that presentation was prior to the receipt of the 'stop.' What is the banker's proper course, to pay, or to refuse to pay?

Answer:　If the order to stop payment is received before the money is actually laid on the counter the cheque should not be paid (*Chambers* v. *Miller* (1862), 32 L.J.C.P. 30); Leading Cases, 4th Ed., page 40).

371 Can a customer stop payment of a cheque which, earlier in the same day, has been paid in by another customer of the same bank and branch for the credit of his account?

Answer: If the customer who paid the cheque in did not ask whether it was paid or not, and the bank did not, by word or act, give him to understand that it was paid, the drawer may stop payment of it at any time before the close of business.

372 A company's cheques have to be signed by two directors and the secretary. An order to stop a cheque is signed by the secretary only. Is the bank justified in refusing to stop the cheque without all the signatures?

Answer: It would be usual to act upon the secretary's instructions to stop the cheque, but to remove the stop the bank should require the instruction of all the signatories, or alternatively should require the issue of a new cheque.

373 Can one of two or more (*a*) trustees, (*b*) executors, (*c*) partners, or (*d*) other joint account-holders, stop payment of a cheque drawn on the account?

Answer: Yes. But to remove such a stop the bank should require the instruction of all the signatories, or alternatively should require the issue of a new cheque.

374 If a cheque which has been credited to a customer's overdrawn account, in reduction of the overdraft, is returned unpaid with the answer 'orders not to pay,' can the bank proceed against the drawer of the cheque?

Answer: Yes, as holder for value to the extent of the amount by which the customer's overdraft was reduced, provided that any necessary endorsement of the cheque is not forged. The cheque should be debited to Unpaid Bills Account and all parties notified of the dishonour.

375 Would a banker be justified in refusing to pay a cheque at the request of the payee, but without the drawer's instructions?

Answer: The only person who can instruct the banker not to pay a cheque is the drawer; but the banker, having received notice from the payee, would endeavour to get into touch with his customer before paying the cheque.

376 A customer having a balance at his bankers is arrested on a charge of fraud. Between the period of remand and trial, the prosecutors' solicitors warn the bankers at their risk not to part with the balance on the accused's account, as it is the proceeds of the fraud. Subsequently and before committal, the accused draws a cheque for the balance. Would the banker be justified, in the circumstances, in refusing payment of the cheque until the result of the trial was known?

Answer: The bank would refuse payment at its risk. The circumstances might be such as to induce the bank to take the risk, but such a decision would not normally be taken without reference to Head Office.

DISHONOUR

377 Is a banker justified in dishonouring a customer's cheque if he has sufficient funds in his hands to pay it, on the ground merely that had the banker paid the cheque there would not have been sufficient balance left on the account to pay the charges incurred to date but not yet due?

Answer: No.

378 An open cheque drawn by A for £100 is presented for payment, and, the balance to his credit at the time being only £80, is returned unpaid with the answer 'Refer to drawer.'

The banker makes no disclosure, but the payee, having from other sources of information ascertained the state of the account, tenders the sum of £20 for the credit of A's account, and again presents the cheque for £100.

Is the banker bound to receive the amount tendered and to pay the cheque? If not, what course should he adopt?

Answer: The banker should accept the £20, and providing he is not claiming lien on A's credit balance, should pay the cheque for £100.

379 A cheque is returned unpaid to another bank with the answer 'Refer to drawer.' On the morning of its receipt by the presenting bank, and before it has been returned to the payee, the drawer calls and desires to take up the cheque, for which he tenders cash. What course should the presenting bank pursue?

Answer: The cheque should be handed to the drawer in exchange for cash, and the bank's customer should be informed.

380 A customer's cheque is returned unpaid with the answer 'Refer to drawer.' On the following day the customer pays in sufficient to meet the cheque, and the banker telephones to the collecting banker, 'X's cheque returned yesterday will now be paid.'

Before the cheque is again presented a receiving order is made against the customer. What is the position of the bank on which the cheque is drawn?

Answer: By telephoning in the words given in the question, the bank has committed itself to the payment of the cheque, but will be unable to debit its customer's account.

381 A bank returns a cheque unpaid, with the answer 'Refer to drawer; please re-present'. Is it the practice of the collecting banker to present the cheque again by return of post, having first given due notice of non-payment to his customer who paid it in, or would the proper course be to return it at once to the customer, leaving him to re-present at discretion?

Answer: The practice is to inform the customer of the dishonour and to re-present the cheque through the usual channels unless the customer requests otherwise.

382 **A,** an agent, pays in a client's cheque for £100 to the **X** bank, of London, for the credit of his principals, **P** & Co., at the **Y** Bank, Lowton. The cheque is returned unpaid to the **X** Bank, who send it by post to the **Y** Bank, Lowton, for the debit of **P** & Co. **P** & Co. immediately wire their agent, **A,** putting him on his guard. **A** replies that, as he had not heard anything of this dishonour, and assuming that the first cheque for £100 was all right, he had already delivered another £100 worth of goods.

 (*a*) Should the **X** Bank have advised the agent, **A,** at the time of the dishonour?

 (*b*) Failing this advice, is the **X** Bank liable for any damages caused by the omission to do so?

Answer: In the absence of any undertaking to do so, the **X** Bank is not bound to advise **A** of the dishonour of the cheque, and incurs no liability to **P** & Co. or their agent by the omission.

383 The **X** Bank receives by post a cheque drawn upon **Y** Bank in the same provincial town, with a request to present it and to telephone fate. The cheque is presented, but not paid, and advice to that effect is telephoned by **X** Bank. Before the close of business, however, **Y** Bank sends the amount of the cheque and asks for the dishonoured cheque in exchange. What course should the **X** Bank adopt?

Answer: The usual course would be to take the money and to telephone to the bank from which the cheque had been received.

384 Within what period must a banker present for payment cheques handed to him by his customer for credit; and, if unpaid, when is the banker bound to return them or give notice to the customer?

Answer: A banker receiving cheques from his customer for credit has the whole of the day on which they are received and of the next business day for presentation if in the same place or to forward them for collection if in different places. When unpaid the rules as to return or notice are as follows: If banker and customer reside in the same place, the cheque must be returned or notice given or sent off in time to reach the latter on the day after dishonour; if they reside in different places the cheque must be returned or notice sent off on the day after dishonour if there be a post at a convenient hour on that day, and, if not, then by the next post thereafter. (See Bills of Exchange Act, sec. 49 (12).) If presentment is made through a Clearing House, the answer to the latter part of the question will depend upon its rules.

The Committee of London Clearing Bankers has decided that if the need to return an article (including a direct debit) for reasons other than technical irregularities is not seen on the day of presentation it may be returned unpaid on the next working day. For sums over £30 advice of non-payment must be telephoned to the presenting branch not later than noon on the working day after presentation.

385 A, having been credited with a cheque for £20 drawn by **B,** has upon its dishonour a balance of £10 only to his credit. How should his bankers treat the dishonoured cheque? If held in overdue bills or a similar account, could they refuse to pay cheques which would absorb the balance? Could they appropriate the balance and still retain a right to sue the drawer of the dishonoured cheque?

Answer: If the bank wishes to retain its rights against the drawer, it should preferably charge the dishonoured cheque to a suspense account. The £10 may be retained and further drawings refused. In this way the right to sue **B** on the cheque is undoubted (See Q. 277).

ANSWER

386 What answer should be written on a cheque that has to be dishonoured in consequence of the service of a garnishee order attaching the drawer's account?

Answer: 'Refer to drawer.'

387 Can a banker or other person who presents a bill or cheque for payment require the banker with whom the bill is domiciled, or on whom the cheque is drawn, to give a written answer if the bill or cheque is dishonoured?

Answer: A rule of the London Clearing House provides that 'No return can be received without an answer in writing on the return why payment is refused.' The rule is not considered to be complied with by an answer written on a slip attached to the bill or cheque returned.

388 Is 'present again,' or 're-present on (date),' a sufficient answer on a dishonoured cheque?

Answer: It is a rule of the London Clearing House that the answer written on an unpaid article shall state the reason why the article is returned. The answers quoted above are therefore insufficient where this, or a similar local rule, applies.

389 A cheque drawn by a customer who has an overdraft is returned with the answer 'Exceeds arrangement.'

Does the answer convey any information respecting the account which it is not desirable to give? Is it a satisfactory or usual answer?

Answer: Such an answer is unusual and improper; it should be 'Refer to drawer.'

390 Does the answer on a cheque
  (a) 'will pay the smaller amount' (when the amounts in words and figures differ),
  (b) 'refer to drawer, please re-present on (date),' or
  (c) 'effects not cleared,'

imply an undertaking by the banker giving the answer to pay the
cheque if re-presented
  (a) for the smaller amount,
  (b) on the date named, or
  (c) after the effects are cleared?

Answer: It is considered that no such undertaking is implied, and
that a second presentation stands on its own merits.

PRESENTATION

391 **X,** who banks at Northtown Bank, receives from **Y** a crossed cheque
drawn on Southtown Bank and, being anxious to obtain prompt
payment of the cheque, resorts to one of the following courses to
ascertain fate:
  (1) The cheque is paid into his account at Northtown Bank with
      the request that it be presented specially to Southtown Bank
      who should be telephoned to enquire advice of fate.
  (2) **X** goes to Southtown Bank and presents the cheque at the
      counter for credit to his account at Northtown Bank, at the
      same time asking whether **Y**'s cheque will be paid.
  (3) **X** sends the cheque by post to Southtown Bank for the credit
      of his account at Northtown Bank and requests Southtown
      Bank to advise him when he telephones the next day whether
      the cheque is paid.
  What is banking practice in each case, and within what time may
the drawee bank pay or dishonour the cheque?

Answer: (1) When the cheque is presented specially through
normal banking channels, Southtown Bank will pay or dishonour it
immediately and will advise fate on receipt of the telephone call.

  (2) Southtown Bank should inform **X** that no answer can be given
until after the close of business.

  (3) When **X** telephones he should be told that an answer cannot
be given to him before the close of business on the day the cheque is
received by Southtown Bank.

392 If a person representing himself to be the payee or holder of an open
cheque or a bill, sends the cheque by post to the bank on which it is
drawn, or the bill to the bank at which it is domiciled, with a request
to send a remittance in return by cash or a draft, should the bank
comply with the request?

Answer: Under sec. 45 (8) of the Bills of Exchange Act presentment for payment through the post is sufficient, where authorised by agreement or usage; but presentment in the circumstances mentioned is not authorised by either agreement or usage, and accordingly the bank should not comply with the request to send cash or a draft.

393 Should a presenting banker, to whom a cheque has been returned unpaid by the drawee banker, allow the latter to recover it by giving cash or a local clearing slip (where these are in use) for it, at any time during banking hours before the presenting banker has returned the cheque to his customer?

Answer: It is usual to do so.

CLEARINGS

394 May a clearing banker hold a cheque for one day before returning it to the presenting banker, or must it be returned on the day of presentation?

Answer: Yes, it may be held but only in the circumstances laid down under the Clearing House rule—
  'Where the need to return an article,
  (i) because of lack of funds; or
  (ii) because payment has been stopped no later than the close of business on the day of presentation; or
  (iii) because the account has been closed; or
  (iv) because the customer's mandate has been determined e.g. by death or garnishee order,
has not been noticed due to inadvertence on the day of presentation then it may be returned unpaid on the next working day. In the case of sums in excess of £30, advice of such non-payment must be given by telephone (not telegram) to the presenting Bank branch not later than noon on the day after presentation.'

CANCELLATION

395 A cheque presented through clearing channels is cancelled by the drawee bank with the intention of paying it. Later in the day, however, the bank finds it necessary to dishonour the cheque which, in accord with established practice, is marked 'Cancelled in error' and returned within the period permitted by the Rules of the Clearing House.

Sec. 63 of the Bills of Exchange Act, 1882, states that 'Where a bill is intentionally cancelled by the holder or his agent, and the cancellation is apparent thereon, the bill is discharged . . . A cancellation made unintentionally, or under a mistake, or without the authority of the holder, is inoperative; but where a bill or any signature thereon appears to have been cancelled the burden of proof lies on the party who alleges that the cancellation was made unintentionally, or under a mistake or without authority.'

Is the paying banker entitled to mark the cheque cancelled in error despite the provisions of this section?

Answer: It is well established that the paying banker is entitled to, and can safely, mark a cheque 'Cancelled in error' in such circumstances, and so long as the signature has not been obliterated so as to make it illegible, the payee or holder cannot raise complaint. Sec. 63 of the Bills of Exchange Act, 1882, does not affect the position. All this is providing, of course, that payment has not previously been advised to the collecting banker.

A bill of exchange accepted payable at a bank may in similar circumstances be marked 'Cancelled in error.'

396   A cheque drawn on the **X** bank is presented by mistake at the **Y** bank and is there cancelled in error. On subsequent presentation at the **X** bank it is dishonoured for want of funds. Is the **Y** bank liable to the holder for having cancelled the cheque?

Answer: No; the cancellation, having been made unintentionally or under a mistake, is inoperative. (Sec. 63 (3) of the Bills of Exchange Act.)

397   Is it legally necessary that the signature of the drawer of a cheque or acceptor of a bill should be cancelled by running a pen through it when such a cheque or bill is paid by a bank?

Answer: No.

NEGOTIABLE OR TRANSFERABLE

398   A cheque is drawn 'Pay **A**' without the words 'or order' or 'or bearer'. Is the cheque payable only to **A** in person, or is it transferable or negotiable by him?

Answer: The cheque is transferable and negotiable. Under sec. 8 (4) of the Bills of Exchange Act, a bill is payable to order which is expressed to be so payable, or which is expressed to be payable to a particular person, and does not contain words prohibiting transfer or indicating an intention that it should not be transferable; and under sec. 73, a cheque is a bill of exchange drawn on a banker payable on demand. The cheque is therefore payable to **A** or to his order, and is negotiable by his endorsement.

399   Is a cheque drawn 'Pay **A** only' not transferable by **A**?

Answer: Such wording has been accepted by bankers as prohibiting transfer although the strict legal position is in some doubt.

The drawing of cheques in this form would seem to place upon the drawee banker the burden of enquiry as to whether he is paying the designated payee and would cause many practical difficulties, for instance where the payee has a joint account or has no bank account. Accordingly the banks agreed in 1958 that the use of this wording should be strongly discouraged.

400   Do the words 'Not negotiable' written across a cheque, without either parallel transverse lines or the name of a banker, render the cheque a crossed cheque within secs. 76 to 82 of the Bills of Exchange Act?

Would the drawee bank be justified in paying such a cheque across the counter?

Answer: The Bills of Exchange Act (secs. 76 and 81) implies that 'Not negotiable' is an addition to an ordinary crossing and there is some doubt as to whether the words on their own constitute an effective crossing. It would therefore seem prudent to regard such a cheque as crossed until a legal precedent is established.

DATE

401   **B** Bank remits for collection to **C** Bank a draft due June 28 drawn on **D**, who banks with **E** Bank. The **C** bank presents the draft to **D** at his office for acceptance, but as **D** wishes it paid at once he gives a cheque dated June 27, drawn on the **E** Bank, to which cheque he adds the words, 'Bill attached.' The **C** Bank presents the cheque with the draft attached on the 27th and the **E** Bank returns the cheque with the answer, 'Bill not due,' explaining that as **D** had added the words 'Bill attached' to his cheque they are bound to see that it is not paid before the due date of the draft. Is the **E** Bank right in thus refusing payment of the cheque?

Answer: No; the cheque is payable on demand.

402 Can a banker legally refuse to honour a cheque or bill dated or accepted on a non-business day?

Answer: He cannot, if the instrument is due and in order.

403 A cheque bearing date November 31, but regular in all other respects, is presented for payment on November 30. Should it be paid?

Answer: Yes, as November 31 is an impossible date.

404 Is a cheque invalid when not dated, or can any holder fill in the date?

Answer: Under sec. 3 (4) (*a*) of the Bills of Exchange Act, a bill of exchange (including a cheque) is not invalid by reason that it is not dated. In *Griffiths* v. *Dalton,* [1940] 2 K.B. 264, (Leading Cases, 4th Ed., p. 30) it was held that the holder of an undated cheque has authority, both by the common law and under sec. 20 of the Act, to fill in a date, but he must do so within a reasonable time.

405 What action should a paying banker take when an undated cheque which is otherwise in order is presented for payment?

Answer: The course adopted by the banker will normally depend upon the amount of the cheque in question, the standing of the drawer and any surrounding circumstances. Although a cheque is not invalid by reason that it is not dated, the bank may, if it so wishes, return the cheque with the answer 'Undated' or 'Date incomplete.' This course can be adopted where circumstances demand caution.

Strictly speaking, the paying banker is entitled to fill in the date if he is 'the person in possession of it' within the meaning of sec. 20 (1) of the Bills of Exchange Act, 1882; but sub-sec. (2) states that, in order that the instrument when completed may be enforceable against any person who became a party thereto prior to its completion against any person who became a party thereto prior to its completion, it must be filled up strictly in accordance with the authority given. It is difficult to see what authority the customer can be supposed to have given to the banker in such circumstances.

406 A cheque, the date of which has been altered from the fourth to the sixth of January, is presented for payment on the tenth day of the same month. Is the drawee justified in requiring the alteration to be confirmed by the drawer's initials?

Answer: By sec. 64 (2) of the Bills of Exchange Act any alteration of the date, is a material one, and the banker should therefore in strictness require its verification by the drawer, but it is doubtful whether in practice he would do so in such a case as the above.

407 As a general rule, how soon after date would a banker return a cheque marked 'Out of date'?

Answer: Most banks regard six months as the appropriate period.

408 A cheque dated October 22 bears at the foot the following: 'This cheque must be presented for payment on or before December 15.' Is the drawee banker justified in paying this if presented after December 15, and if it were so paid would the banker be held responsible for the amount of the cheque?

Answer: The banker would be justified in refusing payment if the cheque were presented after December 15, and he would be responsible if he acted contrary to his customer's instructions. A clause of this kind does not make the cheque a 'conditional order.' (*Thairlwall* v. *Great Northern Railway,* [1910] 2 K.B. 509, Leading Cases, 4th Ed., p. 27.)

409 A post-dated cheque is given by **A** to **B,** who presents it for payment. Can the bankers refuse payment on the ground that the cheque is post-dated, seeing that sec. 13 (2) of the Bills of Exchange Act states that a bill is not invalid by reason only that it is post-dated, and by secs. 10 (1) and 73 a cheque is payable on demand?

Answer: The banker should refuse to pay such a cheque before the date which it bears.

410 On January 25 a customer pays into his account a post-dated cheque dated January 27, which the bank allows him to draw against. On presentation, at the due date, the bank on which the cheque is drawn returns it marked 'Drawer deceased,' he having died the previous day, January 26. The customer has no balance available at the bank and consequently his account cannot be debited, and, further, he is a man of straw.

Can the bank claim against the estate of the deceased drawer, having regard to the facts that the cheque was post-dated and that the drawer was dead on the date the cheque was supposed to be drawn?

Answer: A cheque is not invalid merely by reason of its being post-dated. Assuming there are no other reasons against the bank being a holder in due course, it has a right of recourse against the estate of the deceased drawer.

411   A banker has debited his customer's account with a post-dated cheque, and has subsequently refused payment of a cheque for want of funds. Is the banker liable to an action for dishonour?

Answer: The banker is liable for dishonouring the subsequent cheque. He should not have paid the post-dated cheque.

412   A draws a post-dated cheque in favour of **B,** who at once presents it across the counter, and the bankers pay it, not noticing until after doing so that it was post-dated. They cannot debit **A**'s account until the date on which the cheque is payable. In the meanwhile, can **A** stop its payment, and, if so, what is the bankers' position?

Answer: There is nothing to prevent the customer from stopping payment of the cheque at any time before the date which it bears, and if he does so, the bankers stand to lose the money.

413   A draws a cheque upon his bankers post-dated October 25. It is presented for payment on October 23, and the bankers return it marked 'Refer to drawer.' **A,** on or before October 25, pays in sufficient funds and complains that the reply of the bankers has needlessly damaged his credit. Has he any remedy against his bankers?

Answer: The answer given when the cheque was presented should have been 'post-dated.' In certain circumstances it might be possible for **A** to claim that the answer given by the bank had damaged his credit but normally the difficulty may be overcome in practice if the bank, at the request of **A,** addresses a letter promptly to the payee of the cheque suitably explaining the circumstances.

414   A customer sends through the post to his bankers, for the credit of his account, a cheque which is post-dated. Are the bankers justified in returning it to their customer without presentation?

Answer: The banker may either present the cheque immediately or advise his customer that he is holding it pending instructions or the arrival of the ostensible date. No rule can be laid down in such cases.

415 (a) A customer post-dates a cheque issued in connection with a cheque card.
What action should the paying bank take on presentation?
(b) Would the action be any different if words and figures differ?

Answer: (a) Pay the cheque and advise the customer that the post-dating of such cheques contravenes the spirit of the cheque card system.
(b) No. The cheque should be paid according to the amount in figures, the drawer being advised accordingly. Similarly, other technical irregularities should not be regarded as warranting non-payment.

416 A cheque, dated on a Sunday, is presented the previous Friday. Is a banker legally justified in returning it marked 'post-dated,' or does sec. 14 of the Bills of Exchange Act apply?

Answer: The answer 'post-dated' is correct. The cheque as described does not come within sec. 14 of the Bills of Exchange Act, which relates to bills payable otherwise than on demand.

AMOUNT

417 What is the practice of bankers when a cheque is presented in which the amount expressed in figures differs from that expressed in words?

Answer: Although sec. 9 (2) of the Bills of Exchange Act provides that where the sum payable is expressed in words and also in figures, and there is a discrepancy between the two, the sum denoted by the words is the amount payable, the usual practice of bankers is to return the cheque with the answer thereon 'words and figures differ,' though where the difference in amount is insignificant payment is sometimes made.

418 A customer informs his banker that he intends to perforate all his cheques with amounts for which they are drawn. Does the banker incur risk in paying his customer's cheque without such perforation —or, in paying a cheque, the written and perforated amounts differing?

Answer: If a customer definitely instructs his bankers not to cash his cheques unless they are perforated, the banker would incur risk in cashing unperforated cheques as to the difference in the amounts, see the answer to the preceding question.

419 A cheque for £40, otherwise in order, bears the words 'under £15.' What is the position of the banker to whom this cheque is presented?

Answer: The banker should return the cheque for clarification, or he might incur liability.

420 Is a banker justified in paying a cheque which has the amount written only in words, and not in figures? Can he, or should he, refuse payment on the ground of the cheque being 'incomplete'?

Answer: The cheque is not incomplete, though unusual in form, and should be paid.

421 What is the practice of bankers as to payment of cheques where the figures are inserted in the usual place, but the sum is not expressed in words in the body of the cheque?

Answer: In the absence of special arrangements with the drawer, it is customary for bankers to refuse payment of cheques, the amount of which is expressed in figures only.

422 Is it the usual custom of bankers to pay cheques presented with the word 'pounds' omitted from the body, the amount appearing complete in figures, for instance, 'Sixteen twenty-three pence'? Would the banker be justified in refusing payment?

Answer: If there is any doubt as to the amount intended, or the cheque is so drawn that it could reasonably have been fraudulently raised, it should be returned. Where mechanical methods, however, have been used, such a cheque may be acceptable by special arrangement between the customer and the banker.

423 If a cheque is altered from a larger to a lesser amount, say, from £5 to £3, would a banker be justified in paying it without the alteration being confirmed by the drawer of the cheque?

Answer: Strictly speaking, the cheque should be returned, as this is a material alteration of the cheque within sec. 64 (1) of the Bills of

Exchange Act. As a matter of practice, such cheques are sometimes paid when the alteration in the amount is only of a trifling character.

ALTERATION

424 A and **B** have a joint account, on which both sign each cheque. A draws a cheque for £100, but omits the word 'pounds' after the amount in the body of the cheque. He obtains the signature of **B** to the cheque in this condition, and then adds 'and fifty pounds' to the amount in words, and alters the amount in figures to £150, for which amount he cashes the cheque. Is the paying banker liable to **B** for paying the cheque which had been materially altered after **B** had signed it?

Answer: In *London Joint Stock Bank* v. *Macmillan and Arthur*, [1918] A.C. 777, (Leading Cases, 4th Ed., p. 43), Lord Finlay said: 'If the customer draws a cheque in a manner which facilitates fraud, he is guilty of a breach of duty between himself and the banker, and he will be responsible to the banker for any loss sustained by the banker as a natural and direct consequence of this breach of duty.' In the present instance, though **B** did not draw the cheque, he adopted it in the form in which it was drawn by A, omitting the word 'pounds,' and thus facilitating the raising of the amount. If therefore the raising of the amount in figures was achieved by A in such a manner as not to afford a reasonable ground for suspicion on the part of the banker, it would appear that the latter is not liable to **B**.

425 The date, intended to be October 30, of a post-dated cheque is expressed in Roman numerals, and is thus easily altered to September 30 by the payee or a holder, who, without the drawer's authority, inserts 'i' before the 'x.' In this condition the cheque is paid, before October 30, by the drawee bank. Can the bank debit its customer?

Answer: Unless it can be maintained, by analogy to the *Macmillan* Case (see the previous question), that the customer, by leaving sufficient space before the 'x' to permit the insertion of an 'i', has facilitated the fraud, it would appear that the material alteration has avoided the cheque under sec. 64(1) of the Bills of Exchange Act, and that the customer cannot be debited with it. (See *Slingsby and Others* v. *District Bank,* [1932] 1 K.B. 544, Leading Cases, 4th Ed., p. 27), in which it was held that leaving a space in a cheque after the payee's name, enabling an addition to be made to it, is not a neglect of a reasonable precaution on the part of the drawer.)

426 If a cheque, drawn by two or more persons, whether in their own right or as executors or trustees, or on behalf of a Local Authority or a company, society or club, is altered from 'order' to 'bearer,' by whom should the alteration be signed or initialled?

Answer: It is considered that the alteration should be signed or initialled by all the persons who have signed the cheque.

427 A cheque payable to 'A or order' is presented for payment with the word 'order' struck out and 'bearer' substituted, the alteration being initialled by the drawer. The cheque is returned unpaid, with the answer, 'Requires endorsement or the alteration confirmed by the drawer's *signature.*' Is the banker justified in returning the cheque for this reason?

Answer: It is usual to pay cheques at the counter which have been altered and merely initialled by the drawer, but the banker is quite justified in demanding confirmation of the alteration by the signature of the drawer, as it is often difficult to judge whether an initial is genuine. If the cheque is presented by another banker it would not require endorsement and the onus would be on the collecting banker.

428 A cheque bears a note presumably written on it by or under the direction of the drawer, 'in settlement of hotel account.' The payee strikes out 'in settlement' and substitutes 'on account.'

    (*a*) Should the cheque be paid in this condition by the drawee bank?

    (*b*) If the cheque were paid, could the payee claim the balance of the hotel account from the drawer?

Answer: (*a*) The drawee bank should return the cheque with the answer 'Alteration requires confirmation by drawer.'

    (*b*) Yes, if justly owing, because he evidently did not accept the cheque for the smaller amount in settlement of the larger claim.

429 A cheque crossed 'not negotiable,' when presented for payment, has the words 'not negotiable' struck through, but the alteration is not confirmed. Would the banker be justified in paying the cheque on the ground that the alteration, although unauthorised, is not a material one?

Answer: The alteration is clearly material, and has made the cheque void under sec. 64 (1) of the Bills of Exchange Act. It should therefore not be paid without the drawer's confirmation.

MARKING

430 Can a bank present a cheque to another banker to be marked as good for payment?

Answer: The Committee of London Clearing Bankers have agreed that cheques are not to be presented for marking. If the fate of a cheque is desired to be known, it should be presented specially (in the Town Clearing under the separate regulations) so that it can be paid or returned.

MUTILATION

431 On what ground is it customary for bankers to refuse payment of mutilated cheques and dividend warrants?

Answer: On the ground that the mutilation may perhaps be evidence of an intended cancellation. Unless torn completely in two, the document would usually be paid.

432 A cheque which has been torn completely across, but pasted together, bears on the back a statement 'mutilation confirmed' signed by the presenting banker. Does the presenting banker's statement amount to an indemnity by him to the drawee banker if it should be discovered that the cheque was torn with the intention of cancelling it, and is the drawee banker justified in paying the cheque?

Answer: It is the practice to pay such a cheque on the basis that among bankers such a confirmation is understood to imply an undertaking of indemnity.

TITLE

433 An order cheque is lost in the post during transmission to the payee, and the finder forges the payee's endorsement and passes the cheque to a shopkeeper in part payment for goods purchased. On presentation the cheque is duly paid. Can the drawer recover the amount from the shopkeeper, or can he make the Post Office responsible?

Answer: As no title to the cheque can be made under a forged endorsement, the shopkeeper has, though innocently, converted the cheque, and the drawer can recover the amount from him as damages.

The Post Office cannot be made responsible, unless the cheque was enclosed in a registered envelope, and then only to the extent of the amount covered by the registration fee.

434   If the person to whom the amount of a lost or stolen cheque has been paid by the drawee bank has to refund the money to the true owner of the cheque, either because the payee's endorsement is forged or because the cheque is crossed 'not negotiable,' has he a right of recourse against anyone?

Answer: If he gave value for the cheque, and was not party to any fraud concerning it, he can recover the amount from the person who negotiated the cheque to him.

435   Has the person in possession of a dishonoured bill or cheque upon which the payee's endorsement has been forged, but on which there are subsequent genuine endorsements, a right of recourse against such subsequent endorsers?

Answer: Yes, if he has given value for the bill, and is not party to any fraud concerning it. Under sec. 55 (2) (*b*) of the Bills of Exchange Act, the endorser of a bill is precluded from denying to a holder in due course the genuineness and regularity in all respects of . . . all previous endorsements. Here 'holder in due course' means a person who would have been such a holder but for the forged endorsement, and the sub-section thus gives him a right of recourse by estoppel against the genuine endorsers *subsequent* to the forgery.

436   A dividend warrant issued by a bank and sent by post to a shareholder is stolen in transit. The signature of the shareholder is forged, and the warrant is transferred to a third party for value. Can the third party recover the amount from the bank?

Answer: No, because no one can become 'holder' of a bill, cheque, or dividend warrant under a forged signature. (See secs. 2 and 24 of the Bills of Exchange Act.)

437   A cheque drawn by **A** payable to **B** and crossed 'account payee only' is negotiated for value by **B** to **C,** and is credited to the latter's account at his bank. On presentation it is dishonoured, and on being returned unpaid it is lost in the post in transmission from the drawee bank to **C**'s bank.

Can **C,** as holder for value, sue **A,** notwithstanding
(*a*) the words 'account payee only,' and
(*b*) the loss of the cheque?

Answer: (*a*) The words 'account payee only' probably do not affect either the transferability or the full negotiability of a cheque. In the present case, as it is not suggested that **B** had not a good title to the cheque, it is necessary only to show that the cheque was transferable, and accordingly **C** can sue **A,** as he could even if the cheque were crossed 'not negotiable.'

(*b*) Under sec. 69 of the Bills of Exchange Act, the person who was the holder of a lost bill may, if the bill was not overdue, compel the drawer to give him another bill on indemnifying him against claims by other persons in case the lost bill shall be found; and under sec. 70, in any action on a bill the Court may order that the loss of the bill shall not be set up, provided that an indemnity be given.

438 A banker cashes for a customer a crossed cheque drawn by another customer of his own bank and branch, but afterwards finds that the drawer is not in funds; can he debit the payee's account and return the cheque?

Answer: No. The payment of a cheque is complete and irrevocable when the money is laid on the counter.

439 An open cheque drawn on bank **X** payable to **A** or bearer is lost. The finder takes it to bank **Y,** who give him cash for it, and the cheque on presentation at bank **X** is duly paid. Has the payee, **A,** any claim against bank **Y**?

Answer: If the cheque, at the time when bank **Y** gave cash for it, was complete and regular, and not overdue, and the bank had no notice of any defect in the finder's title, bank **Y** are holders in due course of the cheque (sec. 29 (1) of the Bills of Exchange Act), and their title to it, and to the proceeds of collection, overrides that of the payee (sec. 38).

440 A person who is well known to a banker, but who has no account with him, asks him to cash cheques, some crossed and others uncrossed, drawn on other banks. Is the banker protected in doing so, if the cheques turn out to have been acquired by fraud?

Answer: In *Great Western Railway* v. *London and County Bank,*

[1901] A.C. 414, (Leading Cases, 4th Ed., p. 19), it was held that a person who had no account, but for whom a bank had for many years been in the habit of cashing cheques, was not a 'customer' within the meaning of sec. 82 of the Bills of Exchange Act (now sec. 4 of the Cheques Act, 1957). That section, therefore, does not protect the bank, nor would it even if the person for whom the cheques are cashed had an account, because clearly a banker who cashes cheques for a customer, instead of crediting them to his account, afterwards receives payment of them, not for the customer, but for himself.

If, however, the cheques are complete and regular, and are not overdue, and not crossed 'not negotiable,' and if the endorsements are genuine, and the banker takes them in good faith and without notice of any defect in the title of the person for whom he cashes them, he will be holder in due course under sec. 29 (1), and his title will override, under sec. 38, that of the true owners of the cheques.

But no one can be a holder under a forged endorsement. (See Q. 435 however.)

441 When does a cheque become 'overdue,' so as to prevent a banker or other person who takes it for value from becoming a holder in due course?

Answer: Under sec. 36 (3) of the Bills of Exchange Act a bill payable on demand, including a cheque, is deemed to be overdue when it appears on the face of it to have been in circulation for an unreasonable length of time; and what is an unreasonable length of time for this purpose is a question of fact.

442 A customer is in the habit of sending a clerk to the bank to pay in credits and to obtain cash for wages cheques drawn by himself. One day the clerk brings a cheque drawn on another bank, payable to and endorsed by his employer, and asks for cash for it, which the banker gives him. In the event of the clerk having stolen the cheque, and absconding, who loses the money, the changing banker or his customer? Is not the course of dealing such as to warrant the banker regarding the clerk as the acknowledged agent of his employer; and, moreover, does not the endorsement of the customer render him liable?

Answer: The banker can be considered as the holder of the cheque in good faith and without notice that the transferor's title is defective. Upon obtaining payment of the cheque from the banker upon whom it was drawn he is entitled to the money, and the loss would fall upon the customer.

443 A cheque is made payable to **A** (who is unknown to the collecting bank) and endorsed by him. He wishes to obtain cash for the cheque, and gets a customer of the collecting bank to buy it from him.

In the event of the cheque being dishonoured, who is responsible for the amount?

Answer: The bank can recover from the drawer, or, if due notice of dishonour is given, from either **A** or their own customer.

444 If a bank cashes for a customer, without crediting his account, a cheque (crossed or uncrossed) drawn on another branch of the same bank, what is the bank's position

(a) if the cheque when presented is returned unpaid by the drawee branch for want of funds, or because the drawer has countermanded payment, or

(b) though the cheque is paid by the drawee branch, the customer for whom it was cashed turns out to have had no title, or a defective title, to it?

Answer: (a) and (b) In *Woodland* v. *Fear* (1857), 26 L.J.Q.B. 202, (Leading Cases, 4th Ed., p. 344), it was held that in cashing at one branch a cheque drawn on another, a bank does not act as the bank of the drawer, but takes the cheque in reliance on the credit of the person presenting it, as it might have taken a cheque drawn on another bank; and that it has a right of recourse against him if the cheque is dishonoured. In practice, facilities for the cashing or exchanging of cheques are limited by the arrangement by the British Bankers' Association, dated 1945, under which no member bank will, at any of its branches in Great Britain or Northern Ireland, cash or exchange any cheque, payable order, or draft (or part thereof) without credit to the banking account of the presenter, unless:

(i) it is uncrossed and drawn on the branch at which it is presented, or

(ii) it is presented by the drawer or his known agent, or

(iii) it is payable under a credit established on behalf of the drawer, or

(iv) it is drawn for a sum not exceeding £10 in which case it may, at the discretion of the manager, on exceptional and isolated occasions, be encashed or exchanged.

Items which cannot be included in any of these categories must be paid in full into a banking account.

445   A banker cashes for a customer a cheque drawn on another bank, payable to and endorsed by a third party, without asking the customer to endorse it. If the cheque when presented is dishonoured, can the banker debit the customer's account with it?

Answer: Although the customer, as 'transferor by delivery,' is not liable on the cheque (sec. 58 (2) of the Bills of Exchange Act), the banker would probably be held to have cashed it on his credit, and to be entitled to recover the amount from him. (See *Woodland* v. *Fear* (1857), 26 L.J.Q.B. 202, Leading Cases, 4th Ed., p. 344).

In accordance with the announced practice of the clearing banks the customer should be required to endorse the cheque.

446   A secretary of a company pays in a number of cheques to the credit of the company's banking account, deducts an amount from the total on the credit slip and asks for cash for the amount deducted, the company to receive credit for the remainder. Would the bank run any risk in paying him the amount under the circumstances? He is authorised to endorse cheques on behalf of the company.

Answer: The transaction is quite irregular and might bring liability on the banker.

447   A places a cheque to his credit, and his bankers allow him to draw upon it before the cheque is cleared. **B,** the drawer, owing to a dispute with **A,** stops payment of the cheque. In the meantime **A** becomes a bankrupt, and when debited with the return, his account becomes overdrawn. Has the bank recourse against **B**?

Answer: It is preferable that the banker should not debit **A**'s account but should hold the cheque as a dishonoured bill. It is considered, however, that he would be able to claim as holder for value against **B** in any event, although the course advised avoids any possible doubt.

448   An employee steals from his employers a cheque drawn payable to the employers or bearer, and crossed generally, and obtains cash for it from a bank where he is known, but has not an account. Can the banker defend an action by the employers as true owners of the cheque?

Answer: In an action by true owners of a cheque for conversion, the only defences the bank can set up are (1) that it collected for a customer and can plead sec. 4 of the Cheques Act, 1957—which clearly is not the case here, as the cheque was exchanged and not collected; or (2) that it is a holder in due course. To be a holder in due course the bank must have taken the cheque for value (as in the question), in good faith and without notice of any defect in the presenter's title. In the absence of actual notice the bank can defend the action.

449 A banker takes for his customer's credit a cheque payable to the customer and crossed 'not negotiable,' and advances against it. The cheque is returned 'Payment stopped.' If the drawer has a good defence against the payee, can the banker recover from the drawer the amount he has advanced against the cheque?

Answer: No. If the drawer's defence against the payee adversely affects the latter's title to the cheque, the banker has no better title to the cheque than the customer from whom he received it. (See Bills of Exchange Act, sec. 81.)

COLLECTION

450 A cheque drawn by **A** on the **X** bank, payable to **B** or order, and crossed generally, fails to reach **B,** but comes into the hands of **C,** who forges **B**'s endorsement and receives cash for the cheque from **D,** who takes it in good faith and without notice of the forgery or of any defect in **C**'s title. **D** pays the cheque into his account at the **Y** bank, who collect it on his behalf.

When the forgery is discovered, is (1) the drawee bank **X,** or (2) the collecting bank **Y,** or (3) the person who cashed the cheque, **D,** liable to refund the amount to the true owner, **B**?

Answer: (1) The drawee bank **X** is protected by sec. 1 of the Cheques Act, 1957, having paid the cheque in good faith and in the ordinary course of business, notwithstanding the forged endorsement, and also by sec. 80 of the Bills of Exchange Act, having paid it without negligence in accordance with the crossing.

(2) The collecting bank **Y** is protected by sec. 4 of the Cheques Act, having, in good faith and without negligence, received payment of the cheque for a customer, notwithstanding the defect in the latter's title to it (but see also Q.'s 464 and 467).

(3) If the endorsement had not been forged, **D** would have been

holder in due course of the cheque (sec. 29), as it was not crossed 'not negotiable'; but under sec. 24 the forged endorsement prevents him from having any title to it, and accordingly he is liable to refund the amount to **B**.

C is of course also liable, for what his liability may be worth.

451   (a) John Jones issues his cheque on the **A** bank in favour of William Smith, or order, and crossed generally. This cheque is lodged by Thomas Brown for credit of his own account at the **A** bank, and bears the endorsement 'William Smith.' Is the **A** bank protected in collecting this cheque under sec. 4 of the Cheques Act, 1957? In other words, is a general crossing satisfied by lodgment of the cheque to the credit of *any* account?

(b) If William Smith had also an account with the **A** bank, could they without risk place the cheque to the credit of Thomas Brown, if William Smith had not endorsed it over to him? William Smith may have lost the cheque after endorsing it; could not he make the **A** bank refund to him for crediting it to another person?

Answer: (a) Yes.

(b) The bank could safely place the cheque to the credit of Thomas Brown.

452   A pays into his bankers a cheque, drawn on another banker, payable to and purporting to be endorsed by **C**, and crossed, 'Not negotiable.' Is **A**'s banker safe in taking such a cheque in the face of such a crossing, or is it necessary that **C** should negotiate it through his own banker?

Answer: The words 'not negotiable' do not mean 'not transferable,' and it is considered that when forming part of a crossing they do not put a collecting banker on inquiry, even though the cheque is being collected for a customer who is not the payee; and that accordingly the banker would not, merely on that ground, lose the protection of sec. 4 of the Cheques Act, 1957.

For the meaning of 'not negotiable' see sec. 81 of the Bills of Exchange Act.

453   **M**, a customer of the **B** bank, pays into his account at the **B** bank a crossed cheque drawn on that bank, payable to **J** or order and endorsed by him. **J** is known to keep an account at another bank.

Is the **B** bank justified in declining to credit **M** with the cheque, and in requiring it to be presented by **J**'s bank?

Answer: The cheque is a negotiable, or even if crossed 'not negotiable' a transferable, instrument. The bank would not, in the absence of special circumstances, be justified in refusing to credit **M** with it.

454 **A** wishes to pay crossed cheques, which are payable to **C** Co., Ltd., and endorsed *'Per pro* **C** Co., Ltd., **A'** into the **X** bank, for the credit of **B** with the **Y** bank.

Is the **X** bank liable to the **C** Co., Ltd., for receiving these cheques in the case of any fraud on the part of **A,** through thus dealing with them?

Answer: **X** bank would receive such cheques at its own risk because, if it subsequently transpired that the cheques had been stolen, **X** bank would be responsible to the true owners for conversion and would probably lose the protection of sec. 4 of the Cheques Act, 1957, because it had not acted 'without negligence.'

Although cheques payable to a limited company are negotiable instruments (unless crossed 'not negotiable') and when endorsed in blank by the payee company are payable to bearer, a limited company is presumed to have a banking account into which it normally passes all its receipts. It would be unusual for a limited company to negotiate cheques to third parties without passing the items through its books. Receipts are normally banked, whilst payments are made by separate entry by cash or the issue of a cheque. This is accepted business practice and departures from it cause the collecting bank to make enquiry. The prudent course is to enquire. If a satisfactory explanation is forthcoming, the cheque may be collected. (*Penmount Estates Ltd.* v. *National Provincial Bank Ltd.,* (1945) 173 L.T. 344; Leading Cases, 4th Ed., p. 121.)

455 Should a bank credit dividend warrants drawn payable to '**A,** a/c **A, B** and **C**' to the separate account of **A**?

Answer: Not without the express instructions of **B** and **C**.

456 Is there any risk, or is the collecting banker put on inquiry, in taking any of the following crossed cheques from a customer, H. Smith, for the credit of his private account with them?
   (1) A cheque payable to the executors of John Jones or order, and endorsed 'For self & co-executors of John Jones, H. Smith';
   (2) A cheque payable to the trustees of John Jones, and endorsed

'Trustees of John Jones,
F. Jones,
H. Smith.'

Answer: Without authority or inquiry, a cheque payable to two or more executors or trustees should not be credited to the account of one of them, or a breach of trust may result. In that event the banker would probably not be able to maintain that he dealt with the cheque without negligence, under sec. 4 of the Cheques Act, 1957.

457   A cheque for £200 in favour of **A,** or order, and crossed generally, is presented at the bank on which it is drawn by a person not known but representing himself to be the payee. He requests that £100 be lodged to the credit of **B**'s current account with the said bank, and £100 to the credit of **C**'s deposit account. Can the bank suffer loss by complying with this request?

Answer: No, if **B** and **C** are already customers of the bank.

458   **A** and **B** are partners in the firm of **A & B,** and they have a partnership account. **A** has also a private account. A cheque payable to **A,** and purporting to be endorsed by him, is brought in by **B** for the credit of the firm's account. Is there any risk in so crediting it?

Answer: The bank collecting the cheque for a customer in good faith would be acting without negligence and would be protected by sec. 4 of the Cheques Act, 1957.

459   A customer pays in for the credit of his account an open cheque drawn payable to a firm and endorsed in the firm-name by one of the partners. After the cheque has been collected it transpires that the partner who negotiated the cheque to the customer did so fraudulently. Has the firm any claim against (*a*) the customer, or (*b*) the bank which collected the cheque?

Answer: If the partner who endorsed the cheque had the usual authority of a partner to endorse cheques payable to his firm, then (*a*) provided that the cheque was complete and regular, and not overdue, and that he took it in good faith, for value, and without notice of the fraud, the customer was holder in due course of it (sec. 29 (1) of the Bills of Exchange Act), and his title to the proceeds of collection overrides that of the defrauded firm; and (*b*) the collecting bank acting as the customer's agent is protected by his title (sec. 29 (3)).

460 Would a banker be justified in refusing to collect a cheque crossed otherwise than generally or to himself?

Answer: If a banker received from his customer a cheque crossed specially to any other banker, he should decline to collect it.

461 Banker **A** collected for credit of a customer a cheque upon banker **B**, but crossed specially to banker **C**. The cheque was paid by **B** on presentation, although it bore the special crossing to **C**, and had not come through **C**'s hands to him. The cheque had been intended by the drawer to go to credit of an account with **C**, and the drawer has been called upon to pay the amount a second time. **B**, the paying banker, is of course, liable to him for the loss, but does any legal responsibility attach to **A**, who was merely the collecting banker?

Answer: Both bankers, **A** and **B**, are liable to the drawer of the cheque; banker **B** because he has paid the cheque otherwise than in accordance with the crossing (sec. 79 (2) of the Bills of Exchange Act), and banker **A** because he has collected a cheque which is crossed specially to another bank.

462 A banker observes that a cheque he has received from a customer for credit of his account is irregular. Is it proper for the banker to return such a cheque at once to the customer without presenting it, or should it be presented for the purpose of obtaining the official answer of the drawees?

Answer: It is desirable to return cheques at once to the parties from whom they are received or to communicate with them, when the cheques are observed to be incomplete or irregular, so as to save delay in their collection.

463 A bank's customer pays to his credit a cheque on another banker, which is irregularly drawn. The bank therefore return the cheque to their customer through the post for correction without presentation to the bank on which it is drawn. The cheque is stolen from the post, the endorsement is forged, and payment is obtained. Will the bank incur liability to its customer?

Answer: No. It is usual, however, in such circumstances for the collecting banker to place his stamp across the face of the cheque to minimise the risk of loss.

464 A stranger opens an account by paying in a cheque of which he asserts himself to be the payee. Does he thereupon become a 'customer' of the bank within the meaning of sec. 4 of the Cheques Act, 1957, and is the bank consequently protected by that section in receiving payment of the cheque on his behalf even though he may turn out to have no title, or a defective title, to it?

Answer: The relationship of banker and customer begins as soon as the account has been opened. (*Ladbroke* v. *Todd* (1914) 30 T.L.R. 433, Leading Cases, 4th Ed., p. 21). The stranger can, therefore, be regarded as a customer within sec. 4 of the Cheques Act, 1957, as soon as the cheque has been accepted by the bank for collection.

Whether or not sec. 4 of the Cheques Act will protect the bank, if the new customer has no title to the cheque, depends upon whether the bank acted without negligence in all the circumstances surrounding the collection. For example, failure to obtain references when opening the account would probably be construed to be negligence. (*Ladbroke* v. *Todd* (*supra*)). (See also Q.'s 440 and 467.)

465   What risk does a bank incur in collecting for a stranger an open or crossed cheque drawn on another branch of the same bank?

Answer: The risk is that the stranger may not be the true owner of the cheque, in which case the banker has no defence to a claim by the true owner for conversion.

466   A branch bank sent by post to its Head Office the daily letter, including cheques for collection, specially crossed, which had been credited to the customers paying them in.

The letter was lost in the post. The amounts of the clearings were debited by the Head Office to the branch concerned, and the latter debited a suspense account with the amounts, pending inquiry by the Post Office. The customers were notified immediately, and were asked to request the drawers to stop payment of the cheques.

Should the branch debit its customers' accounts with the amounts of the cheques, on receiving definite information that the letter had been lost?

Answer: Yes. Thus clearing its liability to the customers and making the position clear to them.

467 A opens an account with the **C** bank with a cheque for £100 drawn by **D** on the **B** bank, leaving £50 to his credit, and taking the remaining £50 in cash.

After the **B** bank has paid the cheque, the drawer **D** discovers that the payee has never received it, and that his endorsement has been forged. **D** then claims the £100 from the **C** bank. Can he succeed?

Answer: Providing **C** bank was not negligent in opening an account for **A** without proper references, the protection of sec. 4 of the Cheques Act, 1957, will prevail. (See also Q.'s 440 and 464.)

468 A stranger **A** calls without prior appointment to open an account with **B** bank by depositing several cheques to his credit and asks to be issued with a cheque book immediately. What should the attitude of **B** bank be to this request?

Answer: **A** should be told that a cheque book will be issued when acceptable references have been taken up, and it is indeed prudent to delay issuing the cheque book until the cheques paid in to open the account have been cleared. Should references not be taken up, the protection of sec. 4 of the Cheques Act, 1957, would be lost and if cheques had been paid to the debit of **A**'s account and he had no title to the cheques he had paid in, **B** bank would face a loss.

469 A cheque drawn on the **X** bank payable to **A** and crossed generally 'account payee' or 'account **A**' is paid by **C** into his account at the **Y** bank. It bears an endorsement purporting to be that of **A** and also the endorsement of **C**. The **Y** bank collects the cheque for the account of **C**, and it is paid by the **X** bank.

What is the position of (*a*) the collecting bank, and (*b*) the paying bank, if it turns out that the endorsement of **A** is a forgery, and that **C** has wrongfully acquired the cheque?

Answer: (*a*) Although the words 'account payee' are not authorised by the Bills of Exchange Act as an addition to a crossing, they have been held by the Courts to be a direction to a collecting banker that the proceeds of a cheque so crossed are to be credited only to the account of the payee named in the cheque. A banker who collects a cheque so crossed for an account other than that of the payee has accordingly been held to be guilty of negligence which deprives him of the protection of sec. 4 of the Cheques Act, 1957.

Accordingly banks do not collect such cheques for third parties unless the standing of their customers is undoubted, or a satisfactory explanation is forthcoming.

(*b*) The paying bank is protected by sec. 1 of the Cheques Act, 1957 provided it acted in good faith and in the ordinary course of business. The crossing 'account payee' is not the concern of the paying banker and will not affect his ability to fulfil these requirements.

470 A draws a cheque in favour of **B** and crosses it generally. Both **A** and **B** are customers of the same bank and branch. If the bank credits **B**'s account with the cheque, and pays it, is the payment in accordance with the crossing?

Answer: Yes; the bank must be considered to be acting both as collecting and as paying bank.

471 A man named Hill fraudulently obtains a crossed cheque, payable to Gill, and having altered the payee's name to Hill, and pays it into his account with his bankers, by whom the cheque is presented, they having failed to notice the alteration. The cheque is returned by the drawee bank, with the answer, 'Orders not to pay.' What is the position of the collecting bank as against the drawer of the cheque if they have paid against it?

Answer: The collecting banker has no recourse against the drawer of the cheque, who is released by the unauthorised alteration. (See Bills of Exchange Act, sec. 64 (1).)

WITH RECEIPT ATTACHED

472 A customer seeks to use a cheque bearing a form of receipt intended to be signed by the payee. What reaction should the banker take to such a request?

Answer: Every effort should be made to dissuade the customer, whose attention should be drawn to sec. 3 of the Cheques Act, 1957, whereby 'An unindorsed cheque which appears to have been paid by the banker on whom it is drawn is evidence of the receipt by the payee of the sum payable by the cheque, and to the following view expressed by the Mocatta Committee (1956 (Cmnd. 3)):

'We are of the opinion that in law a simple receipt for a payment by cheque, not linking the payment with the relative transaction, has no greater value as evidence of payment than the paid cheque itself. This is so whether the receipt is printed on the cheque or is issued separately.'

The intention of the Cheques Act, 1957, was to relieve customers from the task of endorsing instruments which are to be collected for the payee's accounts, and it would be a retrograde step to introduce new combined cheque and receipt forms which call for examination by the collecting and paying banks.

If a real need for the facility can be proved by the customer and the bank is disposed in the special circumstances to grant an exception, the receipt form should be limited to a mere acknowledgement of receipt of the money (a narrative receipt connecting the payment with any specific transaction is to be deprecated) and the face of the cheque will have to bear a bold outline letter 'R' at least half-an-inch high and as close to the '£' sign in the amount box as practicable. All such instruments bearing a denoting 'R' on the face of them require examination by both the collecting and paying banks. See Appendix C.

MISCELLANEOUS

473 Is a customer entitled to draw at once against cheques which he pays in for the credit of his account, without waiting for them to be cleared?

Answer: Not unless there is an agreement between the customer and the banker to that effect.

474 ABC Limited have an account at the local branch of **X** Bank and draw a cheque on that account in favour of that bank in connection with certain funds to be remitted abroad. **B** steals the cheque before it is despatched to **X** Bank and sends it to another branch of that bank where he has an account, accompanied by a letter in which he states that the cheque represents money due to him by ABC Limited. The branch collects the cheque for the account of **B** and when the theft is discovered a claim is made upon it.
Has **X** Bank a defence to this claim?

Answer: It is considered unlikely that the bank can avail itself of the protection afforded by sec. 4 of the Cheques Act, 1957.

A cheque drawn in this manner is probably intended to be delivered to the bank in payment for some service to be rendered by the bank, such as the issue of a draft. It should not be collected, or dealt with in any way, without the express instructions of the drawer, ABC Limited.

475   If a cheque drawn payable to 'bill attached' or bearer, or to 'documents attached' or bearer, is presented for payment, is the drawee banker responsible for seeing that the cheque has a bill, or documents, attached to it, and if so, that the bill is, or the documents are, in order?

Answer: It is considered that the banker should see that a bill is, or that documents (more than one) are attached to the cheque, but that he has no further responsibility.

476   Does a banker, who receives a cheque for payment by post from another banker, become the 'agent for collection' within the meaning of the Bills of Exchange Act, sec. 77 (5) and sec. 79 (1)?

Answer: A bank receiving a cheque by post from another bank for payment becomes the 'agent for collection' of the sending bank, whether the cheque is drawn upon the bank or upon some other bank in the town.

477   What is the position of a banker to whom is presented across the counter, by a stranger, a cheque drawn by a customer in favour of a payee unknown to the banker which bears across its face the words 'Account payee only,' but without the transverse lines or the name of a banker which constitute a crossing?
  (*a*) Is it a crossed cheque?
  (*b*) If it is not a crossed cheque, would the banker be in order in paying it across the counter?
  (*c*) If payment is refused, what would be the correct answer to be placed on the cheque?

Answer: (*a*) No. (See sec. 76 of the Bills of Exchange Act, which defines a crossing.)
  (*b*) As the cheque is in so ambiguous and contradictory a form as to impose more than the ordinary risk on the banker who pays it, he would be justified in refusing payment.
  (*c*) The best answer would be 'form of cheque irregular.'

478   Is it right to have alternative payees on a cheque, as, 'pay John Smith or R. Brown or order,' and would a bank be justified in returning a cheque made out in such a manner?

Answer: Alternative payees are permitted (see Bills of Exchange Act, sec. 7 (2)).

479   On the back of a cheque presented for payment appear the words, 'Subject to goods being in accordance with specification,' in the writing of the drawer, but having no signature or initials to it. Is the banker in order in paying this cheque, or does it cease to be a cheque (as being conditional) under sec. 3 of the Bills of Exchange Act?

Answer: The words on the back are in the nature of a memorandum, which may be disregarded by the banker.

480   Is a cheque in the following form a negotiable instrument?
'Pay **A B**, or order . . . pounds by draft at twenty-one days after date.'

Answer: As the instrument requires an act, namely the issue of a draft, to be done in addition to the payment of money, it appears not to be a bill of exchange within sec. 3 (2) of the Bills of Exchange Act, and therefore not to be a negotiable instrument; but as between the drawer and the drawee bank, it appears to be a valid mandate for the issue of a draft to the payee in person.

481   A document is drawn as follows:
'Pay to the order of A. Brown the sum of five pounds at the British Bank, Penzance.
£5.
                                                                                        T. Richardson.'
The bank refuses to pay, saying that it is an irregular document.
The reason given is that it is not addressed to any person, as required by sec. 6 of the Bills of Exchange Act. Is the document in order, that is, duly addressed to the British Bank? Is the bank justified in returning it unpaid?

Answer: The document is not in order for the reason given, and the bank is justified in returning it.

482   Should a bill or cheque drawn 'Pay to . . . or order,' no payee's name being mentioned, be paid without the express authority of the acceptor or drawer?

Answer: No; it should be returned as being incompletely drawn; but in *Chamberlain* v. *Young,* [1893] 2 Q.B. 206, a bill drawn payable to . . . order (without 'or') was held to be payable to the drawer's order.

483   In addition to giving value to the payee of a cheque crossed 'not negotiable,' is it necessary, in order to establish a good title as against the drawer, to be satisfied that the drawer received valuable consideration for it?

Answer: By sec. 81 of the Bills of Exchange Act a person who takes a crossed cheque marked 'not negotiable' can neither have, nor give, a better title to the cheque than that of the person from whom he took it.

Assuming the cheque to be crossed and marked 'not negotiable' by the drawer it is necessary for the holder, in order to establish a good title as against the drawer, to be able to prove that all persons through whom he claims, including the person who took it from the drawer were able to give a good title to it, and if such title depends upon value having been given to the drawer, proof of such value having been given would be required. (See *Great Western Railway* v. *London and County Bank,* [1901] A.C., 414, Leading Cases, 4th Ed., p. 19.)

Value to the drawer would not be necessary in the case of a gift or loan of the amount of the cheque by the drawer to the person to whom he gives it.

484   A sells goods to **B** and receives in payment a cheque drawn by a third party, **C**, payable to **A** and not endorsed by **B**. If **C**'s cheque is dishonoured when presented, can **A** sue **B** for the price of the goods, or is he restricted to his remedy against **C** on the cheque?

Answer: In the absence of evidence to the contrary, **A** is presumed to have taken the cheque as conditional payment only, the condition being that the debt would revive if the cheque were not paid; but if **A** were guilty of negligence with regard to the cheque, such as omitting for an unreasonable time to present it for payment, the cheque would then be treated as absolute payment, and **A** would lose his right against **B**.

485   Is a customer entitled to demand his paid cheques from his banker without giving a receipt for them?

Answer: No. See *Charles* v. *Blackwell* (1879), 5 C.P.D. 7.

ENDORSEMENTS

It will be appreciated that the Cheques Act, 1957, radically amended the requirements in the U.K. for the endorsement of cheques. See the guide notes prepared by the Committee of London Clearing Bankers in September, 1957, (see Appendix C).

Endorsements continue to be required in the case of bills of exchange and promissory notes, but so far as cheques are concerned they are, or may be, relevant only in matters touching upon negotiability.

486 Is a banker, before payment of a cheque drawn on him and payable to bearer, entitled to demand the endorsement of the party receiving the money?

Answer: No.

487 If a person who represents himself to be the payee of an open order cheque presents the cheque for payment, can the banker insist on his endorsing it?

Answer: It is established banking practice to require the payee to endorse the cheque, or to furnish a receipt for the amount thereof.

488 A cheque drawn 'Pay bearer or order' is presented across the counter without any endorsement. Should it be paid without endorsement?

Answer: The word 'order' being printed in the form of the cheque, the drawer, by inserting 'bearer', evidently meant it to be so payable. The cheque may therefore be paid without endorsement.

489 A cheque is drawn 'Pay bearer (J. Smith) or order,' Is it payable to bearer or order?

Answer: The cheque requires J. Smith's endorsement if presented for payment at a bank counter.

490 Should a cheque with the word 'bearer' struck out, but the word 'order' omitted, be regarded as a cheque payable to order?

Answer: Yes. (Bills of Exchange Act, sec. 8 (4).)

491 A cheque is drawn payable to a named payee or order, but the drawer deletes 'order' and initials the deletion, without substituting 'bearer' for it. Should the cheque be considered to be payable to bearer?

Answer: Under sec. 8, sub-secs. (3) and (4), of the Bills of Exchange Act a bill or cheque is payable to bearer which is expressed to be so payable, or on which the only or last endorsement is an endorsement in blank. A bill or cheque is payable to order which is expressed to be so payable, or which is expressed to be payable to a particular person. The mere deletion of 'order' without substituting 'bearer' does not make a cheque payable to bearer.

492 If a cheque is drawn payable to A or bearer, and A, or a subsequent holder, has specially endorsed it, would a scrutiny of the endorsements be necessary if the cheque were presented at the counter?

Answer: No; a bill or cheque drawn payable to bearer remains so payable notwithstanding special endorsements. (See sec. 8 (3) of the Bills of Exchange Act.)

493 A bill drawn payable to A or order is endorsed by A in blank and is delivered by him to B.
   (1) Can B convert A's blank endorsement into a special endorsement in favour of himself or another person?
   (2) If, on the other hand, B leaves A's endorsement as it was, in blank, and adds his own special endorsement in favour of C, is C's endorsement necessary if the bill is negotiated further, or has A's blank endorsement made it payable to bearer?
   (3) If the ultimate holder endorses in blank, can his bankers convert his endorsement into a special endorsement to themselves, for collection?

Answer: (1) Yes; under sec. 34 (4) of the Bills of Exchange Act, which provides that, when a bill has been endorsed in blank, any holder may convert the blank endorsement into a special endorsement by writing above the endorser's signature a direction to pay the bill to, or to the order of, himself or some other person.
   (2) C's endorsement is necessary, because under sec. 8 (3) of the Act a special endorsement controls the effect of a previous endorsement in blank.
   (3) Yes; under sec. 34 (4) quoted above.

494 Should the following be regarded as special endorsements by A in favour of C?
   (1) A, pay to the order of C;
   (2) A, in favour of C;
   (3) C or order, A;
   (4) Please exchange, C, A?

Answer: All these should be regarded as intended to be special endorsements in favour of **C**. All that sec. 34 (2) requires is that a special endorsement should specify the person to whom, or to whose order, the bill is to be payable.

495   A cheque drawn payable to **A** and specially endorsed by him to **B** is lost by **B** without having been endorsed by him. The finder presents it for payment without any endorsement in the name of **B**, and the drawee bank pays it. Can **B** recover from the bank?

Answer: If the cheque was paid over the counter otherwise than to a customer, the bank would find it difficult to claim the protection of sec. 1 of the Cheques Act, 1957, but if paid through the clearing in the normal way the protection of sec. 1 would stand.

496   A bill accepted payable at a bank bears, when presented, several special endorsements, one of which has apparently been blackened out so as to be completely illegible. Following the obliteration appears the discharge of the preceding endorser.

Should the bank demand confirmation that the obliterated endorsement has been cancelled by a person entitled to cancel it?

Answer: The holder of a bill is at liberty to strike out any endorsement which is not necessary to his title and the risk that an obliterated special endorsement may have been detrimental to the holder's title, and may have been cancelled fraudulently, either by him or by some previous holder, is no greater than the risk of forgery of any of the endorsements, against which a banker has no statutory protection in the case of a bill accepted payable at his bank, though he has in the case of a cheque drawn on him.

It is therefore considered that a banker would usually pay such a bill without asking for confirmation.

497   A bill payable to **A** or order is specially endorsed 'Place to my account with the **X** bank, **A**.' Is this a restrictive endorsement, requiring discharge by the **X** bank, and should such discharge state that the bill has been credited to **A**'s account?

Answer: The endorsement is considered to be a restrictive endorsement under sec. 35 of the Bills of Exchange Act, and to render the bill payable to the **X** bank; but the paying bank is not responsible for the application of the money by the **X** bank, nor need that bank state in their endorsement that it has been credited to the account of **A**.

498   A bill payable to **A** or order is endorsed 'Pay to **B**'s account, **A**.' Is a second endorsement necessary?

Answer: As there is no direction to pay to **B**, and the name of **B**'s bank is not stated, the words quoted are considered to be a mere memorandum which may be disregarded by the drawee bank.

499   A cheque payable to **X** 'in full settlement' is endorsed by **X** as follows:
  (*a*) 'in part settlement';
  (*b*) 'received without prejudice.'
Should the drawee banker refuse to accept these endorsements as contravening the expressed intention of his customer in issuing the cheque?

Answer: A creditor may refuse to accept a cheque for a smaller amount in satisfaction of his debt even though he does not return the cheque; and he may then sue for the balance. The payment of the cheque in its existing state would not, therefore, prejudice the drawer. Any condition implied in the endorsement may be disregarded by the drawee bank under sec. 33 of the Bills of Exchange Act and, in any event, the paying bank is protected by sec. 1 of the Cheques Act, 1957.

500   A bill bearing an irregular endorsement bears also the stamp of the presenting bank 'Endorsement confirmed, per pro, the **X** Bank Limited,' signed 'pro Manager' by a person purporting to be an official of that bank.
  Is it customary:
  (1) to accept such a confirmation as implying an undertaking by the **X** bank to indemnify the paying bank against the risk of the endorsement not being that of the payee;
  (2) to ascertain whether the person signing on behalf of the **X** bank has authority to do so?

Answer: (1) Yes; among bankers such a confirmation is understood to imply an undertaking of indemnity.
  (2) Although a signature 'pro Manager' is irregular in form, a manager having no power to delegate his authority, it is usual to assume that the person so signing has the requisite authority from the bank to do so. For this reason a bank manager should always keep the 'endorsement confirmed' stamp in a place of safety.

501 What is the practice of bankers with regard to the payment of cheques and bills purporting to be endorsed (where endorsement is required) on behalf of a principal, whether an individual, a firm, a company or other corporate body, by an agent?

Answer:

(1) An endorsement 'per procuration—,' or 'per pro.,' or 'pp.,' is accepted as indicating that the person making it has authority to endorse on behalf of his principal. But if the endorser adds his capacity, it must be such as to lead reasonably to the conclusion that authority to endorse has been delegated to him.

(2) An endorsement 'for,' or 'pro,' or 'on behalf of' the principal, or 'by,' or 'per' the agent, is not considered to imply that the agent has authority to endorse, and is therefore not accepted, unless the agent adds, after his signature, a description of his position relative to the principal, and unless that position is such that a person holding it would or might normally have authority to endorse.

(3) If the endorser merely writes his principal's name, adding thereto his bare signature, the endorsement will not be in order, because it does not purport to be made on the principal's behalf.

(4) By sec. 33 of the Companies Act, 1948, the name of a limited company is by itself sufficient if placed on the instrument by any person acting under its authority. Where, therefore, the signatory's capacity as shown is adequate to support the presumption that he has authority, it may be accepted even though the name of the company has no prefix such as 'for' or 'on behalf of.' (See also Q. 509.)

(5) A partner may sign the firm-name without any prefix whether he adds his own name or not.

See the examples quoted below.

EXAMPLES

Payee	Regular endorsement	Irregular endorsement
A B	per pro. (or p.p.) A B, C D	pro. per A B, C D (without description)
	A B per pro. (or p.p.) C D (see *Slingsby* v. *District Bank,* [1932] 1 K.B. 544,	

Payee	*Regular endorsement*	*Irregular endorsement*
	for (or pro., or on behalf of) **A B,** **C D,** Agent (or Manager) **A B** by (or per) **C D,** Agent (or Manager) **A B** by (or per) **C D,** Attorney	for (or pro., or on behalf of) **A B,** **C D** (without description) **A B** by (or per) **C D** (without description)
The Duke of Sussex	for (and on behalf of) the Duke of Sussex, **X Y,** Agent	**X Y,** Agent to the Duke of Sussex (because the Agent does not purport to sign on behalf of his principal)
A B & Son	**A B** & Son, **C B,** Partner (or the partner might, and usually would, sign the firm-name, without adding his own) per pro. (or p.p.) **A B** & Son, **C D** for (or pro., or on behalf of) **A B** & Son, **C D,** Chief Clerk (or Manager)	**C B,** a partner in the firm of **A B** & Son (because this does not purport to be the firm's endorsement) for (or pro., or on behalf of) **A B** & Son, **C D** (without description)
A B Limited	per pro. (or p.p.) **A B** Ltd., **C D** for, or pro., or on behalf of **A B** Ltd., **C D,** Managing Director, or Manager, or Accountant, or Secretary, or Cashier, or 'a person duly authorised to endorse cheques on behalf of this Company' **A B** Ltd., per (or by) **C D** (described as above) **A B** Ltd., **C D** Secretary For **A B** Ltd. J. Jones Assistant Secretary	for (or pro., or on behalf of) **A B** Ltd., **C D** (without description) for (or as above) **A B** Ltd., **C D,** their Solicitor (it is not considered that a company's solicitor would usually have authority to endorse) for (or as above) **A B** Ltd., **C D,** Private Secretary (would not usually have authority to endorse) per pro. **A B** Ltd., pro. **C D,** Manager, **E F** [a manager has no power to delegate his authority)

Payee	*Regular endorsement*	*Irregular endorsement*
A B & Co. Ltd.	A B & Co. Ltd. J. Jones Assistant Secretary	
Hightown Corporation	for (and on behalf of) Hightown Corporation (or the Borough of Hightown), C D, Borough Treasurer (or Borough Accountant)	for (and on behalf of) Hightown Corporation, E F, Rate Collector (the late Sir John Paget considered that a Rate Collector would have authority to endorse cheques drawn in payment of rates, but not for other purposes)
Managers of the X School	for (and on behalf of) the Managers of the X School, C D, Chairman	

502 Must the expression 'per procuration,' or 'per pro.,' or 'p.p.,' when appropriate, always precede the name of the principal ('per pro. **A, B**'), or may it appear after his name but before that of the agent ('**A**, per pro. **B**')?

Answer: The usual sequence is 'per pro. **A, B**.' The sequence '**A**, per pro. **B**' was at one time common in Scotland, and occasionally in use by solicitors in England; the practice has now fallen into disuse, although eminent authorities have regarded it as acceptable.

503 Is a banker protected by sec. 1 of the Cheques Act, 1957, in paying cash over the counter for an open cheque endorsed 'per pro'.

Answer: Yes; provided that the payment is made in the 'ordinary course of business.' Whether or not payment is made in the ordinary course of business depends entirely upon the facts of each case.

The practical guidance is that when dealing with a negotiable instrument the banker does not need to view every presentation with suspicion. Business prudence in doubtful circumstances may demand care, but the need for enquiry arises only in exceptional cases. If the appearance of the presenter or the relevant facts, including the amount of the cheque, occasion suspicion, then the prudent course is to institute the necessary enquiries before effecting payment.

504 A cheque endorsed specially to R. B. Richardson is further endorsed by H. Jones, his agent:

H. Jones
per pro R. B. Richardson
Would this endorsement normally be accepted?

Answer: Yes.

505 Can a firm sign or endorse 'per pro.' for another firm or person?
For example—
'per pro. **A,**
B & Co.'

Answer: Yes.

506 How should a bill or cheque which is payable to two or more
individuals, who are not partners, be endorsed?

Answer: Under sec. 32 (3) of the Bills of Exchange Act, where a
Bill or cheque is payable to the order of two or more payees or
endorsees who are not partners all must endorse, unless the one
endorsing has authority to endorse for the others. If one of them has
such authority he may adopt the form 'for self and . . .'

507 How should a bill or cheque payable to a minor be endorsed?

Answer: Under sec. 22 (2) of the Bills of Exchange Act, where a
bill or cheque is endorsed by a minor, the endorsement entitles the
holder to receive payment of it, and to enforce it against any other
party to it. The minor may therefore endorse the bill or cheque
himself.

508 By whom should a bill or cheque be endorsed which is payable to
(1) an individual or firm that has executed a deed of assignment;
(2) an individual or firm that has become bankrupt;
(3) a company that has gone into liquidation?

Answer: The bill or cheque should be endorsed by
(1) the trustee under the deed;
(2) the trustee in the bankruptcy, or, if no trustee has been
appointed, or during a vacancy in the office of trustee, by
the Official Receiver;
(3) by the liquidator.

509 Is the name of a limited company, written on a bill or cheque
payable to the company, a sufficient endorsement, without the
signature of any person expressed to sign on the company's behalf?

Answer: Under sec. 33 of the Companies Act, 1948, a bill of exchange or promissory note shall be deemed to have been . . . endorsed on behalf of a company if . . . endorsed *in the name of* or by or on behalf or on account of the company by any person acting under its authority. In practice, however, the name of the company, by itself, is not accepted. (See also Q. 501.)

510 Are the following endorsements correct:
    (*a*) on a cheque payable to John Brown,
        John Brown
        John Browne (in the same handwriting);
    (*b*) on a cheque payable to James Smith,
        p.p. James Smith
        p.p. James Smythe
            X.;
    (*c*) on a cheque payable to **A** & Co.,
        for   **A** & Co.
              A & Co., Ltd.
                B, Secretary;
    (*d*) on a cheque payable to S. Thomson,
        S. Thompson, described as S. Thomson?

Answer: (*a*), (*b*) and (*c*) Yes, under sec. 32 (4) of the Bills of Exchange Act, which provides that where, in a bill or cheque payable to order, the payee or endorsee is wrongly designated, or his name is mis-spelt, he may endorse the bill or cheque as therein described, adding, if he think fit, his proper signature.

(*d*) Yes, but the more usual mode of endorsement is as in (*a*) above.

511 How may a cheque payable
    (*a*) to the executor (or administrator) of **A**,
    (*b*) to the executors (or administrators) of **A**, be correctly endorsed?

Answer: (*a*) **B**, executor (or administrator) of **A**,
    (*b*) **B**,
        C,   executors (or administrators) of **A**,
or, **B**, for self and co-executor(s) (or co-administrator(s)) of **A**,
N.B.—In Scotland this mode of endorsement is considered to be
       irregular;
or, for the executors (or administrators) of **A**, **B**, executor (or
       administrator) of **A**,
N.B.—Also deemed to be irregular in Scotland.

512 A cheque payable to **B**, executor of **A**, is endorsed with **B**'s name, without description. Is this correct?

Answer: No; **B** should describe himself as executor of **A**.

513 Is a cheque payable to J. Brown & Co., correctly endorsed 'Brown & Co.,' or a cheque payable to Brown & Co., correctly endorsed 'J. Brown & Co.'?

Answer: No; the endorsement will not be considered to correspond with the payee's name if an initial or fore-name is either omitted or added.

514 On a cheque payable to J. Brown & Co., would an endorsement 'John Brown & Co.,' or on a cheque payable to John Brown & Co. an endorsement 'J. Brown & Co.,' be considered to be correct?

Answer: Yes; as with individuals, initials may be expanded to names, or names contracted to initials.

515 A bill of exchange payable to Smith & Co. is endorsed 'Smith, Jones & Robinson.' Is this correct?

Answer: No; the cheque should be endorsed as drawn; but the payees may, if they choose, add their full signature below. (Bills of Exchange Act, sec. 32 (4).)

516 How may a cheque payable to (*a*) Messrs. A. & B. Brown, or (*b*) Messrs. Brown & Smith, be correctly endorsed?

Answer: (*a*) Either 'A. & B. Brown,'
                     or 'A. Brown
                        B. Brown,' in different hand-writings.
           (*b*) Either 'Brown & Smith,'
                     or 'J. Brown
                        F. Smith,' in different hand-writings.

517 What forms of endorsement are permissible on a cheque payable to (*a*) Messrs. Brown, or (*b*) Messrs. J. Brown?

Answer: The endorsement should purport to be that of a firm consisting of at least two persons of the name mentioned.
    Thus (*a*) 'Browns,'
              'Brown & Son(s),'
              'Brown Brothers,'

    'A. & B. Brown,'
    (*b*) 'J. & J. Brown,'
would be considered to be correct but not
    (*a*) 'Brown & Co.'
    (*b*) 'J. Brown & Co.'

If, however, the partners sign their individual names, whatever these may be, and add 'trading as Messrs. Brown,' or 'as Messrs. J. Brown,' the endorsement should be passed.

518 May the equivalent in a foreign language of such words as 'Sons' or 'Brothers,' in the name of a firm to which a cheque is drawn payable, be accepted in an endorsement of the cheque?

Answer: Yes. Examples: **X** & Sons, '**X** y Hijos;' **X** Brothers, '**X** Frères.'

519 Is the endorsement—
        'Robinson & Brown,
        Wm. Smith,'
a valid discharge of a cheque payable to the order of Robinson & Brown, the second name being written immediately under the first and in the same handwriting, the two obviously forming one signature?

Answer: Such an endorsement is irregular, as it does not show that Wm. Smith has any authority to sign for Robinson & Brown.

520 A cheque is drawn payable (*a*) to Mesdames (or Misses) Smith & Jones, or (*b*) to Mesdames (or Misses) Brown. How may it be correctly endorsed?

Answer: The drawer's use of the collective feminine prefix may be considered to indicate that the intended payees are two or more women, probably in partnership.
In case (*a*) the cheque may accordingly be endorsed
    'Smith & Jones,'
  or 'Eva Smith
    Alice Jones,' in different handwritings.
In case (*b*) the endorsement may be
    'Brown Sisters,'
    'Brown & Daughter' (if the prefix is 'Mesdames'),
    'A. & B. Brown,'
    'A. Brown
    B. Brown, trading as Mesdames (or Misses) Brown.'

521 A cheque payable to Mrs. Jones and Sons is endorsed 'Sarah Jones and Sons.' Is this correct?

Answer: The endorsement would usually be accepted.

522 A cheque payable to the order of Mr. J. and Mrs. S. Langdon, is endorsed 'J. and S. Langdon.' Is this correct?

Answer: No. Mr. Langdon and Mrs. Langdon should each endorse the cheque separately.

523 When the name of the payee of a cheque has the prefix Mr., Messrs., Mrs., Miss, Dr., Rev., or a military or other rank, or a title, is it the practice of bankers in this country to accept an endorsement having before the name the same prefix, rank or title as in the cheque?

Answer: The endorsement of the payee exactly as he is designated on the face of the cheque, including any prefix, rank or title, is not accepted.

In the United States, on the contrary, an endorsement must correspond exactly with the order to pay.

Examples of endorsements regarded in this country as regular and irregular are given below:

Payee	Regular Endorsement	Irregular Endorsement
Mr. John Smith	John Smith	Mr. John Smith
John Smith, Esq.	John Smith	John Smith, Esq.
Mrs. Helen Smith	Helen Smith or (Mrs.) Helen Smith	Mrs. Helen Smith
Mrs. John Smith	Jane Smith, wife (or widow) of John Smith Jane Smith (Mrs. John Smith)	Mrs. John Smith
Major Henry Jones	Henry Jones or Henry Jones, Major	Major Henry Jones
The Earl of Hightown	Hightown	Earl of Hightown (but Continental titles are often so signed)
The Countess of Hightown	Mary Hightown	Countess of Hightown (but see above)
The Bishop of Hightown	James Hightown (in some cases the Latin name of the See is used in place of the English name, as in 'Ebor.' for 'York') or James Brown Bishop of Hightown	Bishop of Hightown

524 Is a cheque payable to **A**, trading as the **X Co.**, sufficiently endorsed with the signature of **A** without more?

Answer: No; **A** should describe himself as in the cheque.

525 A cheque payable to **A** is endorsed '**A** for self and co-executors of **B**.' Is this correct?

Answer: No; the endorsement purports to be that of the executors of **B**, not that of **A**, in his private capacity.

526 The endorsement on a cheque presented for payment at the counter of the drawee bank purports to be that of the payee but it so happens that the drawee bank is satisfied that the endorsement is not in his handwriting. Can the cheque safely be paid?

If the payee were the drawer himself, the cheque having been drawn payable to self or order, would the position be different?

Answer: Under sec. 91 (1) of the Bills of Exchange Act, it is not necessary that the payee should endorse the cheque with his own hand but his signature may be written by some other person by his authority. Under sec. 1 of the Cheques Act, 1957, a banker paying a cheque in the ordinary course of business need not show that the endorsement was made by the authority of the person whose endorsement it purports to be. The drawee banker is, therefore, not bound to enquire before paying the cheque, but he may well think it prudent to do so where the amount is large enough to demand caution.

Where the cheque is drawn payable to 'self or order,' the banker would normally call for verification of the endorsement unless satisfied that the customer is in the habit of allowing some other person to endorse for him.

527 A cheque drawn by a firm payable to selves or order is drawn by one partner and endorsed by another, both signing the firm-name. Should the cheque be paid without inquiry?

Answer: It is considered that there is nothing in these circumstances to put the drawee banker on inquiry.

528 How should a married woman endorse a cheque drawn payable to her in her maiden name?

Answer: Either by signing her maiden name, adding, if she chooses, her married name below (sec. 32 (4) of the Bills of

Exchange Act), or by signing, for example, 'Jane Smith, formerly (or née) Jane Jones.'

529   Is a cheque payable to J. Smith correctly endorsed 'J. H. Smith,' or a cheque payable to J. H. Smith correctly endorsed 'J. Smith'?

Answer: No; the endorsement will not be considered to correspond with the payee's name if an initial or fore-name is either added or omitted.

530   May a cheque payable to J. Smith be correctly endorsed 'James Smith,' or a cheque payable to James Smith be correctly endorsed 'J. Smith'?

Answer: Yes; initials may be expanded into fore-names, or names may be contracted to initials. (See also Q. 514.)

531   May a cheque payable to 'Smith' be endorsed 'Smith'?

Answer: No; it is not usual in this country for an individual (unless a peer) to sign without initials or fore-name, but the practice in some other countries is different.

532   May a cheque payable to James McGregor be endorsed 'James MacGregor,' or conversely?

Answer: No; 'Mc' and 'Mac' are not considered to be interchangeable.

533   Is a cheque payable to the initials 'M. G.,' or order, having on the back the initials 'M. G.,' followed by a signature 'M. G. Brown,' correctly endorsed?

Answer: It is considered that the endorsement may be accepted but, where necessary, the cheque may be rejected on the ground that the intended payee is not 'named or otherwise indicated with reasonable certainty,' within the meaning of sec. 7 (1) of the Bills of Exchange Act.

534   Is an endorsement in block letters (JOHN SMITH) a regular endorsement?

Answer: No.

535 Are the following rubber-stamp endorsements acceptable?

Cheque drawn f/o	*Endorsement*
J. Williams & Co., Ltd.	per pro ~~John~~ Williams & Co. Ltd. A. Heath, Director
John Williams & Co., Ltd.	per pro John Williams & Co. (~~Stafford~~) Ltd. A. Heath, Director
John Williams & Sons, Ltd.	per pro John Williams & Son s Ltd. A. Heath, Director
John Williams & Sons, Ltd.	per pro and Sons John Williams/Ltd. A. Heath, Director

Answer: Such endorsements should normally be accepted. It is submitted that they purport to be those of the payee and that the drawee banker need not ask for confirmation merely because a rubber-stamp impression of what is evidently the correct name of the company has been altered.

If there is any factor which might raise suspicion, then the drawee banker should ask for confirmation, but this would be likely to arise only in respect of open cheques presented for payment over the counter.

536 Can a person who is unable to write validly endorse a cheque payable to him?

Answer: Where the endorsement of such a payee is necessary, he can endorse by a mark with words clearly indicating the action in the presence of a witness whose address should be quoted. The usual form is 'X. Tom Blank, his mark' with Y, of High Bridge, North Town, signing as witness. Where such an illiterate payee presents the cheque over the counter for cash, it is undesirable that the paying cashier should be the witness.

Alternatively, the person unable to write may orally authorise some other person to endorse the cheque for him.

(Bills of Exchange Act, sec. 91 (1)).

537 A branch of a bank draws upon its London office a draft in favour of two individual payees.

One payee endorses the draft and presents it for payment, at the same time exhibiting for registration a certificate of the death of the other payee.

Would the bank be in order in paying the draft upon the signature of the payee only?

Answer: The draft must be taken to be in favour of the payees jointly, and consequently the survivor can obtain payment on supplying proper evidence of the death of the other payee without the concurrence of his legal personal representatives.

538 Is it the practice of bankers to cancel their own endorsements on bills presented by them and dishonoured?

Answer: Yes; the cancellation of his own endorsement does not prejudice a banker in proceeding, as holder in due course, against the acceptor, drawer, or prior endorsers.

539 A bill drawn payable to, or specially endorsed to, the **X** bank, London, and accepted by the drawee payable at Manchester, is sent by the **X** bank, without endorsement on behalf of its London office, to its Manchester branch for collection, and before presentation is endorsed on behalf of the **X** bank, Manchester. Is the bank at which the bill is domiciled justified in paying it without the endorsement of the London office?

Answer: The Manchester endorsement would usually be accepted, since both London and Manchester are offices of the same bank.

540 A bill on London, (*a*) drawn and endorsed abroad, or (*b*) drawn in the United Kingdom but endorsed abroad, is presented bearing an endorsement which, though valid, as regards requisites in form, in the country where it was made, is invalid here. Should the bill be paid without confirmation of the endorsement?

Answer: (*a*) Under sec. 72 (2) of the Bills of Exchange Act, the legal effect of the endorsement of a bill or cheque drawn *abroad* is determined by the law of the country where the endorsement is made.

Confirmation of the endorsement is therefore unnecessary.

(*b*) Under the proviso to sec. 72 (2), the endorsement in a foreign country of an *inland* bill is to be interpreted, as regards the payer, according to the law of the United Kingdom. In this case, therefore, the bill should not be paid unless the endorsement is confirmed.

541 What is the practice of bankers in this country with regard to the payment of bills and cheques bearing endorsements, whether in blank or special, in Oriental characters?

Answer: The practice is to require either a notarially certified translation of the endorsement, or a banker's confirmation.

542 What is the effect of the endorsement of a bill, cheque or note 'without recourse' (or *sans recours*)?

Answer: The effect, under sec. 16 (1) of the Bills of Exchange Act, is to render the endorser free from all liability as endorser of the bill, cheque or note, to any subsequent holder.

543 A, the holder of a bill, endorses it for value, 'without recourse,' to **B**. If the bill turns out to be a forgery, has **B** any remedy against **A**?

Answer: **A**, having endorsed without recourse, is not liable on his endorsement to **B**, but his liability is probably the same as though he had transferred the bill by delivery, without endorsing it. Under sec. 58 of the Bills of Exchange Act, a transferor by delivery warrants to his immediate transferee that the bill is what it purports to be. **A** is therefore probably liable to **B** for any damage that **B** may sustain through the bill turning out to be a forgery.

544 If the payee of a cheque specially endorses it 'without recourse,' is the drawee banker or the drawer adversely affected?

Answer: Neither the drawee banker nor his customer the drawer is affected by the endorsement without recourse. The only persons affected by the endorsement would be holders subsequent to the payee, if the cheque were dishonoured.

545 If Bank **X** endorses a bill, without recourse, to its agent, Bank **Y**, for collection, what is the nature of Bank **X**'s liability, if any, to Bank **Y** or to the true owner of the bill, if, after the bill has been paid, it is discovered that one of the prior endorsements is a forgery?

Answer: The effect of the endorsement without recourse is to negative the liability of Bank **X** as endorser, but to leave undiminished its liability, as principal, to indemnify its agent, Bank **Y**, if the latter is sued by the true owner for conversion of the bill. Bank **X**'s direct liability to the true owner for conversion is also unaffected by its endorsement without recourse. If it has to refund the amount to him, either directly or through Bank **Y**, it will have a remedy against its customer on whose behalf the bill was collected.

546 If **A**, the payee of a dividend warrant, when discharging it, writes over his signature 'pay to **B**,' should a signature purporting to be that of **B** be required?

Answer: Yes; this is a special endorsement under sec. 34 (2) of the Bills of Exchange Act, and should be completed by the signature of the special endorsee unless collected through a bank for **B**'s account.

547 Is a cheque issued by a trustee in bankruptcy, or by the liquidator of a company, in payment of a dividend on the claim of a creditor, considered to be a 'dividend warrant'?

Answer: No; such an instrument is a cheque, not a dividend warrant.

BONDS AND COUPONS

548 Is a bond, or a coupon, falling due on a non-business day payable on the following, or the preceding, day?

Answer: On the next succeeding business day.

549 Coupons are advertised as payable at a London bank. If the bonds are lost or stolen, can the owner of them restrain the London bank from paying the coupons if presented in the ordinary course of business?

Answer: The only person whose instructions the banker is bound to obey is his customer. In the absence of these, he must pay the coupons, on presentation and he incurs no liability in so doing, in spite of notice from persons other than his customers. After receipt of such notice, however, a banker would make inquiries before payment.

550 Bonds of a loan having a sinking fund operating by periodical drawings at par, are deposited for safe custody with a banker by his customer with instructions to cut off the coupons as they mature, and collect the proceeds to his credit.

Is it incumbent upon the banker, without further instructions, to examine the published lists of the numbers of the bonds drawn, and to inform his customer in the event of any of the bonds being drawn?

Answer: While there is no obligation on a bank's part to do so by virtue of the mere deposit, it usually performs this service for its customers.

ADVANCES AND SECURITIES
GENERAL

551 A bank agrees to lend to a customer on the understanding that the overdraft will not exceed £2,000 at any one time. When the indebtedness has reached say £1,000, would the bank be within its rights in refusing to pay further cheques? If it is necessary in such circumstances to give the customer notice of reduction of the limit before returning the cheques, what notice would be held to be sufficient?

Answer: Arrangements for overdraft accommodation to a customer should always be made subject to normal banking conditions, i.e. repayable upon demand unless otherwise stated at the outset, and the bank can then cancel, or reduce, the arrangement without notice where changed conditions demand such steps to protect the bank's position. In an emergency where the bank is satisfied beyond doubt that its position would be endangered by the payment of further cheques, demand for repayment of the overdraft can be made and cheques returned unpaid on the same day. Such peremptory action would rarely be taken in practice as a banker would endeavour to give reasonable notice before dishonouring cheques in such circumstances although under no legal obligation to do so. The length of such notice would depend entirely on the facts of the case.

552 An account is opened in the name of the **X** School, upon which cheques are drawn by three members of the committee, under a mandate given by the committee. If the account becomes overdrawn, are the members of the committee who have signed the cheques creating the overdraft personally liable to the bank for it?

Answer: Not unless they have expressly undertaken to be personally liable, or have represented themselves to have an authority which they did not in fact possess to create an overdraft on behalf of the School. There should however be no doubt on the latter point, because the mandate given by the committee ought to express that cheques signed as directed are to be paid whether the account is in credit or overdrawn, or may become overdrawn in consequence of such payment. Under a mandate in this form, if authorised by the constitution or regulations of the School, the property and funds of the School will be responsible for the overdraft, and the officials who sign the cheques will not be personally responsible.

553 A customer borrows £1,000 from his bankers on April 30; how many days' interest should he be charged with on the next balance-day, June 30?

Answer: Sixty-one days. In calculating the number of days, the day on which the money was borrowed is excluded, but the day on which the interest is payable is included. The interest is calculated on a day to day basis on the outstanding daily balance.

554 If a customer whose account is overdrawn cashes a cheque at a branch of the bank other than the branch at which his account is kept, can interest be charged on the amount of the cheque from the date of cashing, or only from the date of the receipt of the cheque at the drawee branch?

Answer: As cash has been delivered to the customer in exchange for the cheque, the bank can charge interest on the amount of it from the date of encashment.

555 The overdraft on the account of a customer who died last month is secured as follows:
  (1) Corporation stocks in name of deceased. No transfer lodged and no notice given to Registrars.
  (2) Quoted ordinary shares in name of deceased. Transfer completed in favour of bank's nominee company but not registered.
  (3) Foreign Government bearer bonds.
  (4) Canadian shares in marking name and endorsed.
The usual form of bank memorandum of deposit was signed by the customer when the advance was agreed in 1965, the documents of title having been held by the bank since 1957. The customer's brother-in-law now claims the securities and all interest, etc. received by the bank since the death of the customer, on the grounds that the customer's wife on her death in 1955 had left all her estate, which included these securities, to her brother (the claimant) subject to the life interest of her husband who was appointed sole executor and obtained probate. Has the bank any rights whatsoever to enable it to retain the securities?

Answer: The interest of the brother is an equitable one and can be overtaken by a prior equity or, of course, a legal title, provided in either case that the party claiming priority acted in good faith and gave value. The bank gave value and its good faith cannot be in doubt. But in cases (1) and (2) the bank has an equitable title which arose after that of the brother to whom the bank will have to release the securities. Even had notice been given to the company in (2) this would not improve the bank's position. The bearer bonds in (3) are a fully negotiable security and thus the bank has an unassailable title to them. The Canadian certificate in (4) lacks one of the essential features of a fully negotiable security in that the holder cannot sue in his own name. Although the market by custom treats such items as negotiable, the bank's claim to a legal title might be defeated. The usual form of memorandum of deposit includes in its charging clause all interest and dividends with the result that in (3), and subject to the validity of the claim in (4), they could be retained, but in the other cases, where the bank's equity can be defeated, they must be surrendered.

BEARER SECURITIES

556 A banker, after having advanced money to a customer against bearer bonds, receives notice that the bonds are the property of a third party. Can he nevertheless retain them as security for the advance made, and if necessary sell them?

Answer: Bearer bonds, if of a description recognised by mercantile custom in this country as being transferable by delivery, are negotiable instruments, and accordingly a valid title to them may be obtained by acquiring them in good faith and for value, even from a person who himself had no title to them. (*London Joint Stock Bank* v. *Simmons,* [1892] A.C. 201, Leading Cases, 4th Ed., p. 225.)

If these conditions were fulfilled in the case put, the banker as pledgee of the bonds can hold them as security for the advance already made, and can sell them after giving reasonable notice to the person entitled to them subject to the pledge. (*Deverges* v. *Sandeman,* [1902] 1 Ch. 579, in which one month's notice or even less, was considered to be sufficient.)

557 A stockbroker whom the bank believes to be entirely credit-worthy has a loan of £10,000 from a banker upon the security of bearer bonds. On settling day he hands to the banker his cheque for £10,000 and receives back the security, the balance on his current account being £8,000 short of the amount of the cheque. In the event of his not paying in to meet the cheque, has the banker lost all claim upon the securities, and could he only sue the stockbroker on the cheque? Would the banker retain his hold on the security (assuming his previous title to be unassailable) if instead of accepting his customer's cheque, he were to require his customer (*a*) to acknowledge that the security is only borrowed, and (*b*) to request that his account be debited by the banker if the security be not returned by the end of the day?

Answer: It is to be presumed that the stockbroker to the knowledge of the banker takes the bearer bonds with the object, not of retaining them in his own custody, but of handing them over to a third person. If this is so, the banker's security is for all practical purposes gone when he parts with the bonds.

STOCKS AND SHARES

558   A bank holds as security for an overdraft shares transferred into the names of its nominees, but without a memorandum of deposit. If the bank wishes to realise its security, is an express authority from the customer necessary?

Answer: No. A mortgagee of shares has an implied power to sell the shares on default by the mortgagor in payment of the amount due at the time appointed for payment, or, if no time be fixed, then on the expiration of a reasonable notice by the mortgagee requiring payment on a day certain. A month's notice, or even less, would be a reasonable notice. (*Deverges* v. *Sandeman,* [1902] 1 Ch. 579.)

A memorandum of deposit, conferring an express power of sale, should, however, always be taken when accepting such security.

559   When certificates of stocks or shares are deposited with a banker as security, with or without a memorandum of deposit, and with or without transfers, is the banker able to give notice of his charge to the companies whose stocks or shares are affected, in order to protect his equitable charge against other possible equities?

Answer: A company incorporated in England under the Companies Acts is prohibited by sec. 117 of the Act of 1948 from accepting notice of any trust, expressed, implied or constructive, affecting its stocks or shares, and the constitutions of chartered, statutory and other companies usually contain a similar prohibition. Companies therefore usually reject (or ignore) notices of charge regarding them as analogous to notices of trust. Such a notice will, however, have the effect, where the company has a lien by virtue of its articles, of preventing the company, after receipt of notice, from itself acquiring a paramount or overriding lien on the shares by making advances to the shareholder. (*Bradford Banking Co.* v.

Briggs (1886), 12 A.C. 29; Leading Cases, 4th Ed., p. 284.) The rules of the London Stock Exchange require a company's articles to contain a provision that its fully-paid shares shall be free from all lien before it is granted a quotation; there is therefore no need to serve a notice of charge upon a quoted company.

560 Does a bank incur any liability to a company when holding a certificate for partly paid shares in that company, with a transfer to the bank or its nominees completed but not registered?

Answer: Not unless and until the transfer is registered, and the shares actually stand in its name or in the names of its nominees.

561 A bank holds some shares in the form of an unrenounced receipted allotment letter in the name of the customer, as the security for an advance. It sends the allotment letter to the secretary of the company, for the purpose of exchanging it for a definitive certificate, at the same time requesting that it may be returned to the bank. Not receiving the certificate back in due course, the bank applies to the secretary, and is informed that the certificate has been sent to the registered holder, who has in the meantime sold the shares. What remedy has the bank against the company?

Answer: Probably none. Where a bank is relying on an allotment letter as security, it is always prudent to have it renounced by the customer and to have registration made in the name of the bank's nominees.

562 What is the usual custom of bankers when a loan is granted, 'with a margin of (say) 20 per cent.'? Should such margin be upon the amount of the loan, or upon the value of the security? In the former case £5,000 would be advanced against securities valued at £6,000, and in the latter case £4,800 only would be advanced against the same securities.

Answer: Whilst it has been customary to calculate the margin on the value of the securities, it is advisable to have the exact intention clearly stated when the loan is arranged so that there can be no room for doubt.

563 Mr. A. obtained the agreement of his bank to provide overdraft facilities to be secured by Stock Exchange securities charged by his wife. Mr. A. subsequently produced the share certificates to the bank and introduced the lady who accompanied him as his wife.

This lady signed transfers and forms of charge which were witnessed by the bank's solicitor at the manager's request. The solicitor added to the forms of charge a statement that the signatory understood the nature and purport of the transaction. One transfer was completed, forwarded to the company and the shares registered in the name of the bank's nominee company. Other share certificates were deposited with the bank, accompanied by a signed but uncompleted transfer. The advance reached the agreed limit, where it became static, and Mr. A. could not be traced. It now transpires that the lady was not A's wife and the signatures on the forms held by the bank are, of course, not those of the real Mrs. A.

What is the position of the real Mrs. A, the solicitor, the company accepting and registering the transfer and the bank?

Answer: The facts here are not dissimilar to those in the case of the *Lord Mayor of Sheffield, etc.* v. *Barclays and Others* ([1905] A.C. 392; Leading Cases, 4th Ed., p. 285). The bank is relying upon a form of charge, the signature upon which has been forged as also has that on the transfers. The company which registered the transfer of its shares has acted upon a signature that was not genuine.

To take the parties concerned in order:

Mrs. A. is the true owner of the shares and must be re-registered as proprietor of those which were transferred to the bank's nominee company. All the share certificates held by the bank must be returned to the true owner. Mrs. A's position is not prejudiced by the fact that some carelessness enabled Mr. A. to obtain the certificates.

No liability can attach to the solicitor; he is entitled to rely upon the genuineness of the introductions, having acted in good faith.

The registering company, having acted upon forged instructions, must restore the true owner's name to the register; it may, however, recover from the bank. The bank's implied warranty of genuineness of the transfer when it was forwarded makes it liable to indemnify the company.

The bank cannot escape liability by arguing that the company could have checked the signature of Mrs. A. from the form which originally transferred the shares into her name.

Unhappily, the bank has no case and must surrender to the true owner all the certificates which it holds.

Had the bank sold the shares registered in its nominee company's name before learning of the position it would still have been liable to make good the loss. The bank purported to act for the true owner, but, as it had no authority from the true owner, it is liable to all who suffered loss as a result. Mrs. A., the true owner, may claim against the company to be reinstated on the register of members. Alternatively she may claim against the bank in conversion for the value of the shares. Whilst in practice she might follow the first course, the company need suffer no loss, as it may claim against the party who submitted the transfer for registration. He in turn could pass the claim back until it eventually reached the bank.

TITLE DEEDS

564 If a banker who has made an advance on current account to a customer on the security of a legal mortgage or a memorandum of deposit of deeds of property receives notice that the customer has created a second charge on the property, what procedure should he adopt?

Answer: He should stop all entries on the overdrawn account, and should open a new account, to which all credits received from the customer (unless expressly allocated by him to the old account) should be placed, and all cheques paid should be debited. The new account should be kept in credit unless separate arrangements are made for fresh borrowing. If, on the other hand, the old account is continued without a break, the effect, under the rule in *Clayton's case*, will be that credits will go in reduction of the debt, and that debits created by cheques paid will rank after the rights of the second mortgagee.

If the customer has several accounts, some overdrawn and others in credit, and the mortgage or memorandum secures, as bank mortgages usually do, the ultimate balance due on all accounts, the accounts should be amalgamated on receiving notice of the second mortgage.

If, however, the mortgage or memorandum imposes an obligation on the banker to make further advances, such advances may safely be made notwithstanding the notice of the second mortgage, and will have priority to that mortgage. (Law of Property Act, 1925, sec. 94 (1) (*c*); extended to registered land by the Law of Property (Amendment) Act, 1926, sec. 5, provided that the obligation to make further advances is noted on the register.)

565 Should a banker stop entries on a customer's account secured by a legal or equitable mortgage on receiving notice that the customer has conveyed the land, subject to the mortgage, to a purchaser?

Answer: Yes, otherwise credits placed to the account after notice will go in reduction of the debt, and debits will be unsecured, as when notice of a second charge is received.

566 A customer to whom his banker has made advances on the security of a mortgage of property to secure the balance of his account from time to time executes a second mortgage of the property in favour of another person, who registers his mortgage as a 'puisne mortgage' at the Land Charges Registry, but omits to give notice of it to the banker.

Does such registration of the second mortgage, without actual notice of it to the first mortgagee, affect him in any way?

Answer: No; sec. 94 (2) of the Law of Property Act, 1925, provides that a prior mortgagee whose mortgage was expressly made for securing a current account or other further advances is not to be deemed to have notice of another mortgage merely by reason that it was registered as a Land Charge, if it was not so registered at the time when the original mortgage was created, or when the last search (if any) was made by the mortgagee, whichever last happened.

If therefore the banker searched immediately following the taking of his mortgage without finding any entry in respect of the second mortgage, the subsequent registration of that mortgage does not affect him unless he makes a search or learns of it in some other way.

567 When a banker who has received notice of a second charge on property mortgaged to him by a customer sells the property under his power of sale, or joins with the customer in selling it, what is his duty with regard to the surplus proceeds (if any) over and above the debt owing to him by the customer?

Answer: The surplus must be paid to the second mortgagee to the extent of the latter's charge. Any balance may be paid to the customer, if a further search of the register discloses no other charges. (*West London Commercial Bank* v. *Reliance Building Society* (1884), 29 Ch.D. 954, in which the Building Society mislaid the notice of second mortgage which they had received, and, having paid the whole surplus proceeds to the mortgagor, were held liable to refund them to the second mortgagee.)

If the banker's mortgage contains a limit on the amount recoverable under it, and the limit is less than the amount of the debt owing to him, he will usually be entitled to retain out of the proceeds only the amount of the limit (plus interest and costs), and must account to the second mortgagee for the surplus over that amount; but if he holds more than one mortgage or other security for his debt, he may be entitled to consolidate them, and the proceeds of their realisation, against the second mortgagee of the one property. On this point legal advice may be necessary. If the right of consolidation exists, and is exercised, the second mortgagee will have a right of reimbursement out of the surplus proceeds of the banker's other securities held for the same debt, but not subject to any second charge; as he will also if the proceeds of the property realised are insufficient to pay off both the banker's debt and his own.

568 Deeds of property are charged to a bank by its usual form of charge to secure an advance of £1,000, the memorandum of charge being worded so as to secure the ultimate balance owing on all accounts. The full amount of the advance is debited to a loan account and credited to the customer's current account. Notice of a second charge is received by the bank when there is a credit balance of £200 on the current account.

(1) On receipt of the notice should the bank at once combine the two accounts?

(2) Is the bank justified in dishonouring cheques drawn by the customer which may be presented after receipt of the notice?

(3) For what amount can the bank rely upon its security after receipt of the notice?

Answer: After notice the second charge only takes precedence with regard to fresh advances and the bank's priority under its first mortgage is restricted to existing advances only. It is therefore necessary to ensure that the existing loan account remains segregated and to charge interest to the current account. The bank has no right to refuse to honour cheques drawn on the £200 standing to the credit of the current account. The first charge will then hold good for £1,000. If or when the loan is called in, or the security realised, the ultimate balance will be the £1,000 less any credit on the current account. Should the current account be allowed to become overdrawn, such overdraft would be a fresh advance and thus postponed to the second charge. The answers to the questions are therefore as follows:

(1) & (2)—No

(3)   —£1,000 if the loan account is properly segregated.

(See also Question 569 following).

569 Arising out of question No. 568 in which it is stated that the deeds of property are charged on the usual bank form for securing the ultimate balance on all accounts—would the charge in the circumstances obtaining provide security for interest due on the loan account?

Answer: The charge, being in standard form, would normally be expressed to cover interest charges. Accordingly interest due, and accruing due, on the loan account will be secured in priority to the second charge. In the example given in the question the current account is in credit, hence the suggestion to apply the interest to that account. The bank's security for any subsequent advances on this current account, apart from any debits which are in respect of interest on the loan account and which are not discharged by the operation of the rule in *Clayton's* case, will be postponed to the second charge.

570 If a lessee fails to perform his covenants, can the lessor sue (*a*) a legal mortgagee of the lease; (*b*) an equitable mortgagee of the lease by deposit?

Answer: Although the assignee of the whole term of a lease becomes the lessor's tenant, or in other words there is 'privity of estate' between them, and consequently either can sue the other on their respective covenants, there is no such privity between the lessor and a legal mortgagee of the lease, whose mortgage must be made either by sub-demise for a term less by one day at least than the term vested in the mortgagor (sec. 86 of the Law of Property Act, 1925), or alternatively by 'charge by way of legal mortgage,' which creates no actual sub-term (sec. 87); nor is there any privity under a merely equitable mortgage. The lessor therefore cannot sue the legal or equitable mortgagee on the covenants in the lease, but if these are left unperformed the lessor may be in a position to enforce a forfeiture of the lease. In that event the mortgagee would be entitled to apply to the Court for relief under sec. 146 (4) of the Act; but relief would probably be granted only on condition of his taking over the lease, including the burden of the lessee's covenants.

POLICIES OF LIFE ASSURANCE

571 A customer left a life policy with his bankers as security for a temporary overdraft, and shortly afterwards was adjudicated bankrupt. The trustee in his bankruptcy claimed the policy, because, he said, the bankers, having no written document concerning it from the debtor, had no right to it. Was the trustee's claim valid?

Answer: No; even though no notice of their charge had been given by the bankers to the insurance company, and though the trustee in bankruptcy gave notice of his interest. (*Re Wallis, ex parte Jenks,* [1902] 1 K.B. 719, Leading Cases, 4th Ed., p. 287 in which it was held that in such circumstances the trustee took subject to the equitable charge affecting the policy.) (See also Question 576.)

572 A customer mortgages a policy of assurance upon his life to a bank as security for advances. The mortgage contains a covenant for payment of future premiums by the assured. The customer becomes bankrupt. Can the bank, after deducting the surrender value, prove against his estate for the value of the covenant to pay future premiums?

Answer: No. (*Deering v. Bank of Ireland* (1886), 12 A.C. 20.)

573 If an insurance company, at the request of the assured, who is unable to continue payment of the premiums, arranges to deduct them from bonuses that have accrued, or may accrue, on the policy, can the company lawfully continue to do so after receiving notice that the policy has been assigned?

Answer: Not without the consent of the assignee, whether the assignment is absolute or by way of mortgage, unless an express power is given to the company by the terms of the policy.

574 Can a policy effected by a husband on his own life for the benefit of his wife and/or children (or by a wife, on her own life, for the benefit of her husband and/or children) be effectively mortgaged?

Answer: If the beneficiaries are not personally named in the policy, but are designated merely as 'wife' ('husband') or 'children,' a subsequent wife (husband) and after-born children will be entitled to benefit under it, and consequently the policy cannot be effectively mortgaged.

If however the beneficiaries are personally named, *and are all of full age,* they can join with the life assured in mortgaging the policy; but if the mortgage is to secure the account of the husband, the wife should have independent legal advice.

Such a policy takes effect under sec. 11 of the Married Women's

Property Act, 1882, and creates a trust in favour of the beneficiaries mentioned in it. Moneys payable do not, so long as any object of the trust remains unperformed, form part of the estate of the assured, and are not subject to his or her debts. Trustees may be appointed by the policy, or by the assured, but if none is appointed the legal title to the policy vests in the assured or his or her executors or administrators, in trust for the beneficiaries. If there are trustees, they should join with the assured and the beneficiaries in mortgaging the policy.

575 After a policy has been mortgaged by a customer to his bank, the bank receives notice of a second mortgage of the policy. The customer's account is accordingly broken, and later the overdraft is repaid by him. Is the bank then at liberty to redeliver the policy to the customer without the consent of the second mortgagee?

Answer: No; sec. 96 (2) of the Law of Property Act, 1925, provides that a mortgagee whose mortgage is extinguished is not to be liable on account of delivering documents of title in his possession to a person not having the best right thereto, unless he has notice of the right or claim of a person having a better right. The bank, as mortgagee in the case put, will have no statutory or other defence if it delivers the policy to anyone except the second mortgagee, of whose charge the bank has received notice.

576 At the maturity of a policy which has been mortgaged by assignment to a bank, can the bank give a good discharge to the insurance company for the whole of the policy money or only for an amount sufficient to pay off the overdraft on the account for which the policy was mortgaged?

Answer: Under sec. 107 of the Law of Property Act, 1925, the receipt in writing of a mortgagee is a sufficient discharge for any money comprised in his mortgage, and a person paying such money to the mortgagee is not concerned to inquire whether any money remains due under the mortgage. In *Hockey* v. *Western*, ([1898] 1 Ch. 350) it was held, under an earlier Act of similar effect, that trustees of a mortgaged fund might, if they chose, pay the fund to the mortgagee without inquiring how much, if anything, was due under the mortgage, but that they were not obliged to pay more than was in fact due.

Most insurance companies, if they have not received notice of any other assignment or charge, will usually pay the whole of the policy money to the bank, without reference to the amount recoverable under the bank's mortgage, or to the amount of the debt owing to the bank. This is generally provided for in the assignment.

If the whole of the policy money is received by the bank, it must, under sec. 107 of the Act, be applied as if it were the proceeds of the exercise of the bank's power of sale, that is, (under sec. 105) (a) in payment of costs incurred in obtaining the money, (b) in discharge of the debt secured and interest, and (c) in payment of the balance remaining to the mortgagor or other person entitled.

MISCELLANEOUS

577 A banker to whom documents of title to goods have been pledged as security for an advance wishes to release the documents to the customer, in order that the latter may sell the goods, and may pay the proceeds to the banker in repayment or reduction of the advance.

(a) How may the banker do this without giving up his rights under the pledge?

(b) What risks does he thereby incur?

Answer: (a) The customer should be required to sign a 'trust letter' or 'trust receipt,' acknowledging the receipt of the documents, and undertaking

(i) to hold them, the goods which they represent, and the proceeds of the goods when sold, in trust for the banker;

(ii) to keep the transaction separate from any other, and to pay the proceeds of sale to the banker immediately on receipt;

(iii) to insure the goods until sold, and to apply the insurance money as proceeds of sale;

(iv) to return on demand the documents or the goods, or such portions as shall remain unsold.

(b) The special risks incident to a transaction of this description are

(i) that the customer may pledge the documents elsewhere (see *Lloyds Bank* v. *Bank of America National Trust,* quoted below);

(ii) that he may fail to pay in the proceeds of sale; although the trust letter amounts to an equitable assignment of such proceeds to the banker, they may perhaps not be traceable in the event of the customer's bankruptcy or (if a company) liquidation;

   (iii) that buyers without notice of the bank's rights may claim
          a right to set off the amount owing by them for the goods
          against money owing to them by the customer;
   (iv)   that if the goods are warehoused in the customer's name
          they may become intermingled with other goods in his
          name in the warehouse.
On the subject of trust letters reference should be made to:
   North Western Bank v. *Poynter,* [1895] A.C. 56, in which it was
held that in giving up possession of goods against a trust letter the
bank had not given up its rights as pledgee.
   Re David Allester Limited, [1922] 2 Ch. 211, (Leading Cases,
4th Ed., p. 230), in which a trust letter was held not to require
registration as a bill of sale, or, if given by a company, as a charge on
a book debt under the Companies Act.
   Lloyds Bank v. *Bank of America National Trust,* [1938] 2 K.B.
147, (Leading Cases, 4th Ed., p. 234), in which documents of title to
goods which had been pledged to the plaintiff bank by a customer
and released to him against a trust letter, were thereupon
fraudulently pledged by him to the defendant bank. It was held that
in dealing with the goods under the trust letter the customer was
acting in the position of a 'mercantile agent' for the plaintiff bank
(or for that bank and himself, according to their respective interests
in the goods); and that consequently his pledge to the defendant
bank was valid under sec. 2 of the Factors Act, 1889.

578 Is a banker liable for
     (1) freight, demurrage and other charges upon imported goods of
          which the bills of lading have been deposited with him as
          security;
     (2) warehouse rent on goods warehoused in (*a*) the customer's
          name, the relative warrants or receipts being deposited with
          the banker, or (*b*) in the banker's name?

Answer: (1) Under sec. 1 of the Bills of Lading Act, 1855, the
endorsee of a bill of lading *to whom the property in the goods passes*
is subject to the same liabilities in respect of the goods as if the
contract contained in the bill of lading had been made with him; but
in *Sewell* v. *Burdick* (1884), 10 A.C. 74, (Leading Cases, 4th Ed.,
p. 227), it was held that as only a special property, not the absolute
property in the goods, passes to a pledgee of the bill of lading, such a
pledgee does not become subject to the obligations of the contract of
affreightment. If, however, the pledgee takes delivery of the goods

under the bill of lading, he thereby acquires both the rights and the obligations affecting them. (*Brandt* v. *Liverpool, Brazil, etc., Steam Navigation Company,* [1924] 1 K.B. 575, Leading Cases, 4th Ed., p. 228.)

(2) (*a*) A pledge of a warehouse warrant, even if purporting to be transferable, or of a warehouse receipt, relating to goods warehoused in a customer's name, would not render the banker liable for the rent payable in respect of them; but if he dealt with them in any way he could do so only subject to payment of rent accrued due. It is, therefore, important to note whether the warehouseman, in his warrant or receipt, claims a lien on the goods not only for the rent on those goods, but for rent on any other goods warehoused in the same name.

(*b*) By having goods warehoused in his own name, the banker would clearly become liable for future rent in respect of them.

579 A loan is made by a banker to a customer against a warehouse warrant for goods warehoused in the name of the customer, the warrant being endorsed by him and accompanied by a letter of hypothecation in favour of the banker. What would form the essential points of a fire insurance policy adequate to cover the banker against loss by fire (1) if the policy is issued in the name of the banker; (2) if it is issued in the name of the customer?

Answer: (1) The banker can take out a policy in his own name, and can then recover, in case of loss by fire, any insurable interest he may have to the full value of the policy.

(2) If the banker is tendered a policy made out in favour of his customer, the banker should obtain the endorsement of the insurance office transferring the interest in the policy to himself. In a policy in favour of the customer *only*, there is no privity between the banker and the insurance office, and the banker's rights would be subject to any defence the insurance company might set up against the customer.

In either case it is essential that the goods should be insured to their full market value, such policies being subject to the 'average clause.'

580 If a customer deposits a fire policy on his stock, and afterwards the stock is destroyed by fire, has the bank a lien on the money payable by the insurance company?

Answer: The bank can have no lien upon, or right to receive, the insurance money, unless it has an insurable interest in the insured goods; and it cannot have such an interest unless the goods have been pledged with the bank, or charged in its favour by a bill of sale, or, if the customer is a company, by a floating charge.

See *Macaura* v. *Northern Assurance Co.*, [1925] A.C. 619, in which it was held that a shareholder in a company, even if the holder of all the shares but one, has not, nor has a creditor of the company, an insurable interest in a particular asset which the company holds.

581   What formalities must be observed in taking an assignment of book debts as security for an advance?

Answer: (1) Unless the book debts are those due at the date of the assignment from specified debtors, or growing due under specified contracts, the assignment, if made by an individual or a firm engaged in any trade or business, must be registered as a Bill of Sale, or it will be void under sec. 43 (1) of the Bankruptcy Act, 1914, in the event of the assignor's bankruptcy before the debts are paid. A bill of sale is not normally acceptable as banking security.

(2)   Notice of the assignment must be given to the debtors in order (*a*) to complete the assignment under sec. 136 of the Law of Property Act, 1925, and to fix its priority, and (*b*) to take the debts out of the 'possession order or disposition' of the assignor under sec. 38 (*c*) of the Bankruptcy Act, in the event of his bankruptcy.

(3)   If the assignor is a company, the assignment will be void against the liquidator and creditors of the company, unless registered with the Registrar of Companies under sec. 95 of the Companies Act, 1948. (See *re Kent and Sussex Sawmills Ltd.* [1947] Ch. 177, Leading Cases, 4th Ed., p. 276.) Such registration is independent of registration as a bill of sale.

582   What is the effect of a mortgage of a ship, or of a share in a ship, made in one of the forms quoted in Schedule (1) of the Merchant Shipping Act, 1894, but not registered under that Act?

Answer: Such a mortgage, although not registered under the Act, is valid between the parties (sec. 33), but, as between one mortgagee and another, registration confers priority, even on a mortgagee registering his mortgage with notice of an unregistered mortgage of earlier date.

Under sec. 95 of the Companies Act, 1948, a charge by a company on a ship, or on any share in a ship, unless registered with the Registrar of Companies, is void against the liquidator and any creditor of the company. Such registration is independent of registration under the Merchant Shipping Act, referred to above.

583 Is there any way of obtaining an effective charge on National Savings Certificates?

Answer: A watertight charge cannot be obtained. National Savings Certificates are not transferable and thus a legal charge cannot be obtained. Moreover, their terms of issue expressly provide that no claim by a person holding a certificate in respect of a loan will be recognised.

However, when dealing with a reliable customer there is little practical risk in relying upon National Savings Certificates as security. Provided the procedure set out below is followed they can easily be realised when required and a valid equitable title is obtained against a trustee in bankruptcy.

The method is to obtain the deposit of the certificates with the standard form of memorandum evidencing the intention of the depositor, together with an official form of request for repayment in favour of the bank signed, but undated, by the depositor. The security can then be realised when required and the proceeds will, of course, be paid direct to the bank. The danger is that, whilst the bank is holding the certificates, the depositor may obtain duplicates or repayment by representing that the original certificates have been lost.

584 Can a bank obtain an effective charge on British Savings Bonds (and former National Development and Defence Bonds) by way of security?

Answer: For reasons similar to those given in the answer to the previous question, a watertight charge cannot be obtained, although a similar procedure may be adopted in dealing with reliable customers.

585 Can Premium Savings Bonds be regarded as acceptable banking security?

Answer: Premium Savings Bonds do not afford complete security because the conditions of issue expressly state that the Bonds are not transferable and the Director of National Savings will not recognise any charge or lien on the bonds. They might be held by a bank as evidence of means but, where appropriate, the depositor could be asked to sign the bank's memorandum of deposit as evidence of intention, together with a signed, undated repayment form.

The Director of National Savings will, on request, confirm the validity of a holding and, in the event of the death of the holder, his personal representatives can claim repayment of the bonds on Form S.B. 4, which can be obtained at any Savings Bank or Post Office. This procedure would have similar weaknesses to those discussed in the previous two questions.

GUARANTEES

586   If a banker omits to give to an intending guarantor information as to the customer's financial position, which, if the guarantor had received it, would probably have induced him not to give the guarantee, does the non-disclosure invalidate the guarantee when given?

Answer: No; see *National Provincial Bank* v. *Glanusk*, [1913] 3 K.B. 335, (Leading Cases, 4th Ed., p. 236); *Royal Bank of Scotland* v. *Greenshields* (1914) S.C., (Leading Cases, 4th Ed., p. 237); but if the banker voluntarily, or in answer to a question, makes an untrue or erroneous representation, and the guarantor relies upon it, the guarantee will be invalidated (*Royal Bank of Scotland* v. *Greenshields*).

In *Westminster Bank* v. *Cond* (1940), 46 Com. Cas. 60; (Leading Cases, 4th Ed., p. 237), the bank was held to be under no duty to disclose to an intending guarantor the fact of an existing overdraft on the customer's account, as no question was asked. In *Cooper* v. *National Provincial Bank,* [1946] K.B. 1, (Leading Cases, 4th Ed., p. 237), a guarantor under two guarantees given by him for the account of a married woman claimed to have them set aside on the ground that the bank had failed to disclose to him that the woman's husband, who was an undischarged bankrupt, had authority to draw on the account, and that the account itself had been improperly and irregularly operated, in that a number of cheques which had been drawn had not been paid because of subsequent orders to stop them. It was held by the Court that the bank was under no duty to disclose the matters complained of, since their contract with the customer did not contain stipulations which were unusual, or which might not reasonably have been anticipated by the surety.

But none of these cases excuse actual misrepresentation. In

McKenzie v. *Royal Bank of Canada,* [1934] A.C. 468, (Leading Cases, 4th Ed., p. 239), Lord Atkin said 'A contract of guarantee, like any other contract, is liable to be avoided if induced by material misrepresentation of an existing fact, even if made innocently.'

587 What is meant by a 'continuing' guarantee?

Answer: A guarantee which is expressed to secure, not a single advance, made once for all, or a series of advances so made, up to a stated limit, but to secure the fluctuating balance from time to time of a current account or accounts, or of the customer's present and future liabilities to the bank, however incurred.

588 Which is the more beneficial form of guarantee to a bank, a guarantee for a customer's liabilities, present and future, (*a*) to the extent of £*x*, or (*b*) with a proviso that not more than £*x* shall be recoverable from the guarantor?

Answer: The latter. A guarantor for part of a debt is entitled, on payment of that part, to prove, in the event of the principal debtor's bankruptcy, for the sum paid, and to receive dividends thereon. On the other hand, when the whole debt is guaranteed, but with a limitation on the amount recoverable from the guarantor, the bank may prove for, and receive dividends on, the whole debt, to the exclusion of the guarantor, and may hold the guarantee against the debt remaining after the dividends have been deducted. (*Re Sass,* [1896] 2 Q.B. 12.) It is however usual to reserve this right of proof for the whole debt expressly in the guarantee, and to provide that sums paid by the guarantor to the bank under the guarantee may be held in suspense, and not be credited to the account guaranteed unless such credit would extinguish the debt altogether.

589 A customer who has an overdraft limit of £1,000 on his current account against securities charged by him asks to have the limit extended to £1,500 against a guarantee by a person who does not wish to be responsible as guarantor for the first £1,000 of the overdraft, but only for the excess from time to time over that figure, with a limitation of his liability to £500. How should such a guarantee be worded?

Answer: If the bank is prepared to accept the condition which the guarantor seeks to introduce, the simplest solution would be to advance the additional £500 on a separate loan account, secured only by the guarantee limited suitably to accommodation taken on such separate loan account.

Where the bank does agree to allow the customer to take all the borrowing on his current account, the guarantee would have to be expressed to cover only the excess of the customer's liabilities to the bank over £1,000 at the time when demand for repayment is made by the bank upon the guarantor, or when the guarantee is determined as to future advances by notice, or otherwise.

If a guarantee is taken in this form, none of the securities for the first £1,000 of the overdraft must be realised unless at the time of realisation demand for payment has already been made on the guarantor, or the guarantee has already been determined, as to future advances, by some means; otherwise the proceeds of realisation will go in reduction of the amount of the principal debt to the possible prejudice of the bank's claim against the guarantor. After demand or determination that amount is fixed by the terms of the guarantee, and will not be reduced by the proceeds of the securities; but, until the guarantor has actually paid the amount due from him, such proceeds should be held in a suspense account.

590 Can a trading company guarantee the banking account of one of its customers, if the memorandum of association does not specially grant this power? It is admitted that by thus assisting its customer the business of the company may be indirectly promoted.

Answer: Power to give a guarantee must be expressly provided in the memorandum of association. Although a trading company has implied power to borrow, it has no implied power to give a guarantee. However, if the objects clause of the memorandum of association does not contain express power, it may be altered by special resolution under sec. 5 of the Companies Act, 1948. Banks often provide a company with a draft resolution to cover all necessary points and should require a certified copy of the resolution, once passed, to be annexed to, or endorsed on, the guarantee when returned after completion.

591 Is it essential that the guarantor's signature of a guarantee should be attested by a witness?

Answer: No, but attestation is useful in case the guarantor should dispute his signature, and it should never be omitted in practice.

592 When signing a guarantee dated July 1, the guarantor amends the document in one or other of the following forms:

(a) 'To remain in force for three months.'

(b) 'My liability hereunder to continue until December 31.'

On what day in each case will the guarantee cease to cover further advances made by the bank to the customer?

Answer: In practice banks do not generally accept amendments to their standard forms, and such amendments should certainly not be accepted at branch level without the guidance of the appropriate controlling department. As to the question, in the unusual event of such alterations being accepted: (a) Since under sec. 61 of the Law of Property Act, 1925, the word 'month' in any contract or instrument means 'calendar month,' the guarantee will cease to cover further advances on October 1, i.e., after the close of business on September 30. (b) At the close of business on December 31.

593 A guarantor, when signing a printed form of continuing guarantee, accompanies it by a letter to the bank stating that his liability is to be restricted to sums which he will from time to time authorise the bank to advance to the customer. Can the bank, in reliance on the printed form, hold the guarantor responsible for advances made without his authority?

Answer: The guarantee and letter must be read together as one document, and consequently the guarantor will be responsible only for advances made with his authority. It would be most unwise to accept such an onerous arrangement.

594 Your customer, Arthur Smith, asks you for an overdraft facility for £400. Two years ago you accommodated him by means of a loan of £500 to assist him with the purchase of a motor car. At that time you took as security a guarantee from his aunt, Mrs. Brown. The guarantee was in the standard bank 'all moneys' form, with a limitation of £500 inserted. The loan of £500 was repaid some time ago. Can you rely on Mrs. Brown's guarantee as security for the proposed overdraft facility? Mrs. Brown is also one of your customers.

Answer: Technically, the existing guarantee will extend to secure the new facility. Nevertheless, you would be very unwise to seek to rely upon it without the written confirmation of Mrs. Brown, even though no doubt you explained to her the 'all-embracing' nature of the guarantee when she signed it. Despite your warning it was probably not within her contemplation that the bank could or would seek to rely upon it at a later date in respect of a completely new and unrelated facility of which she had not been made aware. It smacks of 'sharp practice', to say the least, if you seek to rely on the guarantee without reminding Mrs. Brown of its existence and asking her to confirm that you may continue to rely upon it for the proposed facility.

In any event, the case of *Lloyds Bank Ltd.* v. *Bundy* [1975] Q.B. 326, 4th Ed., (Leading Cases, 4th Ed., p. 14) has emphasised the need for bankers to take special care when taking a guarantee from a customer. It has imposed upon the banker, in certain circumstances, the duty of ensuring that its customer is fully aware of the nature and possible effects of the security document which he or she is asked to sign. In the particular circumstances of this case, even if Mrs. Brown was not your customer, you should obtain her written confirmation that she is aware of the new facility.

595   Brown gives a bank a guarantee for Smith's account for £1,000 which runs: 'That it shall be a continuing guarantee for the benefit of the said bank, however for the time being constituted, until the expiration of three months after notice in writing shall have been given by me, my executors, administrators, or assigns to determine the same.' Brown gives notice of withdrawal of his guarantee when Smith owes £500. Is it safe to continue transactions on the account after notice; may the debit balance be increased; and also will Brown be liable for the whole if it goes up to £1,000?

Answer: In the given circumstances the bank can, if it so wishes, continue the account of Smith until the expiration of the required three months' notice in writing from the guarantor, Brown. The legal effect of the clause requiring three months' notice of determination of the guarantee is beyond question; the account of the customer can be continued for the period of notice and the guarantor will be liable for the balance outstanding at the end of the period.

Whether a bank in practice always relies on this strict interpretation of the clause depends usually upon the facts of the case, but normally it will give some thought to the equitable rights of the guarantor. The right of the guarantor to determine his liability is clearly limited by the stipulation for three months' notice and, where it is laid down as here that on the death of the guarantor three months' notice is necessary from his personal representatives, such provision is binding upon his estate. (*Coulthart* v. *Clementson* (1879) 5 Q.B.D. 42).

It should, of course, be remembered that the bank is entitled to make demand on the borrower at any time and thereafter to refuse further advances, and in exceptional cases this might be the appropriate course of action. However, to stop Smith's account without very good reason when it is overdrawn only £500 may completely upset outstanding business commitments which Smith has entered into, safe in the knowledge that his overdraft limit is £1,000. The bank can hardly, in the circumstances, dishonour cheques issued, or about to be drawn, in respect of such bona fide commitments even if entitled to do so.

In practice, it is usually possible to come to an equitable arrangement between the debtor and guarantor by asking them to call at the bank to discuss the position.

596 What is the effect of the death of a sole guarantor,
    (*a*) if the guarantee makes no provision for that event,
    (*b*) if the guarantee provides that it is to be binding on the guarantor until the expiration of a given period of notice of determination, and, in the event of his death, is to continue to bind his estate until the expiration of such notice given by his executors or administrators?

Answer: (*a*) In the absence of express provision to the contrary in the guarantee itself, the guarantee will be determined as soon as notice of the death of the guarantor reaches the bank.

(*b*) Where the guarantee binds the personal representatives of the deceased guarantor by a clause calling for notice of determination the account of the borrower can be continued unbroken until the expiration of such notice. The validity of this provision was upheld in *Coulthart* v. *Clementson* (1879) 5 Q.B.D. 42, and the liability of the deceased's estate for further advances pending notice from the executors appears to be supported by *Egbert* v. *National Crown Bank* [1918] A.C. 903, (Leading Cases, 4th Ed., p. 247).

597 If a customer whose account is guaranteed takes another person into partnership with him, will the guarantee extend to cover advances made to the partners on an account in their joint names?

Answer: Not unless the guarantee is expressed to secure the account of the customer 'whether alone or jointly with any other person.' It would, however, avoid any misunderstanding if a new guarantee were taken.

598 What is the effect, on a guarantee for the liabilities of a firm, of a change in the constitution of the firm, by (a) the death or retirement of a partner, or (b) the addition of a new partner?

Answer: Under sec. 18 of the Partnership Act, 1890, a continuing guarantee given in respect of the transactions of a firm is, in the absence of agreement to the contrary, revoked as to future transactions by any change in the constitution of the firm.

  Bankers' forms of guarantee usually provide that the guarantee, if given for the account of a firm, shall continue notwithstanding changes in the firm's constitution.

599 When a banker demands payment from a guarantor of the balance of the account guaranteed, should the account be broken to prevent subsequent transactions in it from falling under the rule in *Clayton's case*?

Answer: Unless otherwise provided in the guarantee, the amount of the guarantor's liability is fixed by the demand, and no further advances would be secured. The account should therefore be broken to avoid the operation of the rule in *Clayton's case*.

600 In the case of a joint and several guarantee, does any event that, as regards one of the guarantors, determines the guarantee, in respect of further advances, determine it necessarily as regards the others also, or will the others continue to be liable for further advances?

Answer: This depends on the form of the guarantee. It would be possible to provide that neither notice given by, nor the death of, one co-surety should have any effect on the continuing liability of the others for past and future advances.

  In *Beckett* v. *Addyman* (1882), 9 Q.B.D. 783, Leading Cases, 4th Ed., p. 247, there was a joint and several guarantee in favour of a bank, and after notice of the death of one of the sureties the bank made further advances to the customer. The surviving surety was held to be liable for such further advances.

  In *Egbert* v. *National Crown Bank,* [1918] A.C. 903, (Leading Cases, 4th Ed., p. 247), a guarantee was to continue until the guarantors or their executors or administrators should give the bank notice to make no further advances on the security of the guarantee. This was held to mean that the guarantee was to remain in force until notice was given by all the guarantors, the representatives of any deceased guarantor taking his place.

601 Can a banker safely continue to make further advances to a customer whose account is guaranteed, after becoming aware of the guarantor's mental incapacity?

Answer: In *Bradford Old Bank* v. *Sutcliffe,* [1918] 2 K.B. 833, (Leading Cases, 4th Ed., p. 250), it was held that notice of the insanity of a guarantor determines his liability for further advances. It can be assumed that the position is unchanged by the Mental Health Act of 1959, but see the answer to Question 155 for the difficulty of establishing the fact of mental incapacity.

602 What action should be taken by a banker who discovers that an act of bankruptcy has been committed by a guarantor of one of his customers?

Answer: He should break the account and cease to make further advances under the guarantee, otherwise he will be prevented by sec. 30 (2) of the Bankruptcy Act, 1914, if a receiving order is made against the guarantor within three months, from proving against the estate for any liability incurred under the guarantee after he had notice of the act of bankruptcy.

In proving against the guarantor's estate, if the guarantee is for the customer's whole debt with a limit on the amount recoverable, deduction must be made of sums received from the customer, and, if he also is bankrupt, of dividends declared, even if not yet actually paid, at the date of the proof; but amounts received from the customer or his estate after the date of the proof need not be deducted. (*Re Houlder,* [1929] 1 Ch. 205.) But the bank may not receive more than 100p. in the £ of the principal debtor's debt to him.

603 If a customer whose account is guaranteed becomes bankrupt, should the banker at once call upon the guarantor to pay off the debt, or should he prove against the customer's estate, and after receiving a final dividend thereon, claim under the guarantee for the balance remaining?

Answer: In practice a demand is made upon the guarantor forthwith. If the amount received is sufficient to cover the debt, the banker may leave the guarantor to prove against the customer's estate.

If, however, the amount is less than the debt, the banker should place it to a suspense account and prove for the whole of his debt, returning any ultimate surplus to the guarantor.

604 When making demand for payment from a guarantor under a guarantee expressed to be for all the customer's liabilities incurred on any current or other account or in any manner whatever, can the bank claim the whole amount of the overdraft on one of the customer's accounts, without deducting a credit balance on another account?

Answer: No; only the ultimate balance may be claimed and this is generally provided for in the form of guarantee. In *Re Sherry* (1884), 25 Ch.D. 692, (Leading Cases, 4th Ed., p. 245), Cotton, L.J., said: 'The balance which the surety guarantees is the general balance of the customer's account, and to ascertain that, all accounts existing between the customer and the bank at the time when the guarantee comes to an end must be taken into consideration.'

605 A customer's account is guaranteed by **X** for £2,000 and by **Y** for £1,000. The customer having become bankrupt, dividends are received by the bank which reduce the debt to £1,290. In what proportions should the bank recover this sum from the guarantors?

Answer: Although between themselves the guarantors are liable to contribute to the payment of the debt in the proportion of the amounts of their respective guarantees, i.e. **X** two-thirds and **Y** one-third, each of them, between himself and the bank, is liable to pay, if required, the whole amount to which his guarantee is limited, in case of default by the other guarantor.

In such circumstances the bank may demand £1,290 from **X** and £1,000 from **Y**, but if both pay in full **X** will be entitled to a refund of £430, making his net payment £860, i.e. two-thirds of £1,290, and **Y** to a refund of £570, i.e. making his net payment £430, i.e. one-third of £1,290.

Alternatively the bank may in the first place demand from each guarantor only the amount of his net liability, i.e. £860 from **X** and £430 from **Y**, warning each that if the other fails to pay any part of his share a further demand will be made.

606 **A** and **B** jointly and severally guarantee a customer's overdraft, limiting their liability to £5,000 in all, and **C** independently guarantees the overdraft, limiting his liability to £3,000. What are the rights of (*a*) the bank, and (*b*) the guarantors among themselves, if the customer's debt is £6,000, and nothing is recoverable from him?

Answer: (*a*) The bank may, at its pleasure, recover up to £5,000 in all from **A** and **B** or either of them, and up to £3,000 from **C**, provided that not more than a total of £6,000 is recovered.

(*b*) Among themselves, **A, B** and **C** are liable to contribute to the satisfaction of the bank's claim, not equally, but in proportion to the amounts of their respective guarantees, that is, in the ratio of £2,500, £2,500 and £3,000. They are therefore, among themselves, liable for £1,875, £1,875 and £2,250 respectively. If any one of them has to pay more than his share, he may recover from any other who has paid less.

607   If, in Question 606, after **A** has paid £1,875, **B** £1,750 and **C** £2,000, an unexpected first and final dividend of 25p. in the £, amounting to £1,500, is received by the bank from the customer's estate, how should the resulting surplus of £1,125, after crediting the account with the dividend and the guarantors' payments, be divided among the guarantors?

Answer: The surplus should first be made up, for the purpose of calculation, to what it would have been if the three guarantors had all paid in full, by adding **B**'s and **C**'s deficits, £125 and £250. The result, £1,500, should then be divided in the ratio of the amounts of the guarantees, £2,500, £2,500 and £3,000, and **B**'s and **C**'s deficits should be deducted from the shares allotted to them.

A, having paid in full, will thus receive	£468.75
B, will receive £468.75 less £125	£343.75
C will receive £562.50 less £250	£312.50
	£1,125.00

608   A customer's overdraft limit of £2,000 is secured by (*a*) a charge by the customer on his property worth £1,150, (*b*) a charge limited to £500 by the customer's wife on her property, and (*c*) a guarantee for £1,000 by a friend covering all moneys owing from time to time. If, at a time when the customer's overdraft is £1,400, the guarantor decides to pay off the whole of it (although this exceeds the amount for which he is liable under his guarantee), what are his rights with regard to the other securities held by the bank?

Answer: A guarantor may volunteer to pay off the entire debt, but the initiative does not rest entirely in his hands and it may well be that any attempt to determine liability will be subject to notice of determination contained in the particular guarantee. Where a surety, with the approval of the lending bank, pays off the whole debt, he is entitled to a charge for the amount which he has paid on all the securities held by the bank from the principal debtor, and to a charge on securities deposited by third parties for the proportions due from them to him under his right to contribution.

609 Can a guarantor at any time call upon the customer to pay off the debt, thus freeing him (the guarantor) from liability under the guarantee, and proceed against the customer if he fails to do so?

Answer: Morrison v. *Barking Chemicals Co.,* [1919] 2 Ch. 325, decided that the guarantor cannot do this while the guarantee remains a continuing security; but when it has been determined he can require the customer to repay and so relieve him (the guarantor) of his liability by paying it off (*Ascherson* v. *Tredegar Dock Co.,* [1909] 2 Ch. 401). On himself paying off the debt he can claim reimbursement by the customer.

If the amount to which the guarantee is limited is less than the debt owing to the bank, it is evident that such proceedings by the guarantor will result in diminishing the customer's assets available for payment of the balance of the bank's debt. Some forms of banker's guarantee accordingly provide that until the bank has received the whole amount of its debt the guarantor is precluded from making any claim against the customer in respect of money paid or payable under the guarantee.

610 Has the guarantor of a customer's account the right to be informed by the bank of the state of the account from time to time; and has he a right to inspect the account in the bank's books?

Answer: Although the guarantor has no right to inspect the account in the books or to demand a copy, he is always entitled to information as to the extent of his liability, if at the time of his inquiry the customer's debt is less than the amount to which his guarantee is limited. If the debt exceeds the guarantee, the guarantor should be informed only that the bank is relying on his guarantee to the full extent. On paying off the guarantee he is entitled to know what other securities are held, in order to be able to decide whether or not to offer to pay off the whole debt and take over the securities.

611 A guarantor, during the currency of his guarantee, calls at the bank and asks the manager if the account of the customer for whom the guarantee has been given is conducted satisfactorily, if any cheques have been returned for exceeding the arranged limit, and whether the manager has any knowledge of outside borrowing. Should the manager reply to such questions?

Answer: Not unless the written consent of the customer has first been obtained. The consent should cover specifically the information to be given.

612 When a guarantor pays off the amount to which his guarantee is limited, can he insist upon having the guarantee given up to him?

Answer: If the sum paid by the guarantor liquidates the entire debt owing to the bank by the customer, subject to what is said below, it is immaterial whether the guarantee is given up or not; but where a customer's indebtedness exceeds the amount to which the guarantee is limited, prudence demands that the bank should retain the guarantee as evidence of the guarantor's contract not to claim against the customer or to prove in his bankruptcy as long as any liability remains unsatisfied. In this case, provision that the guarantee may be retained after discharge is useful.

Another important reason for retaining the guarantee arises where there is a risk of fraudulent preference within the meaning of sec. 44 of the Bankruptcy Act, 1914. It might be that a customer who is subsequently adjudged bankrupt has acted in such way that he has preferred the bank to other creditors in order to reduce the liability of the guarantor. (See *In re M. Kushler Ltd.* [1943] 2 All E.R. 22, Leading Cases, 4th Ed., p. 320, and *In Re J. S. Lyons ex parte Barclays Bank Ltd.* v. *The Trustee* (1934) 1952 L.T. 201, Leading Cases, 4th Ed., p. 318). In the event of such untoward development within six months, the bank will be in a much stronger position if it has retained the guarantee in its original form.

613 A bank lends to a customer against the security of a guarantee for £1,000 which contains the express provision that the guarantor will not claim on the borrower's estate until the claim of the bank is met in full for all sums whatever due by the customer to the bank.

One day the guarantor comes into the bank and deposits £1,000 for the credit of the customer whose account is overdrawn £3,000. The guarantor then asks for his guarantee to be cancelled. Should the bank comply?

Answer: If the guarantor wishes to determine his liability, subject to any notice of determination stipulated in the guarantee, the bank may accept the payment of £1,000, applying the proceeds to the credit of a special Guarantee Security Account in order to preserve the collateral position and retain the bank's rights against the customer pending fresh arrangements. In the meantime, the guarantee should be retained to preserve the bank's rights under the other covenants therein.

Here, the bank is entitled to decline the request, pointing out that the deposit of £1,000 in the account of the customer does not without the prior approval of the bank in any way reduce, or determine, the liability of the guarantor under his guarantee.

614 What are the obligations of a branch manager when taking security from one customer in respect of the liabilities of another customer?

Answer: If the customer looks to the bank manager as his financial adviser either expressly or impliedly by or through a previous course of conduct between them, the customer should be referred to his own solicitor or other professional adviser for advice before executing the security in the presence of a solicitor or adviser.

If the customer does not look to the bank or branch manager as his financial adviser and is a person of independent judgment, business experience and understanding (and ideally already known to the branch to have given previous security to a bank for another customer) he can reasonably be expected by the bank to understand the nature of the commitment into which he is entering and the branch is not obliged to cause that customer to seek a solicitor's or other professional advice before executing the security.

If the customer is not looking to the bank manager or branch as financial adviser, but the branch doubt whether both the business experience and understanding of the customer are such that he can reasonably be expected to understand the nature of the commitment, then he should be referred to a solicitor or other professional adviser and execute the security in the presence of that solicitor or adviser.

Similarly, where such a customer appears to be acting under the influence or domination of the party to be secured, or of another person in circumstances in which he is not free to make his own decision to give security, he should be referred to a solicitor or other professional adviser and execute the security in the presence of that adviser.

615 Where arrangements are made for a group of companies to borrow from the bank, it is usual to request interlocking security from the

various companies comprising the group whether or not they fall
within the strict definition of holding company to a subsidiary as
defined in sec. 154 of the Companies Act, 1948. Whilst it is clear
that separate consideration will be required to support security given
between companies which are totally unrelated, what is the position
between companies which stand in relation to one another as
associated companies, for example, and where the affairs of all the
companies in the group are generally supervised by a common
directorate and shareholding?

Answer: In the case of *Charterbridge Corporation Ltd.* v. *Lloyds
Bank Ltd.* (1969) 2 All E.R. 1185, (Leading Cases, 4th Ed., p. 184),
neither Lloyds Bank nor their customers Castleford Ltd., which was
not a subsidiary company, had considered the interests of that
company in isolation but they had it clearly in mind that the security
was to support the activities of the group as a whole. It was held that
a clause in the memorandum of association, which explicitly
authorised the Castleford company to give guarantees and to lodge
security in support, was valid. The words of the learned Judge are of
interest: 'the proper test, I think, in the absence of actual separate
consideration, must be whether an intelligent and honest man in the
position of the director of the company concerned, could, in the
whole of the existing circumstances have reasonably believed that
the transaction was for the benefit of the company'.

MISCELLANEOUS
HOURS OF BUSINESS

616 Can a bank be legally closed on any day not authorised by Act of
Parliament, as, for instance, Tuesday, December 27, after giving 14
or 21 days' notice? Would the fact of giving such notice protect the
banker?

Answer: Any bank closing its doors on a day not authorised by an
Act of Parliament or order in Council would do so at its own risk.
Whether a bank opens its doors or not is a matter for those in
control of its business, and, strictly speaking, it is not illegal for a
bank to close on any day not so authorised; but if a banker does any
act outside the ordinary course of his business he may render himself
liable to pay damages as there is an implied contract that the banker
will repay money, etc., which he has received in the ordinary course
of his business by honouring cheques of persons from whom or for
whose account he has received it.

As to whether 14 or 21 days' notice of closing is sufficient, this is a question of fact. The bank, in seeking to close on a certain day not so provided for must give sufficient notice to all concerned so as to vary the implied contract or give the customer an opportunity of transferring his business to another bank.

In reply to the second part of the question, the banker would be protected if sufficient notice had been given for arrangements to be made to ensure that no one suffered any damage.

617 If a bank leaves its doors open after its customary closing hour, and a cheque is presented and paid, payment of which is stopped by the drawer on the following morning, may not the bank be held to have paid the cheque on its own responsibility, and to be liable for any loss arising to the drawer through its paying after hours and so depriving the drawer of his right to stop payment at the opening time next morning?

Answer: A banker's duty and authority are to pay his customer's cheques only if presented within banking hours. If he pays a cheque at any other time he exceeds his duty and authority, and may be liable for any damage suffered by the customer through the payment.

See, however, *Baines* v. *National Provincial Bank*, [1927] 96 L.J.K.B. 801, (Leading Cases, 4th Ed., p. 62), where a cheque was presented and paid over the counter a few minutes after closing time. The Court held that the bank had acted within its rights in paying the cheque within a reasonable margin of its advertised closing time.

LEGAL TENDER

618 A customer of a bank finds a £5 note on the floor outside the counter, and hands it over to the cashier. A few weeks afterwards the customer calls again, and learning that no application has been made in the meantime by the loser, claims the note. The bank refuses to give it up, contending that it belongs to the bank because it was found on the bank premises. Exclusive of the £5 note the cash balanced correctly on the date the note was found. Who has the better claim to it?

Answer: The finder. In *Bridges* v. *Hawkesworth* (1851), 21 L.J.Q.B. 75, a person entering a shop found on the floor a bundle of banknotes which had been accidentally dropped there by a stranger.

The latter could not be discovered. It was held that, as against everyone but the true owner, the property in the notes was in the finder, and not in the owner of the shop, because the public part of the shop was not in the custody of the shopkeeper.

619 What notes are legal tender in (*a*) Scotland and Northern Ireland, (*b*) the Republic of Ireland, (*c*) Isle of Man, (*d*) Channel Islands?

Answer: (*a*) In Scotland and Northern Ireland, Bank of England notes of denominations of less than £5 are legal tender under sec. 1 (2) of the Currency and Bank Notes Act, 1954.

(*b*) In the Republic of Ireland the only notes that are legal tender are the Legal Tender Notes issued by the Central Bank of Ireland.

(*c*) Isle of Man. All denominations of Bank of England notes and Isle of Man Government notes are legal tender under Acts of Tynwald dated February 15, 1955, and March 21, 1961, respectively.

(*d*) Channel Islands.

   (i) Jersey. All denominations of Bank of England notes and States of Jersey notes are legal tender under Acts of the States dated September 13, 1955, April 28, 1959, and October 13, 1970.

  (ii) Guernsey, Sark, Herm and Jethou. Under an Ordinance of the States, dated October 28, 1970, Bank of England notes of all denominations and States of Guernsey notes of all denominations bearing a date subsequent to July 2, 1966, are legal tender.

 (iii) Alderney. Under an Ordinance of the States, dated October 6, 1970, Bank of England notes of all denominations bearing a date subsequent to July 2, 1966, are legal tender.

Bank of England Notes referred to in sections (*c*) and (*d*) are those notes which at any given time are legal tender in England and Wales in accordance with the Currency and Bank Notes Act, 1954.

620 Are Scottish and Northern Ireland bank notes legal tender in their respective countries or in England and Wales?

Answer: No.

SAFE CUSTODY

621 Is it the custom of bankers to give receipts for articles deposited with them for safe custody only, and if so, does the fact of having given a receipt place the banker under any responsibility which he would have avoided if he had not done so?

Answer: Current practice is to give such receipts if requested, but the banker's responsibility is the same whether or not a receipt is given (see the following question). The banker may, however, incorporate within the wording of the receipt a clause limiting his responsibility for losses not caused by his staff.

622 What is a banker's liability in respect of an article deposited with him by a customer for safe custody,
  (*a*) if the article is lost, stolen, destroyed, or damaged while in his keeping, or
  (*b*) if he delivers it to the wrong person?

Answer: (*a*) The banker has a duty to take care; his liability, if any, depends upon the degree of care exercised, and whether he is found to have been negligent in failing to maintain a sufficiently high standard of care. The standard of care set by the Judicial Committee in *Giblin* v. *McMullen* (1968) L.R. 2 P.C. 317, (Leading Cases, 4th Ed., p. 292) remains applicable today 'that he must take the same care of the property entrusted to him as a reasonably prudent and careful man may fairly be expected to take of his own property of the same description' and as bankers must, in their ordinary business, take precautions which, reasonable in their case, would be exceptional for ordinary persons, the standard expected from them would be that much higher. If standards of care are met, the banker is not liable: therefore customers should be advised to effect their own insurance. (See also Q. 621.)

(*b*) The delivery of an article deposited to the wrong person is a 'conversion' of the article, for which the liability is absolute, independently of the degree of care exercised.

623 Does an authority given to a banker by a customer to allow the customer's solicitor, or other person, to have 'access' to his box deposited, justify the banker in allowing the solicitor or other person to remove the box, or any part of its contents?

Answer: No; it is considered that 'access' does not imply or include removal. A member of the staff of the bank should be present during the period of access to ensure that nothing is removed from the box.

624 Under an authority given by a customer to his banker, to allow a third party to remove a specified article from his box, is the banker bound to see that nothing else is removed?

Answer: Yes; a bank official should be present when the box is opened, and should see that only the specified article is taken away.

625 A customer wishes to leave a sealed envelope (contents unknown) with his bankers for safe custody, with instructions that in case of his death the envelope is to be handed to a third party. Would the bank be in order in acting upon these instructions, or does the death of the customer cancel such an authority?

Answer: The death of the customer cancels the authority, and the title to the envelope and its contents passes to his executors or administrators. Such an authority should therefore not be accepted. On the customer's death his personal representative may inspect the contents of any sealed envelope or locked box deposited with the bank under strict security and in the presence of a bank official. If a will is contained therein, it should be released to the named executor or his solicitor against a receipt, but no other articles or papers may be removed until probate of the will has been obtained.

626 If a banker becomes aware that a customer who has deposited bearer bonds or other articles with him for safe custody has committed an act of bankruptcy, will he be justified in redelivering them to the customer?

Answer: Subject to the relative provisions of the Exchange Control Act, the banker will be protected by sec. 46 of the Bankruptcy Act, 1914, in redelivering the bonds or other articles to the customer, if he does so before the date on which a receiving order is made against the customer, and without notice of the presentation of a bankruptcy petition.

627 If **A**, who is not a stockbroker, deposits, for safe custody, in his own name certificates of stocks or shares registered (*a*) in the name of **B**, or (*b*) in the joint names of **A** and **B**, is it necessary for the banker to have the authority of **B** before redelivering the certificates to **A**?

Answer: No; the banker is responsible for the certificates only to the person in whose name they are deposited.

LIEN

628 What is banker's lien?

Answer: A lien is the right to retain the property of a debtor until he has discharged a debt due to the holder retaining that property, and lien may be particular or general. A particular lien arises from that particular transaction connected with the property subject to the lien. However, banker's lien is a general lien, arising not only out of a particular transaction but also out of the general dealing between the banker and customer, and covers 'all securities deposited with them as bankers by a customer, unless there be an express contract, inconsistent with lien, (*Brandao* v. *Barnett* (1846) 12 Ch. & Fin. 787, Leading Cases, 4th Ed., p. 222.) Bankers lien does not apply to securities deposited with the banker solely for safe custody. To be subject to lien the property must come into the hands of the banker to be dealt with in his business as the banker of his customer.

629   To what articles deposited with a banker by a customer does the banker's lien for money owing to him by the customer extend?

Answer: Whilst the class of securities that may be the subject of lien is not very clearly defined, it would seem from the answer to the previous question that the lien only applies to property owned by the customer with which the banker deals for him in the ordinary course of business, otherwise than for safe custody, unless it be held under special conditions inconsistent with the claim of a general lien, e.g. a share certificate deposited with the bank as cover for a specific advance where the banker is an equitable mortgagee could probably not be held to be subject to banker's lien in respect of a separate advance.

Examples

Probably subject to general lien	*Probably not subject to general lien*
Bills or cheques deposited for collection, or pending discount.	Articles deposited for safe custody.
	Securities received for sale.
Warrants for dividends paid to the banker under mandates.	Securities deposited upon a particular trust, although the trust fails.
Bearer bonds, if the banker cuts off the coupons and collects them.	Bearer bonds held pursuant only to the Exchange Control Act.
	Securities left in banker's hands, after an advance

Securities deposited to secure a specific loan, but left in the banker's hands after the loan had been repaid. (*Re London and Globe Finance Corporation,* [1902] 2 Ch. 416.)

against them has been declined.
Securities deposited to secure a specific loan. (*Cuthbert* v. *Robarts, Lubbock & Co.,* [1909] 2 Ch. 226.)

630 Does a banker's lien on negotiable securities include a right to realise and recoup himself from the proceeds, thus differing from an ordinary general lien?

Answer: As banker's lien has been described as an implied pledge (*Brandao* v. *Barnett* quoted above) it appears that the remedies of a pledgee apply, i.e. power of sale subject to the giving of reasonable notice to the customer and any necessary application to the Court.

631 A provincial broker instructs his bankers to pay through their London office, to the debit of his account, a sum of money to a London broker in exchange for a certified transfer of stock. This is done, and the transfer when received is in favour of a person who is presumably a client of the provincial broker.

If the payment has created an overdraft on the broker's account, have the bankers a lien on the transfer for the overdraft?

Answer: A banker's lien does not extend to securities which he knows to be the property of third parties, and a transfer is not a negotiable instrument. The transfer cannot therefore be retained by the bankers against the client whose property it is, if he has paid the broker for the stock purchased on his behalf.

632 Has a banker a lien on a security, whether negotiable or not, which he has purchased or taken up at the request of a customer, for the amount paid?

Answer: Yes, as against the customer.

633 A country stockbroker instructs his bank to pay, through a London office of the bank, a specified sum of money against delivery of certificates and transfers in the name of **X.**

(*a*) Is the bank justified in debiting the broker's account with the sum named before the delivery of the securities, even if his credit balance is thereby exhausted, and in dishonouring a cheque afterwards presented?

(b) If the debit causes the account to be overdrawn, has the bank a lien on the securities for the overdraft?

Answer: (a) Whether the country branch credit a London office of the bank, and debit their customer, when advising the payment, or whether they await a debit by the head office when the securities are delivered and the money is paid, they are, in either case, entitled to regard an equivalent amount of the customer's credit balance as set aside for the payment, and to dishonour cheques which if paid would leave less than that amount available.

(b) The bank have, as against **X**, the owner of the securities, no lien on them for any liabilities of the broker to them.

634   A banker receives direct for his customer, under mandate, dividends on stock standing in the names of trustees on his customer's behalf. In anticipation of the next dividend he allows his customer to overdraw his account. Before the dividend is received the customer dies. Has the banker any claim on the next dividend or can the trustees claim it?

Answer: No. It belongs to the trustees.

SET-OFF

635   Can (a) a credit balance on an account in the sole name of **A** be set off against an overdraft on an account in the joint names of **A** and **B**;

(b) a credit balance on an account in the joint names of **A** and **B** be set off against an overdraft on an account in the sole name of either?

Answer: The general principle is that, apart from express agreement, there is no right of set-off between joint and separate debts, even in bankruptcy. Thus,

(a) **A**'s credit balance cannot be set off against the joint debt unless
   (i) he has expressly agreed that it may, or
   (ii) **A** and **B** have agreed to be both jointly and severally responsible for the debt in their joint names.
(b) The joint credit balance cannot be set off against a debt in either of the sole names unless both **A** and **B** have agreed with the bank that it may.

636 The account of a firm is overdrawn, but each of the partners has a private account with a credit balance. Can the bank set off these balances against the firm's debt?

Answer: Apart from express agreement, the bank has no right to set-off a partner's private account against an overdraft on partnership account. In bankruptcy the separate estate of each partner (including the credit balance of his separate account) is applicable in the first instance in payment of his separate debts. (Sec. 33 (6) of the Bankruptcy Act, 1914.)

If, however, the partners have undertaken to be severally, as well as jointly, responsible to the bank for the partnership liabilities, the bank may set off their credit balances against such liabilities.

637 Is a credit balance on an account in the name of 'A, executor of X, deceased,' a good set-off against a debit balance standing on the account of X deceased, or conversely?

Answer: Not in either case. A's credit or debit balance as executor is a debt owing by or to the bank to or by A personally, but in the case of X deceased, the debt is owing to or by X's estate.

638 Can a credit balance on the account of A as executor, administrator, or trustee be set off against an overdraft on A's private account, or conversely?

Answer: The money held by A in a fiduciary capacity cannot be set off against his private debt; but if the fiduciary account is overdrawn A is personally liable for the overdraft, and his private credit balance can be set off against it, unless the terms on which the overdraft was arranged are inconsistent with such a right of set-off.

639 A and B are members of a firm for which the X Bank discount a joint and several promissory note, signed by A and B. At maturity the firm's balance is insufficient to cover the note, but A and B both have private accounts, the credit balances of which would partly meet the note. The X Bank give notice to A and B that they have impounded these balances, pending the settlement. (*a*) Can they legally do this? (*b*) In the event of cheques drawn on the private accounts being presented after notice has been given, would X Bank be justified in returning them?

Answer: (*a*) and (*b*) Yes.

40 A has a deposit account with a banker, and is also party to a bill lying overdue and unpaid in the same hands. Can the banker refuse payment of the deposit to **A**, and apply the amount, or so much of it as is needed, in payment of the overdue bill?

Answer: Yes.

41 Is a deposit balance a set-off against the depositor's contingent liability on current discounted bills?

Answer: No, except in the event of a customer's bankruptcy, or, if a limited company, liquidation.

42 Can the trustee in the bankruptcy of a customer who has money on deposit and also an overdrawn current account, claim, by presenting the deposit receipt or passbook, to have the amount of the deposit paid to him, leaving the bank to prove for the whole amount of the overdraft?

Answer: No; the deposit must be set off against the overdraft under sec. 31 of the Bankruptcy Act, 1914.

43 If a depositor, who has also an overdrawn current account, assigns his deposit to another person, and notice of the assignment is given to the bank, can the bank, as against the assignee, set off the overdraft against the deposit?

Answer: Yes; any such assignment, which takes effect under sec. 136 of the Law of Property Act, 1925, is, under that section, 'subject to prior equities,' and one of these is the bank's right to set off, out of the deposit, the amount owing to it on the depositor's other account at the time when it received notice of the assignment.

44 A bank cashes for a deposit account customer a cheque payable to him drawn on another bank. If the cheque is dishonoured on presentation, is the bank justified in debiting his deposit account with it?

Answer: Yes: there is clearly a right of set-off against the deposit in respect of the liability on the unpaid cheque.

45 If, at a time when a customer's overdraft has become repayable according to the terms on which it was arranged, the customer pays in money expressly to meet a cheque which he has drawn, is the bank at liberty to appropriate the money in reduction of the overdraft, and to dishonour the cheque when presented?

Answer: No; the money must be held to provide for the cheque which it was specifically paid in to meet.

646 A customer has a private account, and also other accounts in his name, designated as follows:

(a) Estate Account.
(b) re **B**.
(c) Executor of **C** deceased.
(d) Treasurer of the **D** School.
(e) Treasurer of the **E** Friendly Society.
(f) Annual Fête Account.

If the customer overdraws any of the accounts (a) to (f), will he be personally liable to the bank for the overdrafts, and will the bank have the right to set off against such liability the credit balance of his private account?

Answer: As all the accounts are in the customer's name, and there is (it is assumed) nothing to indicate that the bank has undertaken to rely on any liability other than his for overdrafts created on them, it is considered that he is personally liable for such overdrafts and that the bank would have a right of set-off against the credit balance on his private account.

It does not follow that the bank (except in the case of the Estate Account, if the 'estate' is the customer's own) has a corresponding right to set off credit balances on some of the designated accounts against overdrafts on others of them, or on the private account.

In the case of the **E** Friendly Society the account should not have been opened in the name of an individual, but in the name of the Society.

647 At the maturity of a policy which has been assigned to a bank as security, if the bank receives the whole of the policy money, but its mortgage is limited to a sum less than that owing by the customer, can the surplus be held as a set-off against the balance of the customer's debt?

Answer: Probably it can, against the customer himself, if the policy matured during his life; but not against his personal representatives if the policy matured at his death, because the surplus policy money is a debt owing by the bank to the representatives, and cannot be set off against the debt owing to the bank by the estate of the deceased.

648 Can the credit balance of a guarantor's account be held as a set-off against his liability under the guarantee?

Answer: If the guarantee is payable on demand, no debt is owing by the guarantor to the bank until demand is made (*Bradford Old Bank* v. *Sutcliffe,* [1918] 2 K.B. 833, Leading Cases, 4th Ed., p. 250), and accordingly until then there can be no right of set-off. As soon as demand has been made the right of set-off is exercisable. Some guarantees, however, expressly afford the right of set-off without prior demand.

GARNISHEE PROCEEDINGS

649 Is it usual or necessary for bankers to give notice to their customers of the service of a garnishee order?

Answer: Yes; the customer should at once be informed of the service of the garnishee order, and of the dishonour of any cheques drawn by him that have had to be dishonoured in consequence. If the order attaches the whole balance of his account, less uncleared cheques, the customer should be informed that he may open a new account for future credits.

650 If a garnishee order is issued for the recovery of a judgment debt which, including costs, is less than the amount of the customer's credit balance, may his cheques be honoured to the extent of the surplus, or is the whole balance attached?

Answer: (1) A *garnishee order nisi* issued by the High Court may, according to its terms, either (*a*) attach all debts owing by the bank to the customer without limit, irrespective of the amount of the judgment debt, or (*b*) it may attach only a stated sum sufficient to satisfy the judgment debt and costs.

In case (*a*) the whole balance of the customer's accounts (but not including any cheques credited to it that are not yet cleared) is attached, and no cheques, even if drawn before the date of the order, should ordinarily be honoured. Where, however, the balance on the accounts exceeds the amount of the order plus the likely costs, the bank should use its discretion as to the payment of cheques subsequently presented. In *Plunkett* v. *Barclays Bank,* [1936] 2 K.B.

107, (Leading Cases, 4th Ed., p. 51), it was held that even the credit balance of a solicitor's client's account is attached, unless expressly excluded by the order.

The amount of the uncleared cheques, if any, should be transferred to a new account, to which all future credits should be placed.

In case (b) only the amount specified in the order, plus costs, is attached, and if this is less than the customer's credit balance (after deducting uncleared cheques) his cheques may be honoured to the extent of the surplus. It will usually be convenient in this case to transfer to a suspense account a sum sufficient to satisfy the order, leaving the remaining balance at the customer's disposal.

(2) A *garnishee summons*, issued by the Mayor's and City of London Court, or by a County Court, allows the bank, on or before a date named in it, to pay the amount of the debt plus costs to the Registrar of the Court. In this case also, it will usually be convenient to transfer the amount required to a suspense account, pending the payment.

651 If a customer pays in cash expressly to meet, on re-presentation, a cheque which has been returned on the previous day with the answer 'Refer to drawer: please re-present,' and if a garnishee order is served on the bank before the cheque is re-presented, should the cheque when re-presented be paid?

Answer: (a) If the garnishee order attaches the whole balance of the account the cheque should not be paid, unless the customer provides further cash to meet it.

(b) If the order attaches only a part of the balance, and, after that part has been transferred to a suspense account the balance remaining is sufficient to meet the cheque, it should be paid.

652 Does a garnishee order or summons attach the balance of a deposit account repayable at a stated period after notice?

Answer: Yes; sec. 38 of the Administration of Justice Act, 1956, enables money standing to the credit of deposit accounts to be attached by garnishee proceedings, whether notice of withdrawal has been given or not and whether the 'deposit book' (if production of the book is necessary before withdrawals can be made) has been delivered up or not.

Deposit accounts at banks with two or more branches where withdrawals are permitted at any branch on production of the pass book are not attached.

Unless the customer has given prior notice of withdrawal, service of a garnishee order *nisi* will operate as such notice. In the event of the order being made absolute, payment, to the judgment creditor, of the amount attached may be delayed until the expiry of the required period of notice of withdrawal. The period of such notice is to be calculated as from the date of service of the garnishee proceedings.

Interest accrued to the account but not credited at the date of service of the order is not attached.

653 A bank receives an enquiry from another bank, asking if a specified cheque will be paid if presented; and replies, 'Yes, if in order'. Before the cheque is presented, a garnishee order is received, attaching the whole balance of the account on which the cheque is drawn. Is the amount of this cheque included in the balance attached under the garnishee order?

Answer: Under sec. 45 of the Bills of Exchange Act a bill or cheque must be presented for payment in order to charge the drawer, and under sub-sec. (3) such presentment must be made 'at the proper place,' which is defined by sub-sec. (4) to be the address of the drawee, i.e., in the case of a cheque, the address of the drawee bank.

It is clear from these provisions that until the cheque reaches the drawee bank, the bank cannot debit the account of the drawer, nor can it appropriate to the payment of the cheque any part of the balance standing to his credit, the whole of which, in the circumstances indicated in the question, is attached by the garnishee order.

The reply in the above form might be held to bind the bank giving it to the bank making the inquiry, but a bank can protect itself against similar risks by replying in the terms: 'Would be paid if presented here now and in order.'

654 (*a*) Can a third party, by giving notice to a banker of a claim (other than an assignment) on money deposited with him, impose any liability on the banker if he parts with the money to his own customer after such notice?

(*b*) Is it necessary for the third party to obtain an order of court to restrain the banker from making the payment?

Answer: (*a*) No.

(*b*) Unless judgment has been obtained, in which case a garnishee order could be served, the third party must apply for an injunction restraining the customer from operating his account.

655 On the day when a garnishee order is served on a bank the proceeds of stocks or shares belonging to the customer, which on his instructions have been sold by the bank for settlement on that day, have not yet come to hand. When subsequently received are they attached by the order?

Answer: No, because the proceeds of sale are not a debt due or accruing due from the bank to the customer at the time of the service of the order.

656 Is money paid in by a customer for his credit after the service of a garnishee order on the bank attached by the order?

Answer: No, because such money was not, at the time of the service of the order, a debt due or accruing due from the bank to the customer.

657 Does a garnishee order served on the head office, as being the registered office, of a bank, attach the customer's balance at the branch concerned at the time of service on the head office, or the balance at the time when notification of the order is received at the branch?

Answer: Service of the order on the head office is service on all the branches of the bank within the jurisdiction of the Court making the order or issuing the summons, but it is considered that a sufficient time to allow the head office to communicate with the branch must elapse before the bank will be liable for permitting the account at the branch to be operated upon.

658 When a branch receives notification from its head office of the service of a garnishee order, is a sum paid in on the day of notification at another branch for the credit of the customer's account attached?

Answer: The proceeds of uncleared cheques paid in for the credit of the customer's account will not be attached, but it is considered that cash paid in before service will form part of the attached balance.

659 What action should be taken by a bank, when a garnishee order

affecting a customer's account is served upon it, with regard to
- (a) the customer's cheques presented on that day through the clearings, which have been cancelled and debited to his account, and
- (b) cheques drawn by that customer which have been credited to the account of another customer, before service of the order?

Answer: Unless the balance of the account, after payment of the cheques, is sufficient to discharge the judgment debt and costs, (a) the cheques should be marked 'Cancelled in error' and returned, if this can be done under the rules of the clearing through which they were presented, and if the presenting banks have not been informed that they are paid; and (b) the cheques should be debited to the customer to whose account they were placed, if he was not informed at the time when he brought them in, or at any time before the service of the order, that they were paid.

STOCKS AND SHARES

660 A solicitor instructs his banker to purchase, out of the credit balance of his Clients' Account, stocks and shares in the names of persons who are presumably his clients. When the certificates are received, should the banker deliver them to the solicitor without the authority of the persons for whom they have been purchased?

Answer: Yes.

661 Should a banker act upon the instruction of a solicitor
- (a) to deliver to the solicitor securities deposited by a customer;
- (b) to sell bearer bonds deposited by a customer, and to pay the proceeds of sale to the solicitor?

Answer: Not without the authority of the customer.

662 A transfer of shares is filled up in ink, except the date, which is in pencil. Is this a complete instrument, and could the company be compelled to register it?

Answer: A company would be justified in refusing to register such a transfer.

663 A customer, who has deposited share certificates with a completely executed transfer in favour of the bank's nominees, is permitted to

withdraw some of the shares before the transfer is registered, and the transfer is amended accordingly, the alterations being initialled by the transferor.

Will the company accept the amended transfer for registration?

Answer: Yes, but it would be sounder practice for the bank to obtain a fresh transfer.

664 When a transfer of stocks or shares is completed, is the company justified in refusing to register it if the transferor dies or becomes bankrupt before it is tendered for registration?

Answer: No; but, in the case of bankruptcy, the transaction may be annulled if it amounts to a fraudulent conveyance or a fraudulent preference.

665 Should a banker who has been instructed to pay cash against delivery of a certified transfer of stocks or shares accept a transfer certified by anyone except the secretary or registrar of the company concerned?

Answer: The banker should accept a transfer certified by the Manager, Stock Transfer Certification Office of the London Stock Exchange. This Office will certify all quoted stocks and shares that have their registers in the U.K., Republic of Ireland and Bermuda, together with a small number of other stocks by request of their Registrars.

By arrangement with companies and corporations, the nominee companies of certain banks also certify transfers executed by them, and such certification is usually accepted also.

666 Can a bank accept American or Canadian shares as security when registered in (1) Good Marking Names, (2) other names?

Answer: (1) Yes—providing such securities are properly endorsed in blank they may be treated as bearer security. A Memorandum of Deposit is normally taken which gives the bank an equitable mortgage with the ability to sell the shares.

(2) Yes. (*a*) If the shares are in the depositor's own name the bank proceeds as in (1) above. Care needs to be taken to ensure the endorsements of corporations, societies, etc. are supported by a signed guarantee that the necessary transfer arrangements have been made with the transfer agents or registrars.

(*b*) If the shares are not registered in the depositor's name, they

should be transferred into the name of the bank's nominee
company. A legal charge is thereby obtained thus avoiding the risk
of prior equitable interests.

Care must be taken to comply with exchange control regulations
in all cases.

667 A customer gives instructions to a bank to pay a certain sum in
London in exchange for American railroad share warrants. One of
these is afterwards found to be irregularly endorsed, and the
attestation not in order. In case of loss would the bank be liable to
the customer?

Answer: Within the scope of his business, the banker is bound to
exercise the degree of skill, care and diligence usual in the ordinary
conduct of banking business, and reasonably necessary for the
proper performance of the duties undertaken by him.'

If the irregularity was manifest, the banker would probably be
liable, but not otherwise.

668 Is it necessary to stamp an undated transfer?

Answer: No.

669 A has an advance from a bank, and **B**, a third party, transfers to the
bank Stock Exchange securities as cover for **A**'s advance. Will **B**'s
transfers be sufficiently stamped with a 50p. stamp—nominal
consideration duty?

Answer: Yes.

670 A stockbroker, who has transferred shares standing in his own name
into the names of the nominees of a bank as security for an
overdraft, pays off the overdraft. He asks the bank, instead of
retransferring the shares to him, to transfer them to a third party, on
whose behalf the broker says that he bought them, *ad valorem*
stamp duty having been paid on the occasion of the purchase. The
bank has not previously been aware that the shares were not the
property of the broker himself.

Can such a transfer be properly made by the bank's nominees for
a nominal consideration, by a transfer deed stamped 50p.?

Answer: Before stamping a transfer with a 50p. stamp the Inland
Revenue authorities require a certificate from a bank that the
transfer is excepted from sec. 74 (6) of the Finance (1909-10) Act,

1910. Whether a bank in the above circumstances is justified in signing such a certificate must be left to the bank's discretion in each case. Provided there were no circumstances to put the bank upon inquiry, it would usually do so. If not, the facts must be specified and the ruling of the Inland Revenue authorities obtained.

671 Is a transfer, executed in England, of shares in a company registered and carrying on business in the Isle of Man, liable to English stamp duty?

Answer: Although the Isle of Man is not within the United Kingdom for the purposes of the Stamp Act, 1891, a transfer executed in the U.K. of registered shares expressed in sterling in a company registered in the Isle of Man is liable to U.K. stamp duty.

672 Are foreign bearer bonds (capital and interest not payable in England) subject to English stamp duty when sold or deposited in England?

Answer: No. Sec. 30 of the Finance Act, 1967, exempts bearer securities from stamp duty.

LIMITATION OF ACTIONS

Notwithstanding the answers to specific questions now given it should be appreciated that a claimant is deemed to be under a disability while a minor or of unsound mind. If when his right to pursue his claim last arose he was under any such disability, his claim is preserved until 6 years (in the case of contractual claims) after he ceases to be under a disability or dies, whichever event occurs first. Where there is a claim against the trustee for any fraud or fraudulent breach of trust, or for conversion of trust property, there is no fixed period under the Limitation Acts after which a beneficiary may not claim. In all these cases the banker should refer to Head Office for guidance.

673 When does time under the Limitation Act, 1939, begin to run against the customer in respect of the credit balance of (*a*) a current account, (*b*) a deposit account?

Answer: (*a*) The statutory period does not begin to run until the customer has made demand for repayment upon the bank.

(*b*) If a deposit is repayable at a fixed date, or after a fixed period of notice, the statute begins to run from the fixed date, or from the expiration of the notice, or from the return of the deposit receipt or passbook, if this is made a condition of repayment.

674 When does time under the Limitation Act, 1939, begin to run against a banker in respect of an advance made by him?

Answer: The general rule is that the limitation period does not start to run until the banker makes demand for repayment of the debt.

With an active current account the rule in Clayton's Case applies in the absence of express appropriation at the time so that credits go in reduction of the debit items in the account in order of date even if the earliest of these is already statute barred. Thus the debt on a current account continually renews itself.

Any acknowledgment under sec. 23 (4) of the Limitation Act, 1939, to revive the right of action has to be in writing and signed by the person making the acknowledgment. In practice, a debt due by a customer to a bank is usually acknowledged by payment of interest or by written evidence in the shape of correspondence with the bank but, in the case of a trading borrower, it was decided in *Jones* v. *Bellegrove Properties Ltd.* [1949] 2 All E.R. 198, that inclusion of a debt in the global heading of 'sundry creditors' in the signed balance sheet of the borrower amounted to an acknowledgement of the debt sufficient to meet the requirements of the Limitation Act, 1939.

675 What is a sufficient acknowledgment by a customer or other person indebted to a bank, or by a guarantor, to take the debt out of the operation of the Limitation Act, 1939?

Answer: An admission in writing of the bank's claim is sufficient, signed by the debtor, or on his behalf by an agent having authority to sign it. The appointment of the agent for this purpose need not be in writing.

No amount need be mentioned, but if a definite sum is named, it is that sum only which is acknowledged.

Since the statutory period begins to run afresh from the date of an acknowledgment, the date is highly material, but if omitted it may be proved by oral evidence.

An acknowledgment of a debt binds only the person by whom, or on whose behalf, it is given, and his personal representatives. If there are two or more joint, or joint and several debtors, or a principal debtor and a guarantor, an acknowledgment by one does not keep the debt alive against the other or others. It is otherwise in the case of a payment on account of principal or interest by one of the persons liable.

676 When two or more persons are jointly, or jointly and severally, indebted to a bank, will

(*a*) an acknowledgment of liability, or

(*b*) a payment on account of principal or interest,

by one of them prevent the Limitation Act, 1939, from running in favour of the other or others?

Answer: (*a*) Under sec. 25 (5) of the Limitation Act, 1939, an acknowledgment (see Q. 675) of a debt binds the acknowledgor and his personal representatives, but not any other person.

(*b*) Under sec. 25 (6) of the Act, a payment made in respect of a debt before the expiration of the period of limitation applying under the Act for the recovery of the debt (six or twelve years) binds *all persons* liable for it; but if made after the expiration of the period of limitation, such a payment binds only the person making it and his personal representatives, and does not revive the liability of any other person.

677 Under a guarantee expressed to be payable on demand, when is the banker's right to recover from the guarantor barred by the Statute of Limitations?

Answer: If the guarantee is under hand, six years, and if under seal, twelve years, from the date of demand made by the banker upon the guarantor for payment. This follows from the decision in *Bradford Old Bank* v. *Sutcliffe*, ([1918] 2 K.B. 883; Leading Cases, 4th Ed., p. 250), that under a guarantee expressed to be payable on demand a cause of action against the guarantor does not accrue until actual demand is made.

After demand has been made upon the guarantor, a payment by him on account of principal or interest, or an acknowledgment in writing by him of his liability, would cause the statutory period to run afresh from the date of the payment or acknowledgment.

A payment on account of principal or interest by the customer, if made before the expiration of the statutory period, would keep the debt alive against both himself and the guarantor, but if made after the expiration of the period, such a payment would revive the liability of the customer, but not that of the guarantor.

An acknowledgment made by the customer at any time would bind himself and his personal representatives only.

678 When is a promissory note statute barred, if it is expressed to be payable
    (*a*) on demand;
    (*b*) one day after demand;
    (*c*) six months after date?

Answer: Six years from
    (*a*) the date of the note, or the date of its issue, if later;
    (*b*) the day after demand;
    (*c*) the date of maturity.

679 A banker collecting a cheque with a forged endorsement is liable to the true owner unless he is protected by statute; how long does this liability last?

Answer: The liability would not normally extend for more than six years from the date of the conversion.

680 A coupon payable to bearer is lost, and the amount is paid by the paying banker to the loser against his indemnity.
    If the coupon gets into the hands of a holder for value without notice of the loss, can the holder recover the amount from the banker (*a*) before, or (*b*) after, the expiration of the six years' period of limitation from the date when the coupon was payable?

Answer: The banker, in paying such coupons, is merely the agent of the Government, Municipality, or Company that issued the bonds to which the coupons were attached, and his only responsibility is to his principals. He will therefore not pay a coupon of which the loss has been notified to him unless instructed to do so by the principals.
    As a bearer coupon is a negotiable instrument, the principals will be liable to a holder in due course until the claim is statute barred, but the period may be twelve years instead of six, if the bonds were issued under seal. It must be borne in mind, if the bonds were issued by a foreign government, that such a government cannot be sued in the Courts of this country.

681 A draft, issued by a branch of a bank on its head office, is stolen from the payee. The amount of the draft is paid by the bank's head office, without production of the missing draft, against an appropriate indemnity.
    (1) When does the liability under the indemnity cease?
    (2) When does action in respect of the missing drafts become statute barred?

Answer: (1) The liability under the indemnity is statute barred six years (12 years in the case of an indemnity under seal) after the cause of action first arose against the indemnifier, that is to say, six years after presentation and payment of the missing draft.

(2) Action in respect of the original draft is statute barred as against the banker six years from the date when the cause of action first arose against him, that is to say, from the date of the maturity of the draft, or, if it is payable on demand, from the date of its being drawn.

SUNDRY

682 A customer who works his account close to, and sometimes slightly exceeding, his overdraft limit frequently draws against uncleared effects. Amongst the cheques thus paid in are some drawn on an account in his name at another bank. What is the danger in allowing this to continue?

Answer: The facts indicate the probability that the customer is financing himself by 'cross-firing': the bank is fortunate in having so clear a warning, for the experienced practitioner is more likely to have set up a chain of accounts in varying names, and the difficulty of detecting the practice increases in proportion to the length of the chain. The obvious danger is that eventually one of the banks involved will dishonour a cheque and break the chain.

In the circumstances of the question the customer should be interviewed and, in the absence of a satisfactory explanation, told that the bank will no longer pay against uncleared effects. More generally any payment against uncleared effects for customers with doubtful accounts should be carefully scrutinised.

In all cases where it is clear that cross-firing is taking place it is prudent to consult other banks involved with a view to stopping the practice without loss to any of them. It is advisable to call in your inspection or legal department who can deal with the whole situation.

683 A company account in the name of XYZ Co. Ltd. is opened at your branch with a small credit balance: it is respectably introduced by a firm of local accountants.

Your customers are described as 'general dealers'. Everything goes along quite satisfactorily until, after six months, you suddenly realise that a turnover of some £350,000 has been passed through the account. You invite the directors to discuss the situation with you, but no real explanation of the extraordinary increase in turnover is forthcoming. You suggest that you would like an invitation to come and see their operations on the ground, but they are somewhat evasive and suggest that they are rather busy at the moment and that a visit from you should be deferred for a month or two.

Does this situation call for any comment? If so, what should you do?

Answer: It is unusual for customers not to appreciate visits from representatives of their bank. It may be, if a satisfactory explanation is not forthcoming, that this is a less obvious case of cross firing, a practice that is not confined to overdrawn accounts.

The situation here may be that substantial uncleared balances have built up at four or five different branches or banks, with no obvious explanation for the build up. There is a tendency for this to happen more frequently in times of financial stringency, sometimes with no fraudulent intent but rather as an attempt to find an easy way out of a difficult position.

But the practice is still dangerous for the banks involved, and as in the answer to the previous question payment against uncleared effects should be stopped and head office called in with a view to consulting other banks and branches involved.

684 Mr. A's business is going through a difficult period, his overdraft limit has been frequently exceeded and the branch manager knows that there are several heavy commitments unsettled. Whilst the branch manager is confident that Mr. A will pull through, his confidence is not shared by his Head Office, who have made this clear to him.

Despite this background, the manager indicates, in response to an enquiry from another bank, that his customer is trading satisfactorily and that he considers him good for his trade engagements generally. This opinion carries the usual disclaimer of responsibility on the part of the bank and its officers.

In a few months Mr. A is made bankrupt, and Mr. B on whose behalf the banker's enquiry was made proposes to sue Mr. A's bank for the loss which he has suffered as a result of granting credit to Mr. A on the strength of the opinion given.

What is the bank's position?

Answer: In the well-known case of *Hedley Byrne & Co. Ltd.* v. *Heller & Partners,* [1964] A.C. 465; (Leading Cases, 4th Ed., p. 295), the House of Lords held that a banker did owe a duty of care in giving an opinion for the benefit of a non-customer, but that there was no such duty if the bank expressly disclaimed responsibility. In a recent decision of the Australian Court of Appeal in *Commercial Banking Company of Sydney Ltd.* v. *R. H. Brown & Co.;* (Leading Cases, p. 299), where the facts were similar to those in question, the Australian Court held that the opinion had been given fraudulently and that the bank was accordingly liable, notwithstanding an express disclaimer. In reaching this decision the Court applied the rule in *Derry* v. *Peek* (1889), where it was stated that 'fraudulent misrepresentation consists of a false statement of fact which is either made knowingly or without belief in its truth, or recklessly without caring whether it is true or false with the intention that it should be acted upon and which is in fact acted upon'.

The English courts are not of course bound by this Australian decision, but nevertheless they will almost certainly take note of it. It is perhaps significant that, whilst in the original pleadings in the Hedley Byrne case fraud was alleged, this particular pleading was withdrawn at the trial, with the result that the House of Lords were not required to consider the point upon which the Australian court gave judgment.

In the light of this decision it is probable that Mr. **B** will be able to bring a successful action.

685 You are operating an account at your branch for a manufacturer of suede coats. His turnover is approaching £1,000,000 and you have been persuaded, albeit reluctantly, to operate a limit of £30,000 unsecured, except for a director's guarantee which cannot be relied upon.

You took this decision two years ago when an adequate balance sheet was shown; but no further audited accounts have since been produced, and the customer is clearly overtrading.

There are continual excesses, you dishonour some cheques, credit turnover dries up and cheques from a factoring company appear.

What should the bank do and why?

Answer: An immediate interview is essential as it is obvious that your customer is making material changes in his financial arrangements which may alter your position without taking you into his confidence.

He is factoring his debtors to overcome his immediate cash flow difficulties and whilst this is a perfectly reasonable step to take, it does mean that debtors are removed from the balance sheet in exchange for immediate cash, thus changing the whole complexion

of the balance sheet from the lending banker's point of view. Such
action may in fact improve the customer's trading position but it
does change the basis on which the bankers' original facility was
agreed. Thus an early discussion and consideration of the extent to
which you may be prepared to lend in the light of the changed
position is essential.

686 A banker receives from a third party a remittance for the credit of **A**.
Having no account in the sole name of **A**, he credits the money to an
account in the joint names of **A** and **B**, in respect of which an
authority for payment to either is held.

If **B** withdraws the money, is the banker responsible to **A** for
having placed it under **B**'s control?

Answer: Yes. As the banker had no account in the sole name
advised, he should have held the money in suspense until **A**'s
instructions could be obtained.

687 A warrant for retired pay or pension contains a certificate intended
to be signed by a justice of the peace, a notary public, a com-
missioner for oaths, a minister of religion, a medical practitioner,
or a bank manager, to the effect that the person whose signature as
payee appears on the warrant is living, and, to the best of the
certifier's knowledge and belief, is the person entitled to the
payment.
  (*a*) Should a bank manager refuse to sign such a certificate unless
        the pensioner is personally known to him, and is, to his
        knowledge, living?
  (*b*) If such a warrant, having the certificate already signed by a
        person purporting to be qualified to sign it, is sent to a bank
        for the credit of the pensioner's account, is the bank bound,
        before collecting it, to ascertain by independent inquiry that
        the pensioner is living?

Answer: (*a*) A bank manager would not be justified in signing such
a certificate unless the conditions mentioned in the question were
fulfilled.
  (*b*) In *Gowers and others* v. *Lloyds and National Provincial
Foreign Bank,* [1938] W.N. 106, 54 T.L.R. 550; (Leading Cases,
4th Ed., p. 134), the bank was held to have been justified in relying
upon such certificates without verifying them, although in fact the
pensioner, without the bank's knowledge, had been dead for some
years, and the certificates had been obtained by fraud. As the money

had been paid to the bank under a mistake of fact, the bank, as
agent, was held liable to refund only the balance remaining in its
hands, but not the money which it had from time to time paid to its
principal, though the bank had been mistaken as to the identity of
the principal, supposing him to be the pensioner when in fact he was
not.

688   If money is remitted to a bank by **A** for the credit of **B**, a customer,
and an acknowledgment is given by the bank to **A**, has the bank any
responsibility in the event of a subsequent dispute between **A** and **B**
as to the amount remitted?

Answer: The bank is responsible only to its customer, **B**, for the
amount which it has received on his behalf.

689   **A**, who has an account with a branch at York, pays in money for the
credit of his account at the bank's branch at Leeds. The credit
advice fails for some reason to reach the York branch through the
credit clearing, and **A**, assuming that the amount is placed to his
credit at York, in due course issues cheques against it, which are
dishonoured. Is the bank liable to **A** for damages?

Answer: Yes.

690   Bank **A** pays a sum of money to bank **B** for the credit of a third party
stating at the time of payment that it is made 'under reserve.' A few
days later bank **A** asks for the money to be returned but offers no
reasons for the request. Is bank **A** entitled to enforce the return of
money by bank **B**?

Answer: A payment received by a bank under reserve should not
be credited until the reserve is lifted. It should be placed to a
suspense account and is repayable on demand to the remitting bank
A which need not give any reason for requesting the refund before
the reserve is lifted.

691   Are bankers obliged to give particulars of their charges at the end of
the half-year if called upon to do so? Would not 'Interest and
commission' be sufficient, and in suing for the payment of such
charges can they be called upon to give further particulars in a court
of law?

Answer: The banker should give particulars of charges if called
upon by his customer, and no doubt if the matter were contested,
would be obliged to do so.

692   A bank manager wishes to close a customer's account, but the latter
refuses to withdraw his balance.
(1) Can the bank manager send him a cheque for the balance
standing at his credit?
(2) Is he justified in dishonouring cheques on the customer's
account if presented after the cheque has been sent for the
balance at his credit?
(3) If not, what course is open to the bank manager to enable
him to rid himself of the account?

Answer: A cheque should not be sent for the balance. The usual
course would be to give reasonable notice to the customer that no
more credits would be received for his account, and to honour his
cheques only until the balance was exhausted.

In *Prosperity Limited* v. *Lloyds Bank* (1923), 39 T.L.R. 372;
(Leading Cases, 4th Ed., p. 303), it was held that before closing a
customer's account a banker must give reasonable notice, the length
of which would depend on the nature of the account, and on the
facts and circumstances of the case.

693   What should be the answer of a bank which is asked:
(*a*) by a prospective customer;
(*b*) by a customer of long standing,
not to reply without his express permission to enquiries concerning
him?

Answer: (*a*) The prospective customer should be informed that it is
normal banking practice to answer enquiries from other banks and
certain trade protection societies without reference to the customer
concerned. It could be pointed out to him with advantage that a
refusal to answer might carry an implication detrimental to him. It
would be open to the banker to refuse to accept an account on such
conditions if he thought fit.

(*b*) A banker, having accepted the account, would ignore at his
peril his customer's instructions overriding the customary practice of
bankers. Here again, the possibility of such a course being to the
customer's disadvantage could be stressed. If the banker was not
disposed to continue banking relations under such exceptional terms
it would be open to him to arrange for the account to be closed.

694   An official receiver in bankruptcy wrote to a branch bank requesting
the name and address of the customer to whose account certain
specified cheques had been credited, and the date on which they

were paid in. The reason for the request was that the cheques had been in the possession of a bankrupt, and the official receiver wished to discover how they had been dealt with.

(a) Should the bank give the required information without first obtaining the consent of the customer to whose account the cheques were credited?

(b) Would the bank incur any liability by so doing?

Answer: It is considered (*a*) that the information should not be given without the customer's consent, and (*b*) that if it were given without his consent, and he suffered injury thereby, the bank would be liable in damages.

An official receiver or trustee in bankruptcy may, under sec. 25 of the Bankruptcy Act, 1914, apply to the Court to summon and examine any person whom the Court may deem capable of giving information respecting the debtor, his dealings or property; but this does not justify anyone in giving such information without an order of the Court.

The official receiver or trustee is, of course, entitled, without an order, to full information from the debtor's bankers with regard to the debtor's banking transactions, but not to those of other persons.

For a statement of the qualifications of the contractual duty of secrecy implied in the relation of banker and customer, see *Tournier* v. *National Provincial Bank*, [1924] 1 K.B. 461; (Leading Cases, 4th Ed., p. 6).

695 (*a*) The plaintiff's solicitors in a civil action, or (*b*) the police in a criminal prosecution, procure the issue of a subpoena requiring the attendance of the defendant's bankers to produce in Court a copy of his banking account. The solicitors, or the police, request the bankers to let them have the copy before the hearing, in order that they may prepare their case. Should the bankers comply?

Answer: It is considered that the bankers should not produce the copy before the hearing in Court, unless the customer consents to their doing so. If the solicitors or the police require the information in advance, they should obtain an order of the Court allowing them to inspect the banker's books, under sec. 7 of the Bankers' Books Evidence Act, 1879.

(See *Tournier* v. *National Provincial Bank*, [1924] 1 K.B. 461; Leading Cases, 4th Ed., p. 6; *Williams and Others* v. *Summerfield* [1972] 2 Q.B. 513, Leading Cases, 4th Ed., p. 11.)

696 Is there any specific length of time required by law during which it is necessary to keep old letters, credit and debit slips, cheques, bank ledgers, etc., before destroying them?

Answer: There is no specific length of time required by law, during which it is necessary to keep old letters, credit and debit slips, cheques, bank ledgers, etc., before destroying them. The only ground upon which it is usually thought unnecessary to retain for more than six years bank ledgers etc. is that at the end of that time the debt is statute-barred, but there may be reasons why it may be desirable to preserve evidence of business transactions for a period much longer than six years, and it is impossible to lay down any general rule which will apply to every case. Most banks have their own internal regulations on the subject.

697 Does the imprisonment of a customer affect the conduct of his banking account?

Answer: No. His civil rights are not affected but he will be unable to conduct normal business whilst in prison as he is not allowed to retain his cheque book. He will, however, be permitted by the prison Governor to attend to any essential business and his relationship with the bank will not be affected. He will be inconvenienced rather than incapacitated.

698 Using his cheque card, a customer of **X** branch cashes his cheque for £20 at **Y** branch; but when the cheque reaches the drawee branch there is a credit balance of only £16 to meet it, and no arrangement for an overdraft has been made.
 Can the bank appropriate the £16 in part payment of the cheque?

Answer: On presentation of any cheque, there is a choice of paying or returning it. In this instance it obviously must be paid and the usual course would be to debit the customer's account at the drawee branch with the cheque, creating an overdraft of £4.

699 A customer who, for exchange control purposes, is regarded as a resident of the UK calls at his bank and produces a foreign currency security which had been forwarded to him by lawyers in the United States under the terms of a legacy of a deceased relative. He requests the bank to arrange for the security to be sold on his behalf and enquires of them whether the proceeds of the sale would be 'premium worthy'. What action should the bank take?

Answer: Note A of the Exchange Control Notice E.C.7 which relates to foreign currency securities states that such securities should not be disposed of without the Bank of England's permission. Such permission is normally given by the Bank of England on condition that the securities are to be sold for foreign currency and that the proceeds are offered for sale without re-investment rights, to an Authorised Dealer in the manner described. Therefore, the bank should apply to the Bank of England for such permission to enable them to sell the security on behalf of their customer and the customer should be informed that the proceeds would not be 'premium worthy'.

700 A non-resident customer of the bank who maintains a foreign currency account in the books of the bank's 'foreign' branch calls with cheques value, say, US$10,000, and requests that his currency account be credited with these dollars immediately. What action should the bank take?

Answer: The cheques should be forwarded by airmail by the overseas branch to their New York correspondents with instructions for the bank's nostro account to be credited immediately with US$10,000.

Since the branch's account abroad cannot possibly be credited with this sum until the arrival of the cheques in New York, the bank may decline the request to credit the customer's dollar account immediately since to do so would mean that the customer would be obtaining value even before the bank's account had been credited.

Most banks are now able to arrange for the remittance to be made to the USA and for credit to be obtained within three days and in principle therefore the customer should receive value only after an appropriate transit time, unless he is prepared to meet the bank's claim for interest for the period it is out of funds.

In practice in some banks, however, the customer's foreign currency account would in any case be credited at the time the cheques were lodged, the bank taking due account of the 'uncleared' element in the balance until a suitable time had elapsed, and likewise probably making an appropriate interest adjustment.

CONSUMER CREDIT ACT

Although the Consumer Credit Act became law in July, 1974 its various sections are being brought into effect only gradually and its full effect is still largely untested.

Its impact on day-to-day branch banking business is not expected to be of great significance especially as:

" (i) *Company borrowing is unaffected.*

(ii) *Borrowing of £5,000 and over is unaffected.*

(iii) *Overdrafts may be canvassed from existing account holders free of the canvassing restrictions in the Act.*

(iv) *It is expected that all bank overdrafts will be excluded from Part V which covers the provisions relating to antecedent negotiations, cancellations, the terms and signing of the agreement, the supplying of copies of the agreement, the application of the cooling-off period and the recovery of money borrowed".**

It is thought that branches should experience few problems if Head Office guidelines on personal lending are observed.

The following situations are hypothetical and merely attempt to illustrate some of the areas where difficulties could arise.

701 A gentleman is shown into your office and identifies himself as a Consumer Protection Officer employed by the Local Authority. He says he is investigating a complaint made by Mr. **A,** a former customer, who closed his account in an acrimonious letter about charges. The C.P.O. asks to see Mr. **A**'s account. What do you say?

Answer: First we must establish the nature of **A**'s complaint and whether it relates to borrowing from the branch. If **A** never borrowed or the complaint to the C.P.O. is unrelated to 'credit', the C.P.O. has no powers under the Consumer Credit Act enabling him to see any of the bank's records.

If it transpires that the complaint does concern your branch's relationship with **A** as a borrower and the complaint is that **A** has been overcharged, a possible allegation of an 'extortionate credit bargain' emerges and it matters not when the advance was made or repaid. There is no need for the advance to be one entered into after 1 April, 1977 and thus a 'Regulated Agreement' within the meaning of the Act. The C.P.O. has a legitimate interest in the case.

By arrangement with the Office of Fair Trading, C.P.O.'s will need authority from the Director of Fair Trading to exercise rights of

*Gilbart Lectures on Banking, 1978 by Frank Ryder, LL.B., F.I.B.

entry and inspection, and in normal circumstances it is expected that his visit will be by appointment arranged through Head Office.

In all cases of unexpected visits by C.P.O.'s reference should be made to Head Office.

702   Your customer **B** owns and manages a small garage which involves credit-broking and debt-adjusting in its car dealing side. An overdraft limit is marked for the company. **B** is killed in a road accident and his executrix widow has to take over the business. She has no experience and calls to ask you for advice. What do you say to her?

Answer: It is not part of the bank's business to give legal advice to customers, so an urgent appointment for Mrs. **B** to see her legal adviser is appropriate. However, certain licensing provisions of the Act should be considered and drawn to the attention of Mrs. **B** and her solicitor. Licences under the Act are granted to named individuals and companies. As debt-adjusting is involves, you will have seen Mr. **B**'s licence. If the licence names him only, Mrs. **B** will be entitled to seek deferment of the licence termination which is automatic on the death of Mr. **B**. She will need to make application in the proper form within two months of Mr. **B**'s death.

If the garage business is a limited company, the company's licence is not terminated but any change in the directorate must be notified to the Office of Fair Trading within 21 days.

If by chance Mrs. **B** is named personally as the holder of any licence under the Act, perhaps jointly with her husband, she may, in her capacity as executrix, take advantage of the group licence available to executors. However, before the estate is wound up the new owner of the business must be personally licensed.

703   **C** Ltd., a substantial retailer customer, makes considerable use of the bankers opinion service through your branch and this is borne in mind when the company's charges are assessed. An individual calls at your branch and complains that he has been refused credit by **C** Ltd. as a result of an enquiry made by **C** Ltd. through your branch. He asks for a copy of his file and tenders 25 pence. You find that the individual is a customer of another bank. How do you respond to the aggrieved individual? Do you take any further steps?

Answer: In the opinion of the Office of Fair Trading and Counsel, the bank is not a Credit Reference Agency within the meaning of the

Act, as it does not collect information on its customers *for the purpose of* making the information available to third parties.

The aggrieved individual must be informed that the bank is not a credit reference agency as defined and in no circumstances do the credit reference agency rules apply to the bank.

(It will be appreciated that the status of the bank is at present a matter of *opinion*. Should that opinion be proved wrong in Court, the implications for the bank in opening its files to customers are so serious that the Bankers Opinion service might be withdrawn. It might be suggested that specific charging for opinions in some way changes the bank's status. While there is no reason to believe that reimbursement of costs affects the issue, an action which scrutinised the bank's status might be provoked by such charges. To avoid such possibility, specific charges should be avoided).

704 On 10 April, 1977 you made a Regulated Agreement for a loan to Mr. **G,** the rate of interest being 4% over base rate. On 15 October, 1977 Base Rate was increased by 2% but, through an oversight the notice displayed in the branch was not changed. On 4 February, 1978 Mr. **G** calls and complains that he has been overcharged in loan interest. How would you deal with the situation?

Answer: A technical breach of the order governing variations of regulated agreements has been committed. Section 82 provides that variations (in this case the change of the actual rate charged following the change of base rate) only take effect when notice is given in the prescribed manner. In these circumstances the change of rate does not take effect, not only in the case of Mr. **G**'s loan, but also for every other Regulated Agreement in the Branch where interest is geared to base rate. Not only has Mr. **G** the right to a refund of additional interest charged at the higher rate but he may feel it appropriate to tell his friends.

The oversight can prove costly in cash refunds and in effort required to re-work charges whenever required.

APPENDIX A

UNIFORM CUSTOMS AND PRACTICE FOR DOCUMENTARY
CREDITS (1974 Revision)

International Chamber of Commerce Publication No. 290

GENERAL PROVISIONS AND DEFINITIONS

(a) These provisions and definitions and the following articles apply to all documentary credits and are binding upon all parties thereto unless otherwise expressly agreed.

(b) For the purposes of such provisions, definitions and articles the expressions 'documentary credit(s)' and 'credit(s)' used therein mean any arrangement, however named or described, whereby a bank (the issuing bank), acting at the request and in accordance with the instructions of a customer (the applicant for the credit),

  (i) is to make payment to or to the order of a third party (the beneficiary), or is to pay, accept or negotiate bills of exchange (drafts) drawn by the beneficiary, or

  (ii) authorises such payments to be made or such drafts to be paid, accepted or negotiated by another bank,

against stipulated documents, provided that the terms and conditions of the credit are complied with.

(c) Credits, by their nature, are separate transactions from the sales or other contracts on which they may be based and banks are in no way concerned with or bound by such contracts.

(d) Credit instructions and the credits themselves must be complete and precise.

In order to guard against confusion and misunderstanding, issuing banks should discourage any attempt by the applicant for the credit to include excessive detail.

(e) The bank first entitled to exercise the option available under Article 32b shall be the bank authorised to pay, accept or negotiate under a credit. The decision of such bank shall bind all parties concerned.

A bank is authorised to pay or accept under a credit by being specifically nominated in the credit.

A bank is authorised to negotiate under a credit either

  (i) by being specifically nominated in the credit, or

  (ii) by the credit being freely negotiable by any bank.

(*f*) A beneficiary can in no case avail himself of the contractual relationships existing between banks or between the applicant for the credit and the issuing bank.

A. FORM AND NOTIFICATION OF CREDITS
Article 1
(*a*) Credits may be either
    (i) revocable, or
    (ii) irrevocable.
(*b*) All credits, therefore, should clearly indicate whether they are revocable or irrevocable.
(*c*) In the absence of such indication the credit shall be deemed to be revocable.

Article 2
A revocable credit may be amended or cancelled at any moment without prior notice to the beneficiary. However, the issuing bank is bound to reimburse a branch or other bank to which such a credit has been transmitted and made available for payment, acceptance or negotiation, for any payment, acceptance or negotiation complying with the terms and conditions of the credit and any amendments received up to the time of payment, acceptance or negotiation made by such branch or other bank prior to receipt by it of notice of amendment or of cancellation.

Article 3
(*a*) An irrevocable credit constitutes a definite undertaking of the issuing bank, provided that the terms and conditions of the credit are complied with:
    (i) to pay, or that payment will be made, if the credit provides for payment, whether against a draft or not;
    (ii) to accept drafts if the credit provides for acceptance by the issuing bank or to be responsible for their acceptance and payment at maturity if the credit provides for the acceptance of drafts drawn on the applicant for the credit or any other drawee specified in the credit;
    (iii) to purchase/negotiate, without recourse to drawers and/or bona fide holders, drafts drawn by the beneficiary, at sight or at a tenor, on the applicant for the credit or on any other drawee specified in the credit, or to provide for purchase/negotiation by another bank, if the credit provides for purchase/negotiation.
(*b*) An irrevocable credit may be advised to a beneficiary through

another bank (the advising bank) without engagement on the part of that bank, but when an issuing bank authorises or requests another bank to confirm its irrevocable credit and the latter does so, such confirmation constitutes a definite undertaking of the confirming bank in addition to the undertaking of the issuing bank, provided that the terms and conditions of the credit are complied with:

  (i) to pay, if the credit is payable at its own counters, whether against a draft or not, or that payment will be made if the credit provides for payment elsewhere;

 (ii) to accept drafts if the credit provides for acceptance by the confirming bank, at its own counters, or to be responsible for their acceptance and payment at maturity if the credit provides for the acceptance of drafts drawn on the applicant for the credit or any other drawee specified in the credit;

(iii) to purchase/negotiate, without recourse to drawers and/or bona fide holders, drafts drawn by the beneficiary, at sight or at a tenor, on the issuing bank, or on the applicant for the credit or on any other drawee specified in the credit, if the credit provides for purchase/negotiation.

(c) Such undertakings can neither be amended nor cancelled without the agreement of all parties thereto. Partial acceptance of amendments is not effective without the agreement of all parties thereto.

Article 4

(a) When an issuing bank instructs a bank by cable, telegram or telex to advise a credit, and intends the mail confirmation to be the operative credit instrument, the cable, telegram or telex must state that the credit will only be effective on receipt of such mail confirmation. In this event, the issuing bank must send the operative credit instrument (mail confirmation) and any subsequent amendments to the credit to the beneficiary through the advising bank.

(b) The issuing bank will be responsible for any consequences arising from its failure to follow the procedure set out in the preceding paragraph.

(c) Unless a cable, telegram or telex states 'details to follow' (or words of similar effect), or states that the mail confirmation is to be the operative credit instrument, the cable, telegram or telex will be deemed to be the operative credit instrument and the issuing bank need not send the mail confirmation to the advising bank.

Article 5

When a bank is instructed by cable, telegram or telex to issue, confirm or advise a credit similar in terms to one previously established and which has been the subject of amendments, it shall be understood that the details of the credit being issued, confirmed or advised will be transmitted to the beneficiary excluding the amendments, unless the instructions specify clearly any amendments which are to apply.

Article 6

If incomplete or unclear instructions are received to issue, confirm or advise a credit, the bank requested to act on such instructions may give preliminary notification of the credit to the beneficiary for information only and without responsibility; in this event the credit will be issued, confirmed or advised only when the necessary information has been received.

B. LIABILITIES AND RESPONSIBILITIES

Article 7

Banks must examine all documents with reasonable care to ascertain that they appear on their face to be in accordance with the terms and conditions of the credit. Documents which appear on their face to be inconsistent with one another will be considered as not appearing on their face to be in accordance with the terms and conditions of the credit.

Article 8

(a) In documentary credit operations all parties concerned deal in documents and not in goods.

(b) Payment, acceptance or negotiation against documents which appear on their face to be in accordance with the terms and conditions of a credit by a bank authorised to do so, binds the party giving the authorisation to take up the documents and reimburse the bank which has effected the payment, acceptance or negotiation.

(c) If, upon receipt of the documents, the issuing bank considers that they appear on their face not to be in accordance with the terms and conditions of the credit, that bank must determine, on the basis of the documents alone, whether to claim that payment, acceptance or negotiation was not effected in accordance with the terms and conditions of the credit.

(d) The issuing bank shall have a reasonable time to examine the documents and to determine as above whether to make such a claim.

(e) If such claim is to be made, notice to that effect, stating the reasons therefore, must, without delay, be given by cable or other expeditious means to the bank from which the documents have been received (the remitting bank) and such notice must state that the documents are being held at the disposal of such bank or are being returned thereto.

(f) If the issuing bank fails to hold the documents at the disposal of the remitting bank, or fails to return the documents to such bank, the issuing bank shall be precluded from claiming that the relative payment, acceptance or negotiation was not effected in accordance with the terms and conditions of the credit.

(g) If the remitting bank draws the attention of the issuing bank to any irregularities in the documents or advises such bank that it has paid, accepted or negotiated under reserve or against a guarantee in respect of such irregularities, the issuing bank shall not thereby be relieved from any of its obligations under this article. Such guarantee or reserve concerns only the relations between the remitting bank and the beneficiary.

Article 9

Banks assume no liability or responsibility for the form, sufficiency, accuracy, genuineness, falsification or legal effect of any documents, or for the general and/or particular conditions stipulated in the documents or superimposed thereon; nor do they assume any liability or responsibility for the description, quantity, weight, quality, condition, packing, delivery, value or existence of the goods represented thereby, or for the good faith or acts and/or omissions, solvency, performance or standing of the consignor, the carriers or the insurers of the goods or any other person whomsoever.

Article 10

Banks assume no liability or responsibility for the consequences arising out of delay and/or loss in transit of any messages, letters or documents, or for delay, mutilation or other errors arising in the transmission of cables, telegrams or telex. Banks assume no liability or responsibility for errors in translation or interpretation of technical terms, and reserve the right to transmit credit terms without translating them.

Article 11

Banks assume no liability or responsibility for consequences arising out of the interruption of their business by Acts of God, riots, civil commotions, insurrections, wars or any other causes beyond their control or by any strikes or lockouts. Unless specifically authorised, banks will not effect payment, acceptance or negotiation after expiration under credits expiring during such interruption of business.

Article 12

(a) Banks utilising the services of another bank for the purpose of giving effect to the instructions of the applicant for the credit do so for the account and at the risk of the latter.

(b) Banks assume no liability or responsibility should the instructions they transmit not be carried out, even if they have themselves taken the initiative in the choice of such other bank.

(c) The applicant for the credit shall be bound by and liable to indemnify the banks against all obligations and responsibilities imposed by foreign laws and usages.

Article 13

A paying or negotiating bank which has been authorised to claim reimbursement from a third bank nominated by the issuing bank and which has effected such payment or negotiation shall not be required to confirm to the third bank that it has done so in accordance with the terms and conditions of the credit.

C. DOCUMENTS

Article 14

(a) All instructions to issue, confirm or advise a credit must state precisely the documents against which payment, acceptance or negotiation is to be made.

(b) Terms such as 'first class', 'well known', 'qualified' and the like shall not be used to describe the issuers of any documents called for under credits and if they are incorporated in the credit terms banks will accept documents as tendered.

C. 1 Documents evidencing shipment or dispatch or taking in charge (*shipping documents*).

Article 15

Except as stated in Article 20, the date of the Bill of Lading, or the date of any other document evidencing shipment or dispatch or taking in charge, or the date indicated in the reception stamp or by notation on any such document, will be taken in each case to be the date of shipment or dispatch or taking in charge of the goods.

Article 16

(*a*) If words clearly indicating payment or prepayment of freight, however named or described, appear by stamp or otherwise on documents evidencing shipment or dispatch or taking in charge they will be accepted as constituting evidence of payment of freight.

(*b*) If the words 'freight pre-payable' or 'freight to be prepaid' or words of similar effect appear by stamp or otherwise on such documents they will not be accepted as constituting evidence of the payment of freight.

(*c*) Unless otherwise specified in the credit or inconsistent with any of the documents presented under the credit, banks will accept documents stating that freight or transportation charges are payable on delivery.

(*d*) Banks will accept shipping documents bearing reference by stamp or otherwise to costs additional to the freight charges, such as costs of, or disbursements incurred in connection with, loading, unloading or similar operations, unless the conditions of the credit specifically prohibit such reference.

Article 17

Shipping documents which bear a clause on the face thereof such as 'shipper's load and count' or 'said by shipper to contain' or words of similar effect, will be accepted unless otherwise specified in the credit.

Article 18

(*a*) A clean shipping document is one which bears no super-imposed clause or notation which expressly declares a defective condition of the goods and/or the packaging.

(*b*) Banks will refuse shipping documents bearing such clauses or notations unless the credit expressly states the clauses or notations which may be accepted.

C. 1.1 Marine Bills of Lading
Article 19

(*a*) Unless specifically authorised in the credit, Bills of Lading of the following nature will be rejected:
    (i) Bills of Lading issued by forwarding agents.
    (ii) Bills of Lading which are issued under and are subject to the conditions of a Charter-Party.

  (iii) Bills of Lading covering shipment by sailing vessels.
(b) However, subject to the above and unless otherwise specified
    in the credit, Bills of Lading of the following nature will be
    accepted:
    (i) Through Bills of Lading issued by shipping companies or
        their agents even though they cover several modes of
        transport.
    (ii) Short Form Bills of Lading (i.e. Bills of Lading issued by
        shipping companies or their agents which indicate some
        or all of the conditions of carriage by reference to a source
        or document other than the Bill of Lading).
    (iii) Bills of Lading issued by shipping companies or their
        agents covering unitised cargoes, such as those on pallets
        or in Containers.

Article 20
(a) Unless otherwise specified in the credit, Bills of Lading must
    show that the goods are loaded on board a named vessel or
    shipped on a named vessel.
(b) Loading on board a named vessel or shipment on a named
    vessel may be evidenced either by a Bill of Lading bearing
    wording indicating loading on board a named vessel or
    shipment on a named vessel, or by means of a notation to that
    effect on the Bill of Lading signed or initialled and dated by the
    carrier or his agent, and the date of this notation shall be
    regarded as the date of loading on board the named vessel or
    shipment on the named vessel.

Article 21
(a) Unless transhipment is prohibited by the terms of the credit,
    Bills of Lading will be accepted which indicate that the goods
    will be transhipped en route, provided the entire voyage is
    covered by one and the same Bill of Lading.
(b) Bills of Lading incorporating printed clauses stating that the
    carriers have the right to tranship will be accepted notwith-
    standing the fact that the credit prohibits transhipment.

Article 22
(a) Banks will refuse a Bill of Lading stating that the goods are
    loaded on deck, unless specifically authorised in the credit.
(b) Banks will not refuse a Bill of Lading which contains a
    provision that the goods may be carried on deck, provided it
    does not specifically state that they are loaded on deck.

C.1.2 Combined transport documents.
Article 23

(*a*) If the credit calls for a combined transport document, i.e. one which provides for a combined transport by at least two different modes of transport, from a place at which the goods are taken in charge to a place designated for delivery, or if the credit provides for a combined transport, but in either case does not specify the form of document required and/or the issuer of such document, banks will accept such documents as tendered.

(*b*) If the combined transport includes transport by sea the document will be accepted although it does not indicate that the goods are on board a named vessel, and although it contains a provision that the goods, if packed in a Container, may be carried on deck, provided it does not specifically state that they are loaded on deck.

C.1.3 Other shipping documents, etc.
Article 24

Banks will consider a Railway or Inland Waterway Bill of Lading or Consignment Note, Counterfoil Waybill, Postal Receipt, Certificate of Mailing, Air Mail Receipt, Air Waybill, Air Consignment Note or Air Receipt, Trucking Company Bill of Lading or any other similar document as regular when such document bears the reception stamp of the carrier or his agent, or when it bears a signature purporting to be that of the carrier or his agent.

Article 25

Where a credit calls for an attestation or certification of weight in the case of transport other than by sea, banks will accept a weight stamp or declaration of weight superimposed by the carrier on the shipping document unless the credit calls for a separate or independent certificate of weight.

C. 2 Insurance documents.
Article 26

(*a*) Insurance documents must be as specified in the credit, and must be issued and/or signed by insurance companies or their agents or by underwriters.

(*b*) Cover notes issued by brokers will not be accepted, unless specifically authorised in the credit.

Article 27

Unless otherwise specified in the credit, or unless the insurance

documents presented establish that the cover is effective at the latest
from the date of shipment or dispatch or, in the case of combined
transport, the date of taking the goods in charge, banks will refuse
insurance documents presented which bear a date later than the
date of shipment or dispatch or, in the case of combined transport,
the date of taking the goods in charge, as evidenced by the shipping
documents.

Article 28
(a) Unless otherwise specified in the credit, the insurance
    document must be expressed in the same currency as the credit.
(b) The minimum amount for which insurance must be effected
    is the CIF value of the goods concerned. However, when the
    CIF value of the goods cannot be determined from the
    documents on their face, banks will accept as such minimum
    amount the amount of the drawing under the credit or the
    amount of the relative commercial invoice, whichever is the
    greater.

Article 29
(a) Credits should expressly state the type of insurance required
    and, if any, the additional risks which are to be covered.
    Imprecise terms such as 'usual risks' or 'customary risks'
    should not be used; however, if such imprecise terms are used,
    banks will accept insurance documents as tendered.
(b) Failing specific instructions, banks will accept insurance cover
    as tendered.

Article 30
Where a credit stipulates 'insurance against all risks', banks will
accept an insurance document which contains any 'all risks'
notation or clause, and will assume no responsibility if any
particular risk is not covered.

Article 31
Banks will accept an insurance document which indicates that the
cover is subject to a franchise or an excess (deductible), unless it is
specifically stated in the credit that the insurance must be issued
irrespective of percentage.

C.3 Commercial invoices
Article 32
(a) Unless otherwise specified in the credit, commercial invoices
    must be made out in the name of the applicant for the credit.
(b) Unless otherwise specified in the credit, banks may refuse

commercial invoices issued for amounts in excess of the amount permitted by the credit.

(c) The description of the goods in the commercial invoice must correspond with the description in the credit. In all other documents the goods may be described in general terms not inconsistent with the description of the goods in the credit.

C.4 Other documents.

Article 33

When other documents are required, such as Warehouse Receipts, Delivery Orders, Consular Invoices, Certificates of Origin, of Weight, of Quality or of Analysis, etc., and when no further definition is given, banks will accept such documents as tendered.

D. MISCELLANEOUS PROVISIONS

Quantity and amount.

Article 34

(a) The words 'about', 'circa' or similar expressions used in connection with the amount of the credit or the quantity or the unit price of the goods are to be construed as allowing a difference not to exceed 10 per cent more or 10 per cent less.

(b) Unless a credit stipulates that the quantity of the goods specified must not be exceeded or reduced a tolerance of 3 per cent more or 3 per cent less will be permissible, always provided that the total amount of the drawings does not exceed the amount of the credit. This tolerance does not apply when the credit specifies quantity in terms of a stated number of packing units or individual items.

Partial shipments.

Article 35

(a) Partial shipments are allowed, unless the credit specifically states otherwise.

(b) Shipments made on the same ship and for the same voyage, even if the Bills of Lading evidencing shipment 'on board' bear different dates and/or indicate different ports of shipment, will not be regarded as partial shipments.

Article 36

If shipment by instalments within given periods is stipulated and any instalment is not shipped within the period allowed for that instalment, the credit ceases to be available for that or any subsequent instalments, unless otherwise specified in the credit.

Expiry date.
Article 37
All credits, whether revocable or irrevocable, must stipulate an expiry date for presentation of documents for payment, acceptance or negotiation, notwithstanding the stipulation of a latest date for shipment.

Article 38
The words 'to', 'until', 'till', and words of similar import applying to the stipulated expiry date for presentation of documents for payment, acceptance or negotiation, or to the stipulated latest date for shipment, will be understood to include the date mentioned.

Article 39
(a) When the stipulated expiry date falls on a day on which banks are closed for reasons other than those mentioned in Article 11, the expiry date will be extended until the first following business day.
(b) The latest date for shipment shall not be extended by reason of the extension of the expiry date in accordance with this Article. Where the credit stipulates a latest date for shipment, shipping documents dated later than such stipulated date will not be accepted. If no latest date for shipment is stipulated in the credit, shipping documents dated later than the expiry date stipulated in the credit or amendments thereto will not be accepted. Documents other than the shipping documents may, however, be dated up to and including the extended expiry date.
(c) Banks paying, accepting or negotiating on such extended expiry date must add to the documents their certification in the following wording:
'Presented for payment (or acceptance or negotiation as the case may be) within the expiry date extended in accordance with Article 39 of the **Uniform Customs.**'

Shipment, loading or dispatch.
Article 40
(a) Unless the terms of the credit indicate otherwise, the words 'departure', 'dispatch', 'loading' or 'sailing' used in stipulating the latest date for shipment of the goods will be understood to be synonymous with 'shipment'.
(b) Expressions such as 'prompt', 'immediately', 'as soon as possible' and the like should not be used. If they are used, banks will interpret them as a request for shipment within

thirty days from the date on the advice of the credit to the beneficiary by the issuing bank or by an advising bank, as the case may be.

(c)   The expression 'on or about' and similar expressions will be interpreted as a request for shipment during the period from five days before to five days after the specified date, both end days included.

Presentation.
Article 41
Notwithstanding the requirement of Article 37 that every credit must stipulate an expiry date for presentation of documents, credits must also stipulate a specified period of time after the date of issuance of the Bills of Lading or other shipping documents during which presentation of documents for payment, acceptance or negotiation must be made. If no such period of time is stipulated in the credit, banks will refuse documents presented to them later than 21 days after the date of issuance of the Bills of Lading or other shipping documents.

Article 42
Banks are under no obligation to accept presentation of documents outside their banking hours.

Date terms.
Article 43
The terms 'first half', 'second half' of a month shall be construed respectively as from the 1st to the 15th and the 16th to the last day of each month, inclusive.

Article 44
The terms 'beginning', 'middle', or 'end' of a month shall be construed respectively as from the 1st to the 10th, the 11th to the 20th, and the 21st to the last day of each month, inclusive.

Article 45
When a bank issuing a credit instructs that the credit be confirmed or advised as available 'for one month', 'for six months' or the like, but does not specify the date from which the time is to run, the confirming or advising bank will confirm or advise the credit as expiring at the end of such indicated period from the date of its confirmation or advice.

E. TRANSFER
Article 46
(a)   A transferable credit is a credit under which the beneficiary has

the right to give instructions to the bank called upon to effect payment or acceptance or to any bank entitled to effect negotiation to make the credit available in whole or in part to one or more third parties (second beneficiaries).

(b) The bank requested to effect the transfer, whether it has confirmed the credit or not, shall be under no obligation to effect such transfer except to the extent and in the manner expressly consented to by such bank, and until such bank's charges in respect of transfer are paid.

(c) Bank charges in respect of transfers are payable by the first beneficiary unless otherwise specified.

(d) A credit can be transferred only if it is expressly designated as 'transferable' by the issuing bank. Terms such as 'divisible', 'fractionnable', 'assignable', and 'transmissible' add nothing to the meaning of the term 'transferable' and shall not be used.

(e) A transferable credit can be transferred once only. Fractions of a transferable credit (not exceeding in the aggregate the amount of the credit) can be transferred separately, provided partial shipments are not prohibited, and the aggregate of such transfers will be considered as constituting only one transfer of the credit. The credit can be transferred only on the terms and conditions specified in the original credit, with the exception of the amount of the credit, of any unit prices stated therein, and of the period of validity or period for shipment, any or all of which may be reduced or curtailed.

Additionally, the name of the first beneficiary can be substituted for that of the applicant for the credit, but if the name of the applicant for the credit is specifically required by the original credit to appear in any document other than the invoice, such requirement must be fulfilled.

(f) The first beneficiary has the right to substitute his own invoices for those of the second beneficiary, for amounts not in excess of the original amount stipulated in the credit and for the original unit prices if stipulated in the credit, and upon such substitution of invoices the first beneficiary can draw under the credit for the difference, if any, between his invoices and the second beneficiary's invoices. When a credit has been transferred and the first beneficiary is to supply his own invoices in exchange for the second beneficiary's invoices but fails to do so on first demand, the paying, accepting or negotiating bank has the right to deliver to the issuing bank the documents received under the credit, including the second beneficiary's invoices, without further responsibility to the first beneficiary.

(g) The first beneficiary of a transferable credit can transfer the credit to a second beneficiary in the same country or in another country unless the credit specifically states otherwise. The first beneficiary shall have the right to request that payment or negotiation be effected to the second beneficiary at the place to which the credit has been transferred, up to and including the expiry date of the original credit, and without prejudice to the first beneficiary's right subsequently to substitute his own invoices for those of the second beneficiary and to claim any difference due to him.

Article 47

The fact that a credit is not stated to be transferable shall not affect the beneficiary's rights to assign the proceeds of such credit in accordance with the provisions of the applicable law.

Reproduced by courtesy of and with the permission of the International Chamber of Commerce.

Copyright © ICC 1974
publication no 290
available from

ICC Services S.A.R.L.
38 Cours Albert 1er
75008 PARIS

and from the

British National Committee of the ICC
6/14 Dean Farrar Street
LONDON SW1H 0DT.

APPENDIX B

UNIFORM RULES FOR COLLECTIONS
(Effective 1 January, 1979)

International Chamber of Commerce Publication No. 322

GENERAL PROVISIONS AND DEFINITIONS

(*a*) These provisions and definitions and the following articles apply to all collections as defined in (*b*) below and are binding upon all parties thereto unless otherwise expressly agreed or unless contrary to the provisions of a national, state or local law and/or regulation which cannot be departed from.

(*b*) For the purpose of such provisions, definitions and articles:

1. (i) 'Collection' means the handling by banks, on instructions received, of documents as defined in (ii) below, in order to
     (a) obtain acceptance and/or, as the case may be, payment, or
     (b) deliver commercial documents against acceptance and/ or, as the case may be, against payment, or
     (c) deliver documents on other terms and conditions.

    (ii) 'Documents' means financial documents and/or commercial documents
     (a) 'financial documents' means bills of exchange, promissory notes, cheques, payment receipts or other similar instruments used for obtaining the payment of money;
     (b) 'commercial documents' means invoices, shipping documents, documents of title or other similar documents, or any other documents whatsoever, not being financial documents.

    (iii) 'Clean collection' means collection of financial documents not accompanied by commercial documents.

    (iv) 'Documentary Collection' means collection of
     (a) financial documents accompanied by commercial documents;
     (b) commercial documents not accompanied by financial documents.

2. The 'parties thereto' are:
    (i) the 'principal' who is the customer entrusting the operation of collection to his bank;
    (ii) the 'remitting bank' which is the bank to which the principal has entrusted the operation of collection;

    (iii) the 'collecting bank' which is any bank, other than the remitting bank, involved in processing the collection order;

    (iv) the 'presenting bank' which is the collecting bank making presentation to the drawee.

3. The 'drawee' is the one to whom presentation is to be made according to the collection order.

(c) All documents sent for collection must be accompanied by a collection order giving complete and precise instructions. Banks are only permitted to act upon the instructions given in such collection order, and in accordance with these rules.

If any bank cannot, for any reason, comply with the instructions given in the collection order received by it, it must immediately advise the party from whom it received the collection order.

LIABILITIES AND RESPONSIBILITIES

Article 1

Banks will act in good faith and exercise reasonable care.

Article 2

Banks must verify that the documents received appear to be as listed in the collection order and must immediately advise the party from whom the collection order was received of any documents missing.

Banks have no further obligation to examine the documents.

Article 3

For the purpose of giving effect to the instructions of the principal, the remitting bank will utilise as the collecting bank:

    (i) the collecting bank nominated by the principal, or, in the absence of such nomination,

    (ii) any bank, of its own or another bank's choice, in the country of payment or acceptance, as the case may be.

The documents and the collection order may be sent to the collecting bank directly or through another bank as intermediary.

Banks utilising the services of other banks for the purpose of giving effect to the instructions of the principal do so for the account of and at the risk of the latter.

The principal shall be bound by and liable to indemnify the banks against all obligations and responsibilities imposed by foreign laws or usages.

Article 4

Banks concerned with a collection assume no liability or responsibility for the consequences arising out of delay and/or loss in transit of any messages, letters or documents, or for delay, mutilation or other errors arising in the transmission of cables, telegrams, telex, or communication by electronic systems, or for errors in translation or interpretation of technical terms.

Article 5
Banks concerned with a collection assume no liability or responsibility for consequences arising out of the interruption of their business by Acts of God, riots, civil commotions, insurrections, wars, or any other causes beyond their control or by any strikes or lockouts.

Article 6
Goods should not be dispatched direct to the address of a bank or consigned to a bank without prior agreement on the part of that bank.

In the event of goods being dispatched direct to the address of a bank or consigned to a bank for delivery to a drawee against payment or acceptance or upon other terms without prior agreement on the part of that bank, the bank has no obligation to take delivery of the goods, which remain at the risk and responsibility of the party dispatching the goods.

PRESENTATION

Article 7 .
Documents are to be presented to the drawee in the form in which they are received, except that remitting and collecting banks are authorized to affix any necessary stamps, at the expense of the principal unless otherwise instructed, and to make any necessary endorsements or place any rubber stamps or other identifying marks or symbols customary to or required for the collection operation.

Article 8
Collection orders should bear the complete address of the drawee or of the domicile at which presentation is to be made. If the address is incomplete or incorrect, the collecting bank may, without obligation and responsibility on its part, endeavour to ascertain the proper address.

Article 9
In the case of documents payable at sight the presenting bank must make presentation for payment without delay.

In the case of documents payable at a tenor other than sight the presenting bank must, where acceptance is called for, make presentation for acceptance without delay, and where payment is called for, make presentation for payment not later than the appropriate maturity date.

Article 10
In respect of a documentary collection including a bill of exchange payable at a future date, the collection order should state whether the commercial documents are to be released to the drawee against acceptance (D/A) or against payment (D/P).

In the absence of such statement, the commercial documents will be released only against payment.

PAYMENT

Article 11

In the case of documents payable in the currency of the country of payment (local currency), the presenting bank must, unless otherwise instructed in the collection order, only release the documents to the drawee against payment in local currency which is immediately available for disposal in the manner specified in the collection order.

Article 12

In the case of documents payable in a currency other than that of the country of payment (foreign currency) the presenting bank must, unless otherwise instructed in the collection order, only release the documents to the drawee against payment in the relative foreign currency which can immediately be remitted in accordance with the instructions given in the collection order.

Article 13

In respect of clean collections partial payments may be accepted if and to the extent to which and on the conditions on which partial payments are authorized by the law in force in the place of payment. The documents will only be released to the drawee when full payment thereof has been received.

In respect of documentary collections partial payments will only be accepted if specifically authorized in the collection order. However, unless otherwise instructed, the presenting bank will only release the documents to the drawee after full payment has been received.

In all cases partial payments will only be accepted subject to compliance with the provisions of either Article 11 or Article 12 as appropriate.

Partial payment, if accepted, will be dealt with in accordance with the provisions of Article 14.

Article 14

Amounts collected (less charges and/or disbursements and/or expenses where applicable) must be made available without delay to the bank from which the collection order was received in accordance with the instructions contained in the collection order.

ACCEPTANCE
Article 15
The presenting bank is responsible for seeing that the form of the acceptance of a bill of exchange appears to be complete and correct, but is not responsible for the genuineness of any signature or for the authority of any signatory to sign the acceptance.

PROMISSORY NOTES, RECEIPTS AND OTHER SIMILAR INSTRUMENTS
Article 16
The presenting bank is not responsible for the genuineness of any signature or for the authority of any signatory to sign a promissory note, receipt, or other similar instrument.

PROTEST
Article 17
The collection order should give specific instructions regarding protest (or other legal process in lieu thereof), in the event of non-acceptance or non-payment.

In the absence of such specific instructions the banks concerned with the collection have no obligation to have the documents protested (or subjected to other legal process in lieu thereof) for non-payment or non-acceptance.

Any charges and/or expenses incurred by banks in connection with such protest or other legal process will be for the account of the principal.

CASE-OF-NEED (PRINCIPAL'S REPRESENTATIVE) AND PROTECTION OF GOODS
Article 18
If the principal nominates a representative to act as case-of-need in the event of non-acceptance and/or non-payment the collection order should clearly and fully indicate the powers of such case-of-need.

In the absence of such indication banks will not accept any instructions from the case-of-need.

Article 19
Banks have no obligation to take any action in respect of the goods to which a documentary collection relates.

Nevertheless in the case that banks take action for the protection of the goods, whether instructed or not, they assume no liability or responsibility with regard to the fate and/or condition of the goods and/or for any acts and/or omissions on the part of any third parties entrusted with the custody and/or protection of the goods. However, the collecting bank must immediately advise the bank from which the collection order was received of any such action taken.

Any charges and/or expenses incurred by banks in connection with any action for the protection of the goods will be for the account of the principal.

ADVICE OF FATE, etc.

Article 20

Collecting banks are to advise fate in accordance with the following rules:

  (i) Form of advice—All advices or information from the collecting bank to the bank from which the collection order was received, must bear appropriate detail including, in all cases, the latter bank's reference number of the collection order.

 (ii) Method of advice—In the absence of specific instructions the collecting bank must send all advices to the bank from which the collection order was received by quickest mail but, if the collecting bank considers the matter to be urgent, quicker methods such as cable, telegram, telex, or communication by electronic systems, etc. may be used at the expense of the principal.

(iii) (a) Advice of payment—The collecting bank must send without delay advice of payment to the bank from which the collection order was received, detailing the amount or amounts collected, charges and/or disbursements and/or expenses deducted, where appropriate, and method of disposal of the funds.

(b) Advice of acceptance—The collecting bank must send without delay advice of acceptance to the bank from which the collection order was received.

(c) Advice of non-payment or non-acceptance—The collecting bank must send without delay advice of non-payment or advice of non-acceptance to the bank from which the collection order was received.

The presenting bank should endeavour to ascertain the reasons for such non-payment or non-acceptance and advise accordingly the bank from which the collection order was received.

On receipt of such advice the remitting bank must, within a reasonable time, give appropriate instructions as to the further handling of the documents. If such instructions are not received by the presenting bank within 90 days from its advice of non-payment or non-acceptance, the documents may be returned to the bank from which the collection order was received.

INTEREST, CHARGES AND EXPENSES
Article 21
If the collection order includes an instruction to collect interest which is not embodied in the accompanying financial document(s), if any, and the drawee refuses to pay such interest, the presenting bank may deliver the document(s) against payment or acceptance as the case may be without collecting such interest, unless the collection order expressly states that such interest may not be waived. Where such interest is to be collected the collection order must bear an indication of the rate of interest and the period covered. When payment of interest has been refused the presenting bank must inform the bank from which the collection order was received accordingly.

If the documents include a financial document containing an unconditional and definitive interest clause the interest amount is deemed to form part of the amount of the documents to be collected. Accordingly, the interest amount is payable in addition to the principal amount shown in the financial document and may not be waived unless the collection order so authorises.

Article 22
If the collection order includes an instruction that collection charges and/or expenses are to be for account of the drawee and the drawee refuses to pay them, the presenting bank may deliver the document(s) against payment or acceptance as the case may be without collecting charges and/or expenses unless the collection order expressly states that such charges and/or expenses may not be waived. When payment of collection charges and/or expenses has been refused the presenting bank must inform the bank from which the collection order was received accordingly. Whenever collection charges and/or expenses are so waived they will be for the account of the principal, and may be deducted from the proceeds.

Should a collection order specifically prohibit the waiving of collection charges and/or expenses then neither the remitting nor collecting nor presenting bank shall be responsible for any costs or delays resulting from this prohibition.

Article 23

In all cases where in the express terms of a collection order, or under these Rules, disbursements and/or expenses and/or collection charges are to be borne by the principal, the collecting bank(s) shall be entitled promptly to recover outlays in respect of disbursements and expenses and charges from the bank from which the collection order was received and the remitting bank shall have the right promptly to recover from the principal any amount so paid out by it, together with its own disbursements, expenses and charges, regardless of the fate of the collection.

Reproduced by courtesy of and with the permission of the International Chamber of Commerce.

Copyright © ICC 1978
publication no 322
available from

ICC Services S.A.R.L.
38 Cours Albert 1er
75008 PARIS

and from the

British National Committee of the ICC
6/14 Dean Farrar Street
LONDON SW1H 0DT.

APPENDIX C

COMMITTEE OF LONDON CLEARING BANKERS

TEXT OF CIRCULARS TO BRANCHES (*as subsequently amended*)

September 23, 1957

CHEQUES ACT, 1957
The Cheques Act, 1957, applies to all banks in England, Scotland, Wales and Northern Ireland and comes into operation on October 17, 1957. Broadly, the effect of the Act is that on and after that date paying banks need not concern themselves with the endorsement or absence of endorsement upon any cheque or analogous instrument and the same applies to collecting banks unless ostensibly there is, or has been, negotiation of the cheque or instrument, for which purpose endorsement is still required.

The protection afforded to collecting banks, which heretofore has been limited to crossed instruments, is extended by the Act to open instruments.

The Act introduces a completely new system relative to endorsement and the banks must feel their way with due regard on the one hand to their own safety and protection, and on the other to the public interest. The intention of the Act is to relieve customers from the task of endorsing instruments which are to be collected for the payees' accounts and to save them and the banks the trouble caused by the return of a large number of such instruments for correct endorsement.

With these considerations in mind the following instructions have been framed for the guidance of all branches of the clearing banks. The instructions however must be regarded as prepared upon an experimental basis pending practical experience of the working of the new system. It may be necessary later to tighten the procedure at certain points, but in the meantime it is desirable that customers should, as far as practicable, derive the benefit of the new legislation without being put to unnecessary inconvenience, consistent with prudent regard for the proper and reasonable protection of the banks.

1. PAYING BANKS
   (a) *Cheques and other instruments presented in the clearings,*

or specially presented, and 'house debits.'

It will not be necessary to examine instruments for endorsement unless the instruments are:

> combined cheque and receipt forms marked 'R';
>
> travellers' cheques;
>
> bills of exchange (other than cheques);
>
> promissory notes.

In these cases endorsement or discharge will be required as heretofore.

(b) *Cheques and other instruments cashed at the counter (including those cashed under open credits).*

The banks have agreed to continue to require endorsement or receipt in all cases where at present it is the practice to look for this. It is felt that the public interest would best be served by a continuance of the present practice. The Mocatta Committee attached importance to the endorsement of cheques encashed over the counter as possibly affording some evidence of the identity of the recipient and some measure of protection for the public.

2. COLLECTING BANKS

(a) With the exception of the instruments referred to in the Schedule to this circular, cheques and other instruments collected for the account of the ostensible payee will not require examination for endorsement, or in the case of dividend and interest warrants for discharge.

(b) Cheques and other instruments payable to a bank to be applied after collection for the credit of a customer's account, e.g., when dividends are mandated to a bank, will not require endorsement or discharge by the payee bank.

(c) Endorsement or discharge will be required as heretofore if the instrument is tendered for the credit of an account other than that of the ostensible payee. If a cheque is specially endorsed to the customer for whose account it is tendered for collection no further endorsement will be necessary.

(d) The banks will not be concerned with the completion of the discharge at the foot of a dividend or interest or redemption warrant unless the instrument is being collected for the account of a third party. If, as a result of the Act, such warrants cease to be printed with a space for the payee's signature, they will nevertheless require endorsement if negotiated. (It is understood that the Bank of England intend to omit the space from warrants in respect of Government, etc., Stocks issued by them.)

(e) If the payee's name is mis-spelt or he is incorrectly designated, the instrument may be accepted for collection without endorsement or discharge unless there are circumstances to suggest that the customer is not the person to whom payment is intended to be made.

(f) The instruments referred to in the Schedule to this circular will require endorsement or discharge as heretofore.

(g) Instruments payable to one or more of a number of joint account holders may be collected for the credit of the joint account without endorsement or discharge. For this purpose joint accounts include accounts of partners, trustees, etc.

(h) Instruments payable to joint payees will require endorsement or discharge if tendered for the credit of an account to which all are not parties.

(i) The foregoing sub-paragraphs of this paragraph also apply when the account is domiciled with another branch of the collecting bank or with another bank.

3. CLEARING BANKS ACTING AS COLLECTING AGENTS FOR NON-CLEARING BANKS, THE POST OFFICE, OR TRUSTEE SAVINGS BANKS

Instruments received from a non-clearing bank, the Post Office or a Trustee Savings Bank need not be examined for endorsement or discharge. It may be assumed that any requisite of endorsement will have been seen to by the non-clearing bank, the Post Office or the Trustee Savings Bank as the case may be, to whom the collecting bank will be entitled to have recourse.

4. EXCHANGING CHEQUES AND OTHER INSTRUMENTS

Cheques and other instruments exchanged at the counter will require endorsement or discharge as heretofore.

5. EXCHANGE CONTROL MARKINGS

All markings in connection with the exchange control must in future be placed upon the face of the instrument.

6. COMBINED CHEQUE AND RECEIPT FORMS

Cheques and other instruments bearing receipts which paying banks have agreed to continue to examine have been dealt with fully in the

Committee of London Clearing Bankers' circular dated September 2, 1957. All such instruments without exception will bear a denoting 'R' on the face of them, and they will require examination by both the collecting and paying banks as heretofore.

SCHEDULE

Combined cheque and receipt forms marked 'R'.

Bills of exchange (other than cheques).

Promissory notes.

Drafts drawn on the Crown Agents, High Commissioners for the Union of South Africa, Pakistan and India, the Commonwealth Relations Office and other paying agents.

Travellers' cheques.

Instruments payable by banks abroad.

September 2, 1957
COMBINED CHEQUE AND RECEIPT FORMS
In due course instructions will be issued by the banks as to modification of banking practice in regard to the endorsement of cheques and other instruments, consequent upon the passing of the Cheques Act, 1957.*

On and after October 17 next, banks paying cheques and instruments other than bills of exchange and promissory notes will be under no legal obligation to examine endorsements. Nevertheless, the banks informed the Mocatta Committee on Cheque Endorsement that in suitable cases by arrangement with customers they would continue to examine receipts on cheques.

1. NEW ARRANGEMENTS
The banks, however, pointed out to the Mocatta Committee that they could not undertake to examine receipts on cheques without limit or regardless of circumstances. Therefore, before any request for the *extension* of the use of endorsed receipts is acceded to, it has been agreed by the banks that the bank concerned must be satisfied that there is real need on the part of the customer for the facility. An endeavour should be made to limit any extension of the facility to a receipt form merely acknowledging receipt of the money; a narrative receipt connecting the payment with any specific transaction is to be deprecated and discouraged. The insurance companies have already intimated an intention to reduce to a minimum the use of this instrument, but receipts will still be required by them in some cases, particularly in connection with the settlement of claims when endorsement by the payee is required to show that the amount is accepted in full settlement of a claim.

2. EXISTING ARRANGEMENTS
The banks have also agreed to encourage *reduction* in the use of endorsed receipts as far as possible. In this connection each bank has undertaken to approach all customers concerned and to suggest to them that sec. 3 of the Act should render an endorsed receipt unnecessary unless, as in the case of some of the insurance companies, local authorities and building societies, the circumstances are exceptional.

Customers' attention should be drawn to sec. 3 of the Act, which states:

*See Circular of September 23 at page 269.

'An unindorsed cheque which appears to have been paid by the banker on whom it is drawn is evidence of the receipt by the payee of the sum payable by the cheque,'

and to the following view expressed by the Mocatta Committee:

'We are of the opinion that in law a simple receipt for a payment by cheque, not linking the payment with the relative transaction, has no greater value as evidence of payment than the paid cheque itself. This is so whether the receipt is printed on the cheque or is issued separately.'

It is hoped that, with the co-operation of customers, the number of these instruments in use will be considerably reduced.

3. DISTINCTIVE MARKING OF COMBINED CHEQUE AND RECEIPT FORMS
On and after October 17, 1957, banks will not accept responsibility for examining receipts, as such, on cheques and other instruments unless the instrument is marked on its face in the position indicated on the specimen cheque [reproduced below], with a bold *outline* letter 'R' at least half-an-inch high. The letter 'R' must be as close to the '£' sign in the 'amount' box as practicable, but some discretion may be given to printers to determine the size of the letter as long as the minimum requirement is observed.

There may be in use special instruments which, as now printed, cannot be stamped or overprinted in the prescribed position. In such cases an alternative position *in proximity to the amount* must be selected, but every effort should be made to standardise the instruments when new stocks are printed.

Arrangements must be made forthwith to ensure that existing stocks of combined cheque and receipt forms, whether held by customers or by the banks, are overprinted or stamped with a rubber stamp in the agreed manner as soon as possible, except in cases where the customers agree that any existing arrangements may be discontinued.

It is essential that such instruments as are issued be marked well before October 17 to allow for delay in presentation.

These arrangements also apply to instruments in the form of a receipt payable by their bankers issued by building societies and others.

4. PROCEDURE
   (a) ALL customers who use combined cheque and receipt forms must be approached forthwith to ascertain whether

they require the facilities to be continued, notwithstanding the provisions of sec. 3 of the Act.

(*b*) Customers who agree to discontinuance of the facility as from October 17 should so confirm in writing. The instruments will not then be marked with an 'R' and on and after that date the form of receipt may be ignored whilst existing stocks are in use.

(*c*) Customers who require the facility to be continued must be informed of the arrangements which must be made to mark the instruments.

5. OPERATION OF SIGNATURE TO RECEIPT AS ENDORSEMENT

Receipts should continue to indicate that the signature thereto is intended to act as an endorsement.

X. Y. Z. CO. LTD.   75-12-34

.... 19..........

BLANK BANK LIMITED

Pay... or Order

R £

For and on behalf of X. Y. Z. CO. LTD.

....................................ACCOUNTANT.   ....DIRECTOR.

⑈089384 ⑈75⑈1234⑈ 03456789⑈

𝕽𝖊𝖈𝖊𝖎𝖛𝖊𝖉 *from*

X. Y. Z. CO. LTD.

the sum stated on the face hereof.

Signature................................

2D. STAMP
IF £2
OR OVER

Date................................

The signature to above receipt is also intended to act as
an endorsement.
No further acknowledgment is required.

(*N.B. It will be appreciated that stamp duty is no longer required on cheque forms or on receipts.*)

INDEX

The references are to the Questions

279

283

284

285

290

294

COLLECTION OF CHEQUE
  see *Collecting Banker*

302

305

* an irregular endorsement

310

315

319

326

334

345

347

348